PROTECT YOURSELF
in
REAL ESTATE

Robert Irwin

McGraw-Hill Book Company

New York   St. Louis   San Francisco   Auckland   Bogotá

Düsseldorf   Johannesburg   London   Madrid   Mexico

Montreal   New Delhi   Panama   Paris   São Paulo

Singapore   Sydney   Tokyo   Toronto

For Hannah and Leo

Library of Congress Cataloging in Publication Data
Irwin, Robert, 1941–
  Protect yourself in real estate.

  1. Real estate business.   2. House selling.
3. House buying.   I. Title.
HD1379.I66   643   76-56375
ISBN 0-07-032064-0

1234567890   KPKP   786543210987

The editors for this book were W. Hodson Mogan and
Joan Zseleczky, the designer was Elliot Epstein, and the
production supervisor was Teresa F. Leaden. It was set in
Baskerville by Monotype Composition Company, Inc.

Printed and bound by The Kingsport Press.

Contents

TWO
Protect Yourself when You Sell by Owner

THREE
Protect Yourself when You Buy

FOUR
Protect Yourself when You Buy a Condominium

FIVE
Protect Yourself when You Buy Rental Property and Become a Landlord

SIX
Protect Yourself when You're a Tenant

SEVEN
Protect Yourself when You Buy Bare Land from Developers

Preface

"If you haven't yet been cheated in real estate, you will be!"

I first heard that statement more than a dozen years ago when I began buying property and working as an agent. The speaker was Leo, a broker who had been in business for more than thirty years and who was well known for his honesty and integrity.

At the time I was surprised not by the words, but that they should come from Leo. I had seen him give up commissions to sellers and buyers who felt they were being cheated, even when they weren't. He always put the reputation of his business above his own personal gain.

"Real estate is a wilderness," he continued. "You'll meet plenty of honest people, and I include brokers, buyers and sellers, and renters. But you'll also meet the other kind, the hunters. If you don't know what you're doing, they'll seek you out and gobble you up!"

I laughed at his choice of words, but in subsequent years I saw their wisdom. I've seen sellers tricked into selling for less than the fair price of their property (a particular hazard in today's market, where values are changing so rapidly). I've seen buyers hoodwinked into paying more than they should out of an unwarranted fear that they might lose the property to some other buyer. Then, of course, there are many who are cheated simply because they don't know their rights.

This is not to say that real estate is totally unregulated. All states, many counties and cities, and, to a lesser extent, the federal government have enacted real estate laws. In practice, however, the selling of real property is rarely conducted in a courtroom. It is most often conducted in a vacant house or an agent's car. A seller contacts a broker or buyer direct and relies on what that person says to start a transaction. Buyers often put their life savings into houses that cost $50,000 or more and commit themselves to 30-year loans with no more investigation than is involved in buying a refrigerator or an encyclopedia. I have seen buyers purchase condominiums without even knowing what the word meant. I have known others to take "free" rides to bare land truly out in the wilderness and then purchase while under the influence of a battery of high-pressure salespeople.

The reason is that renting, buying, and selling real estate are *easy* in the United States. Even the Constitution guarantees these rights in the Fifth Amendment: "No person shall be . . . deprived of life, liberty or *property*, without due process of law; nor shall private property be taken for public use without just compensation" [italics added].

But just because it's easy doesn't mean you can't get into trouble. Real estate, particularly today, is a sophisticated field, and every transaction is complex and loaded with perils. Even for the person who is infrequently involved with real estate, the questions remain: *Am I making or losing money? Am I bargaining successfully? Are the terms of this deal to my advantage or to someone else's? Could I get a better deal if I knew a little bit more? Am I being intimidated because I don't know enough? Should or shouldn't I sign?*

If you're buying, selling, or renting, to whom should you turn for the answers?

Certainly not to the other party to the deal. Even if you're involved with honest people, there is always a conflict of interest between buyer and seller, landlord and tenant. A good deal for a buyer is often a bad deal for a seller. A terrific deal for a seller may mean the buyer is getting swindled.

What about the broker? Most brokers are honest and competent. But remember, a broker is not like a salaried worker. A broker gets paid only when there's a sale. You, on the other hand, don't want just a sale; you want the *best* deal.

Ultimately, you're going to have to rely on yourself. No one else is going to be as concerned about your interests as you are. In real estate you need to protect yourself.

This book is unique in that it is written for real estate consumers— buyers or sellers, landlords or tenants—who want a reliable guide for protecting themselves. It is a practical reference that can be read from cover to cover or consulted for help in a specific area. It is designed to show how to avoid paying too much for closing costs and commissions. How to avoid being taken on a sales price. How to handle an agent so as not to be cheated or intimidated. How to know when you're being told the truth. How to know when you've got a good deal, and when to walk away. And how to get out of a bad deal if you fall into one. It also contains information on how to invest your money to get a better deal when buying a house, a condominium, investment property, or bare land.

If you're not fortunate enough to have a broker like Leo, you'll find this book a true friend. It will clear a path for you through the real estate wilderness and help you to keep from becoming a victim.

Robert Irwin

DISCLAIMER

The reader should take careful note of this disclaimer. This book should not be construed as providing legal or tax advice. The reader should not rely on any legal or tax material herein. The purpose of this book is to describe real estate practices today while pointing out the many abuses that occur and reporting the manner in which individuals are successfully combating them. For all legal and tax advice, the reader should consult a competent attorney.

ONE

Protect Yourself When You Sell through an Agent

1

How to Handle a Broker

A real estate broker, or agent, can be your best helper or most cutthroat enemy when it's time to sell your home. The agent is a bit like the trusted and loyal counselor of a king of centuries ago. If the counselor gave good and honest advice, the king prospered. But if the advice was bad and deceitful, the king stood to lose much of his domain. The agent, like the king's counselor, has great influence over your financial fortunes because he or she is aware of your most confidential finances, your most personal money needs and desires. The person in this position of trust and loyalty even has a special name—*fiduciary*.

When you engage an agent to sell your house, you establish what's known as a *fiduciary relationship,* which means, simply, that the broker must act in your behalf and under your control. In general, brokers or agents are honest, decent, and competent and are worthy of trust and loyalty. But not always. Licensing and training are not uniform throughout the United States. In some areas they are strict, in others, superficial. Consequently, some agents just don't know what they are doing. Often such agents will try to cover their lack of knowledge with bravado and aggressiveness. Some fewer agents are unscrupulous and downright dishonest. These are always ready to profit from their client's insecurity or lack of knowledge.

What if your broker doesn't fulfill his or her fiduciary relationship either through lack of knowledge or through plain dishonesty? What if your broker performs acts which do not result in your getting the best deal you could? Or what if your broker performs acts which are to your detriment or which injure others, as is possible? How can you tell which brokers will stray from the path? Or when? To whom should you turn? What can you do to protect yourself?

This and following chapters will help to answer these questions.

Finding a broker who will list your house is easy; discriminating between an honest, loyal broker who will work hard for you and a con artist or high-pressure salesperson who will do nothing for you is a bit more difficult. First it's important to understand some terms:

AGENT

An agent is a state-licensed person employed by you to perform a specific act—sell your home. You usually agree to pay this person a percentage of the selling price, a commission, and to pay nothing if the house does not sell.

BROKER

The word *broker* is used interchangeably with the term *agent*. In the theatrical world artists have agents; in the world of real estate, homeowners have brokers. A broker must be licensed in every state of the union, the District of Columbia, Guam, the Virgin Islands, and many of the Canadian provinces. Generally, a broker must pass a rigorous examination on real estate law and practice before a license is issued. In most states, a broker must establish an office or place of business, apply for a local business license, and in general be available to the public.

SALESPERSON

This term will also be used interchangeably with *agent*. In many states one of the requirements for a broker's license is one or more years of on-the-job training. To get this training, an individual can become an apprentice to a broker for the stipulated period of time. The individual must also obtain a license and pass an exam that is usually much simpler than that for a broker. While a salesperson, an individual is under the tutelage of a broker (although it is not always clear whether the person is an employee or an independent contractor). Salespersons cannot sign listings or sales agreements for themselves, but usually they can sign or initial such agreements for the broker. Salespersons are, in a certain sense, working on a trial basis, and everything they do is supposed to be under the watchful eye of the broker. Most brokers watch their salespeople closely, for a serious error could cause the state licensing commission to revoke not only an offending salesperson's license, but that of the supervising broker as well.

Salespeople have much the same business relationship to their broker as you, the property owner, have to the broker. Usually they receive no salary, although they may get an advance on future sales commissions, often called a *draw*. When they make a sale, they split the commission with their broker. The usual split is either 60 percent for the salesperson and 40 percent for the broker or 50–50.

Many times, even after fulfilling the time requirement for a broker's license, a salesperson will remain as a salesperson. There are several reasons. Some individuals may find it impossible to pass the rigorous broker's exam; some may not have the capital necessary to establish their own office; some may need the coaching and support offered by the broker.

Just how brokers think of their salespeople is suggested by one personal interview form designed to be used in screening applicants. The qualities a broker should look for in a good salesperson were listed on the form in the following order:

1. Personality
2. Ambition
3. Speaking ability
4. Aggressiveness
5. Judgment
6. Courtesy
7. Appearance
8. Honesty and integrity
9. Sales experience
10. Age
11. Automobile
12. Economic stability
13. Personal ownership of real estate
14. Availability

It speaks for itself that honesty and integrity are eighth on the list after personality, aggressiveness, and ambition. Real estate offices tend to have a very high turnover—as high as 200 to 300 percent a year. Many brokers feel that failure to find the "right" person (presumably one who would fit such requirements) accounts for this.

REALTOR

This term is *not* synonymous with the word *broker*. *Realtor* is a registered trademark of the National Association of Realtors and can only be used by its members. In most areas only a broker can be a Realtor, but a sales-person can join the association as an Associate Realtor. In California, it is against the law for anyone to use the designation Realtor who is not a broker. In at least seven states and several localities, however, both salespeople and brokers use the designation.

LISTING

This is a contract by which an owner "hires" an agent to sell or lease property. It usually indicates what price and terms are to be obtained by the broker, gives the duration of the contract, and spells out the commission the broker is to receive.

It's easy to find a broker. Just go through the telephone directory yellow pages under "Real Estate" and call any office. You will find it difficult to get off the phone without first giving your name and address and promising to allow the prospective broker to pay you a visit. If you really want to get into the swing of things, a much more challenging approach is to put a "For Sale by Owner" sign in your front yard. This is guaranteed to produce a long line of salespeople coaxing or coercing you to give them a listing. I know of one individual in a suburb of Los Angeles who claims that he had no less than sixty-five calls from agents within a two-day period after putting his sign out.

Probably a better method, although by no means guaranteed to get you a *good* broker, is to talk to friends who have recently sold their homes and, if they were satisfied with the transaction, find out which broker they used.

Whichever method you use, there are certain clues that will help you avoid a con artist and get a broker who will work hard in your interests:

1. *Find out how long the agent has been actively working in your area.* It doesn't matter if the person you are dealing with works for a large nationwide chain or operates a one-person office. Real estate is largely a business built on reputation. If, in this highly competitive field, your agent has lasted for many years in your area selling many of your neighbors' houses, you could reasonably conclude that he or she has a good record of sales and fair play and should be seriously considered when you decide to sell.

2. *Find out whether your broker is a Realtor.* The National Association of Realtors requires all members to pledge adherence to a code of ethics that calls for fair play and honesty for all parties to a transaction.

Being a Realtor is really a minimum requirement for your broker candidate. To understand why, it is necessary to understand the benefits to a broker of becoming a Realtor. Realtors through their local real estate boards operate multiple listing services (MLS). These services provide an exchange of listings between members, a necessity in many cases for staying in business. With the exception of Pennsylvania, it is not usually possible for a broker to have access to these listings without being a member of the National Association of Realtors. Many brokers therefore join the organization and become Realtors not so much out of a desire to adhere to its high principles as out of a need to receive its listings.

3. *Verify the truthfulness of your prospective agent.* I knew of a salesman, let's call him Joe, who would go to a prospect's house and tell the owner that he regularly sold three to four houses a month (in fact he sold less than a fourth that number), that he had been in the business for half a dozen years (in truth, less than a year), that he had special connections with lenders and thus could get loans for buyers that wouldn't normally qualify for them (no agents have such special connections unless they make the loan themselves or have a private individual make it). Joe went on to guarantee that he could get the owner a quick sale at a price many thousands of dollars above market value.

Many owners were taken in by Joe's line. They would regard him as a close friend, invite him over for dinner (which invitations he always accepted), and seek his financial advice. Ultimately they would list with him.

Joe's game was to get as many listings as he could and then put them on the MLS, hoping that every so often one would sell. His listings would sit a month or two with no prospects even looking at them because they were so overpriced. Then, when the sellers would begin to get worried and question Joe, he would send a notice out to the cooperating agents: "Seller desperate. Submit any offer!!!" He might also get the sellers to drop the price a thousand dollars "to get the ball rolling."

Other agents would occasionally respond to this tactic and come in with an offer usually much lower than the actual market value of the house. Now Joe would twist the screws. As a trusted financial adviser, he was able to tell the sellers that their house was a "dog"; after all, no one had even come by to look at it until this particular offer appeared. Joe would tell the sellers that they'd better grab the offer or be prepared to wait six months before another one came along. They might not be able to sell at all unless they accepted this offer, Joe would hint.

The poor sellers by now had been conditioned to a sale. The minute the house was listed, they began looking for another house and soon had a dream home in mind. All their friends knew they were going to be moving. The husband had prepared his employer by asking for his vacation early so that he could help with the move. The kids were all excited. Joe had gotten his sellers psychologically primed to move. More often than not, they signed the bad offer.

An agent who lies or exaggerates unreasonably to get you to sign a listing will probably do the same thing when it's time for you to sign a sales agreement. You'll end up with a bad deal because you didn't have the facts.

Probably the most difficult thing in the world is to tell when someone is lying (or grossly exaggerating, which is just as bad). If you're one of those who can look a person straight in the eye and tell this, you're set. If not, here's a simple test you may find useful.

Engage your prospective agent in a fairly extended conversation during which you ask some of these questions or make some of these comments. The agent's response will tell you a lot.

A. *"I'm sure I can get $_____ (here quote a price at least $5000 above the going rate for homes in your area)—don't you agree?"*

An honest broker won't. An honest broker will tell you, gently, that your house is overpriced. A con artist will quickly agree, trying to get your listing at any price and then after a few months of no buyers hope to knock you down to a low price.

B. *"Several other agents I talked to said they could sell my house within one week after it's on the market. Can you?"*

No agent can guarantee a sale to a buyer who has yet to be found. An honest agent will admit this and tell you that all he or she can do is work hard for you. A con artist will assure you that your house will be sold immediately. Such a bad agent may even offer to prove it by accepting a one-week listing.

Unless the agent's already talked you into a ridiculously low price, the chances are that your home won't be sold in a week. However, by getting a listing, the agent hopes to exclude other brokers from working on your property and to gain the inside track with you when the week is up. Some agents may even bring a few buyers through to prove they're working hard.

If an agent wants you to sign for one week and you think a sale may really be made, try giving an *open listing* (discussed in Chapter 3). This entitles the agent to a commission if he or she sells your home, but does not keep you from selling it yourself or listing with other brokers.

C. *"My house is perfect and it's in the perfect location for a sale—don't you agree?"*

Any agent will be hard-pressed to disagree with a seller about the merits of a home and its location, particularly when the seller chose to live there in the first place. Nonetheless, if you did have the perfect home, you wouldn't need an agent. And an honest broker will point that out as well as carefully mention a few of the drawbacks to the house and the location that the typical buyer might notice.

D. *"I would probably list with you now, but I have a friend who's just gotten a license and I'd like to give _____ (name of person) first chance at the listing."*

An important thing to remember about honest and professional agents is that they don't knock their competitors. Good brokers will try to convince you to list by emphasizing the good job they will do. The most a good agent might do is point out that you would be better off listing with an *experienced* broker, rather than with your friend, who is obviously inexperienced.

Con artists, on the other hand, will go out of their way to knock a competitor. The emphasis will be not so much on what a good job they will do, but on what a bad job your friend will do. They may even go so far as to say that they have heard of the office your friend works for and that it's been involved in a lot of shady deals.

Stay away from such agents. They will probably ridicule your house to half the buyers who see it in hopes they will buy some other listing the agents have. The net result is that probably half your potential buyers will be scared away.

E. *"I guess I'd better list (with you) because the last broker I talked to said I needed a license to sell my house by owner."*

Honesty involves not only actively telling the truth, but also pointing out an obvious falsehood, particularly when it affects an agent's client, or principal.

All the con artist has to do here is keep silent, not actively lie or even exaggerate—just keep silent. You, presumably, have heard some false information from someone else (you never need a state real estate license to sell your own home), and by not informing you of the truth, the agent can hope to get a quick listing.

An honest broker, however, will be happy to take your listing, but will also inform you that it's not being taken because you can't sell by yourself. This agent will correct your misunderstanding.

An omission of this sort is a serious matter and should immediately disqualify an individual from consideration as your agent. If such an important fact is omitted now, similar omissions to a buyer or to you later on in the transaction may have disastrous effects (see Chapter 6).

4. *Beware of an agent who tries to list your home by deception.* The following is a method acted to near perfection by a saleswoman I met called Gail. Gail would call and say that she had a buyer for your home. Would you agree to a twenty-four-hour listing just so this buyer could see the premises?

Most people who were thinking of selling would go along with this ploy. After all, they figured, what could they lose?

Gail would have them sign an exclusive agency agreement (see Chapter 3) and then waltz a couple through their home. The "buyers" would ooh and ahh at this and that and then leave. Gail would call back a few hours later and say the buyers were interested, but it would be a few days before they decided. Would the sellers agree to extending the listing for a short while?

Why not, most sellers would reason.

A few days would go by and Gail would call back. She would tell the sellers that her buyers just couldn't make up their minds, but she had a couple of other buyers she'd like to try out. How about listing for a few weeks?

Often the sellers would agree. After all, Gail certainly seemed to have her finger on active buyers, they would reason.

When Gail arrived to get the listing, she would tell the sellers they might as well sign a full three-month listing so that she could put the house on the multiple listing board. This would mean just in case her buyers didn't work out, other cooperating brokers could work on the house too. This way the sellers *wouldn't lose any time.*

Gail always appeared sincere, showed enthusiasm, and really seemed sorry about not having already sold the house. Often the sellers went along and signed. If they did, they had been "taken."

Gail never had a buyer. The couple she waltzed through were her brother and his wife. They never intended to buy, but had a standing agreement with Gail that for a fee they would parade through a house for fifteen minutes pretending.

She never had other buyers, either. She just orchestrated the ruse to fool the sellers into listing with her. And her bag of tricks did not end here. In Chapter 6 we'll see how she finagled sellers into signing sales agreements.

Such tricks are illegal in most areas, as is paying an unlicensed person (Gail's so-called buyers) a fee for helping in a sale (although a *finder's fee* for locating a buyer for a broker is often allowed). The difficulty comes in proving that the whole thing was a trick. The brother and sister-in-law will swear they really wanted to buy. Only if the agent has tried this ploy on many sellers and the total facts are uncovered will justice be done, but that is a job for the state real estate commissioner and/or the local district attorney.

What are the chances that an agent who pulls Gail's stunt really does have a buyer for your house? Unless your home is unique, no other like it anywhere, the chances are very slim. Why would any broker go to the trouble of getting a shaky listing and potentially losing a good buyer on your home, when he or she could show that same good buyer other already listed homes similar to yours in your area?

While it's true that on occasion brokers do have buyers just for one home, treat such situations with much suspicion. If you do agree to a twenty-four-hour listing, make a point of *not extending it* no matter what the circumstances. And certainly wait several weeks before you decide to give the final listing to this broker and then only if you find that this broker is the most qualified for the other reasons listed here.

5. *Make sure your broker will work actively on your property.* It's really true that advertising is the key to real estate sales. In its simplest form advertising may be just a sign on your property. On the other extreme it can involve continuing newspaper ads and even plugs on the radio. You want your broker to advertise actively. Too many brokers are just listers. They're out to get as many listings as possible; then they put them on the multiple listing board or spread them around the office and let others try to find buyers. They believe in the motto "Those who list, last" (the salesperson who gets many listings will last a long time in the business).

Residential real estate is basically a *volume* business. Consider this: When a salesperson sells a $45,000 home, the commission is figured thusly:

$$\begin{array}{rl} \$45,\!000 & \text{Selling price} \\ \times 0.06 & \text{Commission rate} \\ \hline \$2700 & \text{Total commission} \end{array}$$

If one office listed the home and another sold it, which is often the case, the commission is split between them, usually on a 50–50 basis.

$$\begin{array}{rl} \$2700 & \text{Total commission} \\ \times 0.50 & \text{Split between offices} \\ \hline \$1350 & \text{Each office's share} \end{array}$$

Now the salesperson has to split again with the broker:

$1350 Commission
×0.50 Split between broker and salesperson
$675 Final commission to salesperson

The Department of Labor estimates that a typical family of four needs around $16,000 a year to live adequately in today's economy. Our salesperson, at an average of $675 per commission, would need 23.7 sales per year or about two each month in order to make a living at real estate.

Of course, if the salesperson both listed and sold the property, the commission would be higher. Nonetheless, these figures illustrate why many salespeople are so desperate to get listings.

You shouldn't be interested in filling some agent's quota of listings; you should be interested in finding an agent who will not *just* list, but will work to see your house is sold. Don't be impressed by agents who tell you how many houses they have listed over the last year. Find out how many of those listed were actually sold.

The volume nature of the real estate business is one reason many sellers will list only with brokers personally and not with salespeople. They feel that the higher commission available to the broker offers greater inducement for the broker to work harder and to advertise more. Others prefer to list with salespeople representing large offices. They feel that the firm's size will enable it to spend advertising dollars and that, in some cases, its well-known name will draw in buyers.

As a seller, it is worth your time to make a list of all the brokers with whom you are considering listing. Then turn to the real estate advertising section of your local paper and see how much advertising they do. You may be surprised.

After checking the ads for three or four days, particularly on the weekends, you may find that the large office advertises few homes. On the other hand, the small office may take out a full page of ads with photos of almost every house it has listed. A quick check of the local paper can be extremely helpful in determining just how active your broker or your salesperson's office really is.

However, just because a particular house isn't advertised doesn't mean the office isn't working on it. It's a fact of the real estate business that buyers very rarely purchase the home they see advertised and call the agent about. What you should look for is extensive advertising of a variety of homes in your price range. This use of the media will be most productive in turning up potential buyers.

6. *Avoid the high-pressure agents.* Usually you can tell these agents by the fire in their eyes and the fierce determination exhibited by their walk and general demeanor. The high-pressure salesperson often believes that unless a seller lists during the first meeting, the listing (and the agent's time) is lost. Consequently these agents turn on the pressure immediately and usually refuse to leave until you've signed a listing agreement. They are determined persons, determined to coerce you into listing, not necessarily by lying, exaggerating, or pulling tricks, but by sheer force of personality. The usual method is fear.

If you can be bullied, the high-pressure salesperson will bully you. You will be shown that you don't know anything about real estate and that the agent knows everything, even to the point where the agent is more capable of deciding on price, terms, and the decision to list than you are. Sellers who cave in to this sort of person are often basically insecure and afraid to stand their ground. Usually the high-pressure agent will challenge your knowledge of real estate terminology, forms, appraisal method, market value, advertising, or any of a dozen different areas. And the moment you admit you don't know, the agent will sneer in mild contempt and say something like, "It's understandable, because you're not in the business, not a professional." The implication, of course, is that the agent is.

If you suddenly feel the wind taken out of your sails, you're in for a rough time. This bully will smile condescendingly as you try to explain what you want done, and you may find your ideas getting confused and your words muddled. In the end, the bully will lead you over to the listing agreement and hand you a pen, and you will know that the agent will think you are a "damn fool" if you don't sign.

Some of the more aggressive high-pressure salespeople will not let up once they have you on the run. It is not uncommon for them to insist on a 7 percent commission when 6 percent is the rule "because your house is so run down and in such a poor location that an extra incentive is needed for salespeople to work on it." They might for the same reason insist on a six-month listing where three months is standard. If you hesitate, such high-pressure agents might go so far as accuse you of trying to cheat them out of a salable listing or their rightful commission.

The answer to this sort of agent, of course, is not to give a damn what he or she thinks of you. It's your property, and you have the right to be as ignorant and incorrect as you want. It is the agent's duty, after all, to help you to enlightenment, *not to intimidate you.* The minute you feel intimidated by an agent—and if it happens, there'll be no mistaking the feeling—ask the agent to leave in no uncertain terms. Don't ever list with high-pressure agents. Staying away from them will save you a lot of unhappiness and self-recrimination in the end.

This brings up another type of high-pressure agent, the one who won't leave.

A friend I'll call Gunther once put up a "For Sale by Owner" sign and talked with all the agents that came by. He loved to reminisce about one agent whom he referred to as "the squatter." This man arrived after lunch one day and tried to talk Gunther into listing. Within forty-five minutes everything was said that could be said, and Gunther told the agent he'd call him if he was interested. But the squatter didn't leave. He walked around the house several times, then sat down on the living room couch and continued to talk real estate.

Not knowing what was up, Gunther humored him, answered questions, and thought up others to ask. He offered coffee; it was accepted. They continued to chat while the squatter tried the other high-pressure technique, intimidation, to get Gunther to sign.

Around four o'clock, Gunther realized the man wasn't ever going to leave. Gunther's daughters were coming home from school soon and he didn't want them to find him arguing with an agent. He simply told the squatter to take his listing form and get out.

The man didn't budge. He kept talking, appeared not in the least offended, and smiled with every other breath.

Lesser men might have caved in at this point and signed something, even a twenty-four-hour listing, just to get rid of the agent. But Gunther was up to the task. He gently, but firmly, took the man's arm, led him out of the house and off the property. Gunther liked to recall how the agent's eyes bulged wider and wider as he was led off, still talking, still smiling.

7. *Avoid the part-time agent.* In almost all states, licensing requires that an agent actively participate in selling property. "Actively," however, is usually defined as establishing a place of business. It does not specify the amount of time spent. Consequently, a great many agents, both salespeople and brokers, work at a regular job during the day and sell property in the evening hours and on weekends.

You do not want to give your listing to a part-time agent. The reason is simple: The agent who is any good at the business will be able to make a living at it full-time. In reply to this argument, part-time agents will often say that they are just getting started, that they will go full-time in the very near future.

As the seller, you should ask yourself if you want to list with someone who when getting started in a business is not willing or not able to give it a full-time commitment. Remember that the amount of time that a part-time agent is working at a regular job may be time lost in the sale of your house.

These seven hints may not guarantee that you will get a good broker, but they should keep you away from the bad apples. Remember, the way agents treat you when they are trying to get your listing is the same way you'll be treated when an offer to purchase comes in. The time to find a good broker is at the beginning, not when you're too committed to change.

One last point should be made, and this has to do with a gut feeling that some people have about other people. Suppose a young saleswoman comes to your door and wants to list your home. She says it's her first listing and if you give it to her she'll work extra hard.

Why not try? If she seems honest and has great enthusiasm and her office advertises heavily, I would give her a chance. A new, young salesperson may make a quicker sale than that wizened old broker who's been in business so long and remembers the old days so well that he can no longer communicate with today's young buyer.

2

How to Know What Your Highest Sales Price Is

Once you've found yourself a good broker (or perhaps along the way) you're going to arrive at a price, the amount for which you plan to list your home. Normally agents, as part of their job, will give you a free valuation of your home and will then expect you to accept the amount they arrive at as your listing price. Even an honest agent, however, is not necessarily an appraisal expert. Virtually all persons who receive a sales license consider themselves appraisal experts. (There *are* appraisal experts, and they usually belong to the International Society of Real Estate Appraisers or the American Institute of Real Estate Appraisers.)

Your interest is to be sure that you get the most money possible out of your property without pricing it out of range of potential buyers. Remember, how much you want, or feel you deserve, or need to get has no bearing on the price your house will bring on the open market. The best way to protect yourself against a bad appraisal is to make a good one yourself. This is surprisingly easy for most residential property.

I knew one broker who used an unusual technique to appraise tract homes. Donald would take a pad of paper and walk along the inside walls of the house, with the owner following, carefully measuring room sizes. Then he would take a chip of paint from a ceiling to check condition of the paint. He would next check all the appliances to see whether they worked. Then he'd go to the yard and carefully note on his pad the exact number of bushes and trees and make a little X for each rose bush. He would take outside measurements, measure cellars and attics, and write down the exact size of the lot.

When he was finished, he and the owner would sit around the kitchen table while he tabulated his figures. Finally Don would take a blank piece of paper and write an amount on it. He would hand it to the owner and say, "That's exactly for how much you should list your house."

Needless to say, few owners dared disagree with him.

When I once asked Don about his method, he mentioned a tract area and said, "Every house on those blocks will go for _____," and he named a figure for the area. "There hasn't been one sold for more or less in the last six months. I know how much a house is worth before I walk in

TABLE 1
SAMPLE APPRAISAL SHEET

House at 2234 Maple Street

| | Actual selling price | | $45,000 |
| House sold 8 months ago—add 5% for appreciation | | | 2,250 |

	Subtract for worse *features* in your *house*	Add for better *features* in your *house*
Repair		
Weird or freakish design		
Lot size	$1,000	
Freeway nearby		
Busy or noisy street	—	$1,000
Landscaping	—	300
Room size		
Quality of building material		
Garage instead of carport		
Swimming pool	5,000	
Air conditioning	—	
Carpets	—	500
Other items		
Broken driveway	—	600
Children's permanent playhouse in yard	150	
	$6,150	$2,400

$45,000	Selling price of subject house
+2,250	Add 5% for appreciation
−6,150	Subtract for worse features in your house
+2,400	Add for better features in your house
$43,500	The amount your house should *sell* for
$47,000	Listing price of subject house
−45,000	Selling price of subject house
2,000	Add to your selling price
43,500	
$45,500	The amount for which your house should be *listed*

the front door. But I give the sellers a little song and dance—it gives them confidence in me and makes them think they're getting their money's worth."

Although Donald was bitten by the acting bug, he was not basically dishonest nor was he acting against the owner's interests. He was using the most common form of appraisal—the comparison method. He was comparing the price of a known sold house with that of a potential sale. Of course, he was dealing with an area where all the houses were identical, which simplified his job. Nonetheless, the comparison method is one which every homeowner should use to verify the agent's appraisal.

The comparison method relies on the fact that there are homes *similar* to yours which have sold recently in the same general area. You compare prices on those other sales to arrive at your own price. It takes time, so you should begin well before you plan to list. Here's how it works:

First it is very important that you find homes that have sold recently and that are very similar to your home. For example, they should have the same number of bedrooms and bathrooms and the same general design. Next you must learn both the price these homes were listed for and the amount for which they actually sold. (The listing price of a home usually indicates the top potential market value. The first offer that buyers make is usually the lowest potential market value. The selling price is closest to actual market value.) Agents who belong to a multiple listing service can usually supply you with this information. If your agent cannot, you can check with former buyers or sellers; but beware, those who have recently bought a house tend to minimize the price they paid. You can also call the real estate office that handled a nearby sale, and an agent there will often give you the information. The old practice of going down to the county or city recorder to check tax stamps is usually time consuming and inaccurate—some buyers purposely buy extra stamps to confuse anyone examining the records.

It is important to get as many other houses for comparison as possible. Six is not too many; two or three is probably too few. Once you know the listing and selling price, you should physically examine the selected houses, if possible. Often, during a sale, there will be a period of a few days to a week or even longer when the house is unoccupied. A friendly former owner, new buyer, or agent often will let you in.

Once you're inside, take a piece of paper and *compare* your house with the subject house as you go through. First, write down the actual selling price. Next, add 5 percent for appreciation for each six months since the subject house sold. Houses in urban areas across the United States have been appreciating at a rate of approximately 10 percent a year for the past several years. Now *add* a money bonus for items which make *your* house worth more, that is, for negative features of the subject house. These may be poor repair, weird or freakish design, a smaller lot, closeness to freeway or shopping center, busy or noisy location, etc.

Next, *subtract* a money penalty for items that make your house worth less, that is, for better items in the subject house, such as higher-quality materials, better landscaping, a swimming pool, refrigerated air conditioning, or better-grade carpets. The amount you add or subtract depends on your good judgment and your ability to be objective. Try to think of what the typical buyer might be looking for. You need only an approximation for these figures.

Now add up the figures and see how much, by comparison, your house should sell for. Finally, *since most houses sell for less than the listing price,* find the difference between the actual selling price and the listing price on the subject house. Add this amount to your appraisal, and you've got the price at which you should list your home.

Now do the same for as many other houses as are available. Throw out any comparisons that are unreasonably high or low. Average them out and you'll come up with your listing price. If it differs from the price your broker gave you, ask for an explanation of the difference. If you've done a good job, the agent will probably end up agreeing with your price!

Some agents may present you with a *market comparison sheet,* such as the one illustrated below. It is really a simplified version of the market comparison methods we've just discussed, and its primary advantage is that it aligns all the properties examined on one sheet for easy comparison. Its weakness is that it overlooks much information and overcondenses other data. If all the houses around you are identical in appearance, the market comparison sheet can be a helpful guide. If, however, there are differences, this sheet's value to you decreases in direct proportion to the uncommonness of your property.

There are some disadvantages to the comparison method of appraisal. Just how reliable it is depends to a great extent on how many properties are readily available for comparison. If you can't find any good comparisons at all, you can throw the method out the window. Also, values occasionally change more rapidly than our figures indicate. Finally, there may be some special influence of which you are unaware, such as a seller's desperate need to get out quickly, that would affect another house's price.

If you don't have the time or the inclination to use this method of appraisal, there are ways to get others to do the appraisal for you, for free. You can tell a nearby savings and loan association, tell them that you are planning to sell your home and that you want to make a maximum loan on it to the potential buyer. In many cases, the lending

TABLE 2
MARKET COMPARISON SHEET

Home Address	Sold	For sale now	Sq. ft.	Bdrms	Baths	List price	Sales price	Days on market	Cash to loan	Second	VA/FHA
3507 Johns St.	x		1600	3	2	53,900	53,000	20	x		
723 Maple St.	x		1650	4	2	57,000	54,000	47		x	
10061 Fremont St.		x	1490	3	1	48,000	?	21	x	x	x

NOTE: An x denotes whether a house is currently for sale or has been sold, and whether the seller is willing to accept or has already accepted cash to loan, a second trust deed, or VA/FHA financing.

institution will send out a competent appraiser to determine the maximum amount the association will loan on your property. When the lender calls to tell you the maximum loan, ask what percentage of the sales price it is. If it's an 80 percent loan, divide the amount by 4, multiply by 5 and that's your market value. If it's a 90 percent loan, divide by 9, multiply by 10, and you've got it again. Because of abuse of this tactic, many lending institutions won't send a representative out until a bona fide buyer has signed a sales agreement.

Some sellers like to ask each broker who comes by how much their house is worth. Then they take an average figure. I don't like this method. It is unscientific and inaccurate. It could well be that half the agents who stopped by were duffers who couldn't appraise a dog house. What's an average of their appraisals worth?

Another appraisal method used on residential properties is mentioned here only because an agent may toss it at you and you don't want to look ignorant and lose your psychological advantage. It is the replacement method and is quite simple. You find out the number of square feet in your home (length of house times width) and then multiply by the current building costs per square foot in your area. You can find the latter by checking with any insurance company that gives fire insurance on homes. Insurance companies make it their business to know up-to-date building costs.

Once you have the cost of your building, you must add on the value of your land. This, again, can be found by the comparison method. If you don't want to go through the work indicated earlier, you can call several brokers, describe your lot and area, and ask whether they have any lots like it for sale. Their answers will give you a rough idea of your lot's price.

The trouble with the replacement method is that you may find that your house costs more to replace than you can sell it for. The reason for this is the fantastic increase in building costs in recent years. This accounts for the fact that new homes of comparable size and material usually cost much more than their used counterparts. Used homes are catching up in price and may do so in a few years, but they have not yet caught up.

A third method of checking your broker's appraisal is by paying the federal government to do it. The only difficulty here is that it takes a bit of time, anywhere from three to twelve weeks. You can get an appraisal from the Veteran's Administration (VA) or the Federal Housing Administration (FHA) through the Department of Housing and Urban Development (HUD). Seeking an appraisal by these organizations does not require you to get a loan insured by them; it in no way obligates you.

To get a VA appraisal on your home, you should contact a bank, a savings and loan association, or a mortgage banker. They will have you fill out a request for determination of reasonable value and forward it to the VA for processing. They will also collect your check for $50, which is the current fee for the service. An appraiser will be out within one to twelve weeks, depending on the VA's backlog of requests, and shortly thereafter you will receive a certificate of reasonable value or CRV. This is the maximum amount the VA appraiser feels your home is worth. The VA guarantees loans on the basis of this appraisal, and should you ask a higher price for your house, a buyer seeking to purchase using a VA loan would have to make up the difference in cash. It is possible for you as a seller to apply directly to the VA for your appraisal, but lenders often have a direct line to the appraiser assignment desk and can usually get results faster.

To get an FHA (or HUD) appraisal, the procedure is the same; just see your banker, savings and loan association, or mortgage banker. The fee is also $50.

If after reading this far you are still concerned that your property appraisal may be inaccurate, there is a final step you can take—consult a professional appraiser. Appraisers are usually listed under the heading "Real Estate Appraisers" in the yellow pages of your phone book. Look for appraisers who are members of the International Society of Real Estate Appraisers or the American Institute of Real Estate Appraisers. Be sure you negotiate a fee beforehand, and remember that it sometimes helps in the price to request a simple value figure and not a detailed appraisal.

Valuation of your property is based on three things: utility, demand, and scarcity. Some things satisfy a great need (utility) and are in great demand, but are also abundant, like air, and consequently have little monetary value. The value of your home depends on its *utility,* that is, its ability to satisfy the need for housing for a broad spectrum of buyers; the *demand,* that is, buyers with the necessary cash and ability to qualify for loans; and *scarcity,* that is, a lack of available houses. Today we are experiencing a sellers' market. Demand for homes is high and few are available; consequently values are rising rapidly. When you set the price on your listing, be sure it's today's high price and not yesterday's low one.

3

Eleven Listing Dangers

Once you've decided on your agent and your price, you will be asked to sign a listing agreement. This is a formal agreement that empowers the agent to find a buyer for your house. You've made the first formal step toward a sale, a process that is summarized as follows:

				Closing	
Step 1	*Step 2*	*Step 3*	*Step 4*	*Step 5*	*Step 6*
List	Find a buyer	Sign a sales agreement	Open escrow	Fulfill escrow requirements	Record deed to buyer

Protecting yourself in the first step will be discussed here. Subsequent chapters will consider the other steps.

Very often the agent will have an impressive form already filled out. It will have the agent's logo and office name at the top, and all that will be needed will be your signature at the bottom. "Just sign," the agent may say, "and I'll take care of the rest."

Stop! Don't sign anything until you've checked it over very carefully and, if possible, have your lawyer look it over. There are numerous danger areas for the seller in a listing agreement. Be sure you understand the agreement and that its terms are to your benefit. Here are some questions to ask yourself:

1. *Is the listing the type you really want?*

There are at least five different types of listing agreements. The type which sellers universally seem to prefer, and of which brokers universally despair, is the *open listing*.

The open listing is just what it says it is—a listing which is open to all brokers. A seller usually signs a document called a *nonexclusive agency* agreement. It entitles the agent to receive a commission if he or she brings in a buyer on the terms specified. The agent is not, however, entitled to a commission if another broker or the owner sells the property. The owner is not limited to only one agent; the listing can be given to as many agents as he or she likes.

It is easy to see why sellers prefer this type of listing: Sellers give the least commitment, and because they can list with as many agents as they can find, they feel they are getting the most service from the brokers.

This is an illusion. Don't disparage the broker who won't take an open listing; watch out for the agent who seeks it. Unless you have such a tremendous house that the first broker who gets it is sure to get a sale (in which case you really don't need an agent), the only reason the agent is taking it is the hope that after a while you will break down and give an exclusive listing (discussed next). Although a seller may give open listings to a dozen, two dozen, even a hundred brokers, none of these is likely to work very hard. Consider: Why should they spend time and money on a listing when it might be sold out from under them by another broker or even the seller?

The *exclusive listing* is the type brokers want and sellers hesitate to give, for the wrong reasons. An exclusive listing means that while the listing is in force only the one agent who has it and no other agents may sell the house for a commission. Sellers often falsely reason that this is limiting the exposure of their property. But remember, it is better to have one agent working hard on your house than a hundred who take your listing, put it in the back drawer of a file cabinet, and forget about it. Further, in most cases agents will share their exclusive listings with other brokers in the belief that half an earned commission is better than none at all.

There are two types of exclusive listings. The first is called the *exclusive agency listing*.

An exclusive agency listing means that while only one broker has the right to sell your home for a commission, you retain the right to sell it *by yourself* without paying a commission. This sort of listing leads to unhappy misunderstandings and on occasion, downright cheating. Usually, under the terms of this listing, if the agent is the *procuring cause* (is responsible for finding a buyer), he or she is entitled to a commission. This usually means that even if the agent only drives by your house and points it out to a buyer, you still may have to pay the broker a commission if that buyer subsequently comes back alone and buys from you. It is understandable that in such a situation, sellers often do not want to pay the broker. "Prove you found the buyer," they will often say. To overcome this problem, many agents will on a regular basis (at the end of every week or month) present to the seller a list of the names of people to whom they have shown the house. Nonetheless, if the seller still refuses to pay the commission, the broker's only alternative is to sue the seller. This costs money and, given the different circumstances of each case, does not guarantee the broker will win or ever get the money.

Some sellers have been known to deliberately get the names and phone numbers of a broker's potential buyers (or prospects) and later call them up and offer to lower the selling price a few hundred dollars if they'll buy direct from the seller. It is easy to see why few brokers will take an exclusive agency listing. If you can get your agent to take it, good for you. You're in the driver's seat. But don't expect your agent to work too hard on a piece of property that you might sell yourself.

The other type of agency agreement is the *exclusive right to sell.* You can easily tell if this is the agreement your broker wants you to sign because it will usually have those exact four words in it. Quite simply it means that no matter who sells the property, you or the agent, you agree to pay a commission.

If you've done your homework and gotten a good broker (see Chapter 1) this is the best listing you can give! It is the type of listing that gives an agent the most protection and the most incentive to work, which should assure you of a quicker sale.

A *multiple listing* is a variety of an exclusive right to sell. In a multiple listing you usually give the broker the right to a commission regardless of who sells your home, and in addition, you authorize and instruct the broker to put the listing on the multiple listing service, that is, to share or "co-broke" it with other brokers, all of whom belong to a multiple or listing sharing service. Many brokers and sellers feel that this is the most effective type of listing. It has the benefits of a single broker, yet allows many other brokers to participate. It does have a disadvantage, however. Your broker must split the commission, usually in half, if another broker sells your property. Quite frankly, agents are less likely to spend advertising money and their own time on a listing which may yield them only half a commission. The drawbacks of a multiple listing are similar to those of an open listing.

Not all brokers belong to a multiple listing service. If you want your house put on the multiple, be sure you ask whether your agent is a member. Usually your listing form will mention in bold letters that it is a multiple listing.

One other type of listing commonly used is the *net listing.* A net listing can be in the form of any of the other listings described. Its special feature is that the commission, instead of being a percentage of the sales price, is simply whatever the broker can get for the property over and above a net price to you. For example, if you give an agent a net listing for $40,000, in any sale the agent makes, you get the first $40,000 of the actual sales price and the broker gets the balance. If the house sells for $40,500, the broker gets $500. But if it sells for $50,000, the broker gets $10,000!

Beware of net listings. They are used occasionally in investment property. If an agent suggests using it in selling your home, however, your home is probably way underpriced and the agent is trying to get more than the normal listing fee. Some unscrupulous agents will occasionally find sellers who are convinced that their house is worth a price tens of thousands of dollars below market value. This is particularly true these days, when prices have risen so quickly. Rather than tell the seller the true market value, such an unscrupulous broker will take a net listing, sell the house at market value, and pocket the difference. If your broker suggests a net listing in selling your house, you better hang onto your pocketbook.

Net listing should not be confused with *netting out,* which is a term used to describe the amount sellers want to receive on a sale. Sellers might say they want to net out $40,000 on their home. The broker now figures out how much the house must be sold for in order to receive the usual 6 percent commission ($42,550).

2. *What are your responsibilities when you sign a listing?*

You agree to pay a commission to a designated broker who brings in a buyer *ready, willing,* and *able* to purchase on the terms you've agreed upon. You also normally agree to allow the broker to procure this buyer in any legitimate way and to accept a deposit for you. (See danger 9 below.)

Ready, willing, and *able* are the key words. They are generally taken to mean the following: *Ready* means that the buyers are ready to show that they are in earnest by putting up a substantial deposit in cash (usually over $500); *willing* means that at the appropriate time the buyers have made an offer to purchase in writing; *able* means that the buyers have the cash or the ability to borrow to pay the full purchase price.

If you decide not to sell, you normally are not obligated to pay a commission unless the agent procures the buyer for the *same price* you have listed for and under the *same terms* of your listing agreement. For example, if you list for $40,000 and the offer is for $37,500, the agent has not fulfilled the listing agreement. Or, if you asked for all cash to you from the sale and the agent brings in a buyer who wants to pay

10 percent cash down, obtain an 80 percent mortgage, and have you carry back a 10 percent second mortgage, again the agent has not fulfilled the exact terms of your listing agreement.

This does not mean you can sell for different terms and thereby avoid a commission. Normally the agent will have a commission clause in the sales agreement. When you sign that agreement, you automatically agree to pay the commission.

You don't agree to sell your house—you can't be forced to sell if you don't want to just because you signed a normal listing agreement. If, however, you decide not to sell while the listing is in force, you may have to pay the agent a commission anyhow if he or she lives up to the broker's end of the agreement. (Beware of any listing agreement which empowers the agent to sign a sales agreement for you!)

3. *Is the listing in writing?*

At this time, the following twenty-two states require that a listing must be in writing to be enforceable: Arizona, California, Hawaii, Idaho, Indiana, Kentucky, Louisiana, Michigan, Minnesota, Mississippi, Montana, Nebraska, New Jersey, New Mexico, North Dakota, Ohio, Oklahoma, Oregon, Texas, Utah, Washington, and Wisconsin (plus the District of Columbia and the province of Ontario, Canada). In the other states, a verbal listing may still be given. Beware of verbal listings. They breed misunderstanding. In a state where they are still allowed, it is usually possible for you to list your property merely by telling a broker that he or she can find a buyer for you at a specific price. If the agent subsequently finds a buyer who is ready, willing, and able to buy and you haven't revoked the verbal listing, it might cost you a commission.

It is always best to have everything in writing. Parties to any contract, even a listing, tend to forget what they have agreed upon, particularly after a period of time. Having a written record helps to eliminate disagreements.

4. *Does the listing have an expiration date?*

Most exclusive rights to sell will have a clause which says something like, "This listing to expire on _____" (a date is written in here). Others will say, "30-60-90 days from the above date." The agent will cross out the inappropriate numbers and have you, the seller, initial the spot.

This clause is for your benefit. It means that the broker has only a specified amount of time to find a buyer. If the broker fails, you have the option of getting another broker, rehiring your former one, or taking your house off the market.

Some listing agreements don't have expiration dates. In such a case you should *write in* a specific date. If you don't, the listing may be presumed to run on indefinitely until canceled. You may forget to cancel and be stuck for a commission long after you had decided not to sell. Ninety days is the longest you should give a listing. If a broker works hard during that period, yet there is still no sale, you can then give another ninety days. If the broker doesn't work hard, you'll want a different broker anyhow.

5. *Is the listing dated in your presence?*

Occasionally agents, particularly when you are putting a house on multiple listing, will leave out the date. They may say nothing, pretending it's an oversight, or they might ask it to be left out until they get to the office and have the agreement retyped. They may intend to keep the listing for themselves for a few days or a few weeks before they let it go on multiple and let other brokers work on it, hoping not to have to split the commission. If you want all the brokers to work on it, be sure the listing is dated.

Another reason is that the listing could conceivably be for a much longer time if not dated. For example, if the listing contains a clause, "Listing to expire 90 days from the above date," and the date is not put on the listing until thirty days after you sign, the agent has effectively extended the listing another month.

6. *Can you guarantee that the broker will work hard for you?*

None of us can really guarantee the action of another individual. Nonetheless, there are some safeguards we can take. Most listing agreements contain a clause which may read something like, "Agent agrees to work diligently to procure a purchaser, including advertising of property at his or her discretion, and that these endeavors shall constitute a good and sufficient consideration for this agreement." Many sellers take this to mean that the broker has agreed to advertise their property. This is not so. This agreement is included in the listing to make it *bilateral* rather than *unilateral* (see Chapter 4) and is inserted to prevent you from arbitrarily canceling the listing. This clause does not guarantee that your broker will advertise your property or even work hard at selling it.

Some sellers have taken to adding their own clause or addendum to the listing. This often specifies the amount of advertising the agent agrees to perform in exchange for receiving the listing. It might include a reference to the property with a note that in consideration for taking the listing, the agent agrees to advertise in a certain newspaper so many times per month (perhaps four or five times), with each ad identifying the property by location, price, and terms. Some buyers add that the agent must run a photo of the property with the ad in at least one issue a month.

It is not clear whether such a condition would allow a purchaser to avoid paying a commission to a broker who did not run such an ad, yet found a buyer, or would allow a seller to cancel a listing to a broker who did not run the ad. Nonetheless, it would give the agent a moment's thought before deciding to forget about your property. And it would give you, the seller, a tremendous bargaining position in case the broker refused to work hard.

7. *Do you understand the terms of the listing agreement?*

The agent, under a listing, must obey instructions. However, since it is often the agent who writes in the instructions, a seller's protections here can be severely inhibited, unless the seller carefully checks over the terms of the sale. It is difficult for an average seller to know whether the agent is writing in something appropriate to what the seller wants unless he or she knows something about real estate financing. Since it is not within the realm of this book to discuss financing, it is suggested the seller consult one of the many books on this subject that are widely available. I consider an excellent choice to be *How to Buy and Sell Real Estate for Financial Security,* by my favorite author (New York: McGraw-Hill, 1975). In general, however, an inexperienced seller will probably do best to check each item the broker puts down, ask for an explanation, and add up the figures to make sure the arithmetic is correct.

For example, the agent may write on the listing agreement, under terms, "10 + 10 and 80 percent." This is a kind of shorthand that means the seller will accept 10 percent cash down and will take back a 10 percent second loan and the buyer will have to come up with an 80 percent loan for the balance. Don't let the agent use this shorthand. Make sure that everything is written out so that you can understand it. And make sure that you really are willing to take back part of the selling price in the form of a loan before it is put in the listing agreement. Once it's down in writing and you sign, you're probably committed to it.

8. *Does the listing have an automatic extension?*

Most exclusive rights to sell include a *carry-over* clause. This is inserted to protect the broker from deceit by the seller. The clause usually states that if the seller goes through with a sale to a prospect *originally procured* by the broker, the seller must pay a commission, even *after* the listing expires. This is only fair, and it protects brokers who may have worked hard and found a buyer, only to have the buyer and seller agree to wait until the listing expires before they finish the sale and then split the commission between them.

Be sure this clause contains an expiration date, such as "within six months after expiration of this listing" (three to six months is standard). If there is no expiration date, you might be liable for a commission to buyers who came back on their own even a year after a listing expired.

Some unscrupulous brokers have included a different type of carry-over clause in their listings. It states that the listing will continue in force after the agreed-upon termination date, until canceled by the seller. Don't allow such clauses in your listing. If your agent hasn't sold your home in ninety days, you'll very likely want a new agent.

9. *Are you getting the lowest commission rate?*

Many sellers want to know what the "official" commission rate is. An honest broker will answer that it is the rate most houses are listed for in the area. It is important to remember, however, that there is no one commission rate that is specifically ordained by law. The agent gets as much as he or she can from the seller.

It may often happen that an agent will say something to the effect of, "I won't work on any listing for less than . . ." (and here name a percentage figure). I see nothing wrong with this. The agent is merely stating his or her lowest price and giving the seller the option of accepting or refusing it. Nonetheless, many sellers still feel the need to know what a "typical" agent's rate is.

The typical rate around the country for residential property is probably 6 percent. Fifteen years ago it was 5 percent, and many agents are now insisting on 7 percent. There is nothing wrong with trying to get a higher rate (although I certainly wouldn't pay it!) unless an agent tells you it's the law and you have to pay it. If this happens, escort that agent out the door and have no more to do with that company.

If you are not sure about the rate in your area, call several real estate offices. You'll find out the going rate pretty quickly.

Should you insist on less than the going rate—4 or 5 percent instead of 6 or 7 percent?

The answer must be, in general, no! The reason is simple. You get what you pay for. Your goal is to sell your house, and you need an agent's services to do it or you wouldn't be signing a listing. It is foolish now to try and beat down the wages of the very person who you are asking for help. If you were the agent and had a dozen listings at 6 percent and one at 4 percent, to which one would you devote the least amount of time? The $400 or $500 you may save by a smaller commission rate may be more than eaten up by a longer wait for a sale and then a lower offer.

The exception to the above rule is when you have a very marketable piece of property, a "perfect home" that'll sell itself. If you don't want to take the time or bother to sell by owner or if you're unsure of handling the transaction, by all means haggle over the commission. A commission of 2 or 3 percent is more than enough for a home that will sell itself. Just be sure you do have the "perfect house" (see Chapter 13).

10. *Who gets a forfeited deposit?*

Almost all listing agreements empower the agent to accept a deposit on the purchase of the home for the seller. Make sure you specify that the deposit is to be received in *cash* or *cashier's* or *banker's check* only. Many listing agreements will simply say the agent is empowered to receive a deposit (unspecified) or a deposit that may be cash, personal check, or promissory note.

You want to be sure your buyers are ready to buy your house, and the way they present evidence of this is by offering hard cash. A personal check may be drawn on insufficient funds or payment may be stopped. A promissory note is just a promise to pay, and you'd have the expense of taking the buyer to court if you had to collect on it.

But, there's another reason to insist on cash or a banker's check. It often happens that a buyer will have only a personal check on hand or will only be able to give a promissory note. If you've allowed the agent to accept these in the listing agreement and they're not good, it's usually up to *you* to collect. If you haven't allowed the agent to accept them and he or she does, it's usually up to the *agent* to collect. This forces agents, out of self-protection, to screen buyers carefully and select only those who are qualified.

The big problem with deposits, however, comes when a deal falls through, that is, when a buyer is found, a sales agreement is signed by both buyer and seller, and for any of a thousand reasons, the buyer backs out of the deal. The deposit is usually forfeited. The question is then: Who gets it?

It's amazing the number of threats and bad words that can pass between an agent and a seller over a $500 deposit. To avoid these, it is best to specify who gets the deposit in the event of forfeiture right in the listing agreement.

Some brokers have recently taken to inserting a clause specifying that the agent receives the full amount of a forfeited deposit. This is blatantly unfair. The deposit is on a house owned by the seller, and the seller should be entitled to it. On the other hand, the agent may have expended considerable time and money procuring the buyer, and the sale may have fallen through because of conditions beyond the agent's control. A happy compromise is to agree in writing in the listing that any forfeited deposit is to be split evenly between seller and agent, but under *no circumstances* is the broker to get more than the agreed-upon commission.

Finally, a deposit is often forfeited because of the worst possible circumstances for the buyer—illness, a death in the family, loss of employment. Under such circumstances, I recommend that the entire deposit be returned. In most cases a good agent will go along with this.

After all, you're trying to sell your house, not make money out of some-one else's suffering and misery.

On the other hand, buyers may just change their minds for no apparent good reason. They may arbitrarily decide they no longer like the house or want to buy. If this happens, by all means keep the deposit. These buyers need to be taught a lesson about the seriousness of real estate dealings.

11. *Did you get a copy of the listing agreement?*

Almost all listing agreements contain the statement "Seller acknowledges receipt of a copy of this listing agreement." Some agents, however, don't supply you with a copy of what you have signed. They may not offer it, or they may say they need one, the office needs one, and there aren't enough to go around. Or they may say they'll take the agreement back to the office, have it run off on a copying machine, and send a copy to you.

Don't let them leave until you get a copy. Only two copies are needed —one for the agent and one for the seller. If the agent wants more copies for the office, let the agent run those off on the copying machine. The reason an agent may not want to leave you with a copy is you may get to reading the fine print and not like what you see, particularly if there is a clause inside against your interests. No honest agent will object to your keeping a copy. He or she will want you to look over what you've signed.

Remember, if you sign a statement that you've received a copy, and then you don't get one, you have little recourse. If there is a dispute and the matter should get to court, the agent can swear you received a copy, and your signature is there to back up the claim.

Finally, be sure the agent actually signs your copy. Don't accept a carbon of the agent's signature. It takes only a moment for the agent to resign on your copy, and that signature is your guarantee that the agent will live up to the terms of the listing.

12. *Have you tried to hide anything from your agent?*

The agent will want to know of any *liens* on your property. These are outstanding loans, taxes, judgments—anything encumbering or tying up the title. Give the agent the *exact amount* now due on any loans you have; don't approximate. The agent will want to know the dimensions of your lot. Get the plot plan you received when you bought your home so that the agent can put down the *exact dimensions*. The agent may want to know whether any zoning changes have been recently passed or are pending. Give the agent the full information you have and make sure it's put into the listing. The agent will want to know whether there are any boundary disputes with neighbors or anyone else. Tell the agent of any such disputes and make sure they are noted. This will also help the agent get them cleared up before a sale.

And most important, if there are any conditions about your house which could be considered dangerous, such as faulty wiring, bad plumbing, or a broken roof beam, make sure the agent knows *in writing*. The agent may insert in the listing agreement a statement about the defect, such as, "Owner will fix bad electrical plug in kitchen before closing."

If, for some reason, your agent neglects to ask about such items, bring them up yourself. Don't hide any problems.

What you, the seller, are doing here is relieving yourself of responsibility in the event a deal goes sour. If you tell the agent and the agent doesn't tell the buyer, it's probably the agent's fault. It may even be the agent's fault if you didn't tell and the agent forgot to ask something obvious, but don't take any chances. Tell all and be safe. You'll save money, heartache, and perhaps even a lawsuit in the long run. (See Chapter 12 for more details.)

CHECKLIST OF LISTING DANGERS

1. Is the listing the kind you want (open, exclusive agency, right to sell, multiple, or net)? Has your attorney looked it over?

2. Do you know your responsibilities?

3. Do you have the listing in writing?

4. Does the listing have a definite expiration date?

5. Is the starting date written in your presence?

6. Does the broker agree to work hard for you?

7. Do you understand all the terms of the listing? Are they written in plain English?

8. Are you sure the listing doesn't have an automatic extension?

9. Are you getting the lowest commission rate possible?

10. Do you get at least half the deposit if a buyer backs out of a deal?

11. Are you getting a signed copy of the listing agreement?

12. Are you sure you gave your agent *all* relevant information?

4

What to Do with the Broker Who Won't Work

After you've signed a listing agreement with an agent, you may discover that some disturbing things are happening. No buyers come by to see the house for weeks or even months. Or buyers come by, but when you talk to them you quickly discover that your house is much too expensive for them, or not nearly as elaborate as they want, or not even the type of house they're looking for. When you check the papers, you discover that your home is almost never advertised. Or when you call the agent's office pretending to be a buyer looking for a house just like yours, you are told by a salesperson that no such house is on the market, but others are available.

All these situations are symptoms of an agent who isn't doing the job properly. You've signed the listing agreement in good faith, assuming the broker would now actively find you a buyer. Instead, the broker has put your listing on the back burner or doesn't care enough about it to send by qualified prospects. If the right buyer stumbles into the agent's office and demands your home, you might get a sale. Otherwise, it's a desperation wait for you.

Many brokers who don't actively work on their listings are simply incompetent. However, occasionally there's a reason for this inactivity. The broker may be trying to wait you out. Quite simply, this means the agent has decided that either your price is too high or your terms are too rigid. This agent knows that as time goes by without a sale, you will get more desperate. There is nothing more exhausting than uncertainty, and when you are uncertain about the sale of what is probably the biggest investment you will make in your lifetime, your home, you may find yourself accepting a lower price and less advantageous terms than you normally would. It is positively amazing how down in the dumps and ready to sell at any cost sellers can be when six weeks have gone by without so much as one real buyer having come by. But let just one buyer nibble and suddenly those sellers are alert and ready to protect their investment. By not showing your home, or by showing it to the wrong people, an agent may be waiting until you're depressed enough to lower your listing price or terms.

I once knew a broker, Van, who carried this to extremes. He would carefully judge the people who gave him listings. If they were not in good shape financially and needed a quick sale to get out of debt, Van would purposely not show their property. He would wait until he judged they would grasp at any straw. Then he would say something like this: "Since it's obvious that no one wants to buy your home and since when I took the listing I told you it would be sold quickly, I feel partly responsible. I feel it is only my duty to buy your house myself. Of course, I can't give you the full price because then I wouldn't be able to resell it. But if you really want to get out, here's my offer." Somehow Van's offer was always many thousands of dollars below market value. Once he bought the property, he would begin showing it to legitimate buyers and soon make a sale for a handsome profit. Van is an exception, but every so often brokers like him do crop up.

Although what Van did is basically immoral, it probably wasn't illegal. There is nothing wrong with a broker buying a listed piece of property as long as the seller is made fully aware of who's buying and all the terms and conditions of the sale. In this case, the sellers didn't care who was buying or at what cost. They only wanted out.

I wouldn't do business with Van and neither should you. The best way to avoid him is to follow the guidelines in Chapter 1 on getting a good broker.

If you've already got a broker who's a lemon, there are certain things you can and can't do to make your broker work.

Your first thought may be to get out of your listing and try to sign with someone else. A listing agreement, however, is a legal contract, and it may be very difficult to break. In theory, it would have been wise for you to have had your lawyer present when you signed, for he or she might have provided an escape hatch for you. However, in common practice, lawyers are rarely called in when a seller gives a listing. There are some actions you can still take.

1. *Tell the agent your feelings.* This is extremely important. Don't overlook the fact, simple though it may seem, that the agent may be unaware you expected harder work.

2. *Contact the agent a second and if necessary a third and fourth time.* It's an old adage that the squeaky wheel gets the oil. Become a squeaky wheel.

Bother the agent to the point where it becomes easier to work on your house than to have to argue with you.

3. *If these actions don't work, it's time to think about getting another agent.* Tell your broker you are dissatisfied, that you don't feel that his or her service will procure you a buyer and you want your listing back. If you're obstinate and won't be swayed by the broker's sweet words urging a second chance, you probably will get your listing back. A sour seller isn't going to do a broker much good. However, if you gave a multiple listing, the consent of the listing service may be needed to get your listing back. See suggestion 8.

4. *If the broker won't give back the listing, the easiest thing for you to do is to wait for your listing to expire.* Rarely are listings given for more than ninety days. This period is probably half gone by the time you discover you need another agent. It's seldom the case that a seller can't wait another six weeks.

5. *If you must sell immediately, find out from your lawyer whether there's any way to break the listing contract.* If there is, a letter from the attorney to the agent is usually sufficient.

6. *Find out whether your listing has a bilateral clause.* This might read something like, "As good and sufficient consideration for this agreement, I, (agent's name), agree to advertise, share this listing with other brokers, and otherwise expend my efforts to procure a buyer." In some states the clause includes the mention of $1 given in consideration by the broker to the seller. The importance of this clause is that it imposes a duty on the broker to advance the sale of the property in exchange for the listing—it makes the listing a two-way or bilateral agreement. Should your listing have no such clause, the broker is not obliged to advance the sale. (This is a unilateral or one-sided agreement.) If you don't have such a bilateral clause in your listing, you may be able to get out of the agreement simply by writing a notice of cancellation. If, however, your broker can show that he or she has already tried to find a purchaser, the listing might become bilateral in effect without the clause. Show your contract to your attorney and ask that this be checked out for you. Don't try to decide for yourself—it could cost you lost time and money.

7. *Find out whether your broker must advertise.* If you have inserted a paragraph in the listing (as mentioned in Chapter 3) in which the broker is obligated to advertise your property a specific number of times each month in a certain newspaper, you may have another out here. Again, check with your attorney. You may be able to bluff your agent into giving up the listing by pointing to the clause and threatening to go to court. But be prepared to follow through if the agent calls your bluff.

8. *Consider the threat of bad publicity.* Should your attorney advise you that you have no out from the listing, you are probably stuck with waiting out your broker. You still, however, have one alternative, but you should consider carefully before resorting to it. It will cost you time and a lot of effort and in the long run may get you nowhere. Your last alternative is to use publicity or the threat of it.

Real estate is very sensitive to public opinion. Agents are normally very concerned about their reputations. Complaining loud enough and long enough may get the broker to give your listing back just to avoid the bad publicity.

There are three sources to which you can complain, but from which the results are uncertain. It is very likely you can complain to the better business bureau or chamber of commerce in your city. These organizations, on your behalf, may call the broker and if not chastise the agent, at least ask for an explanation. This takes time on the broker's part and can be embarrassing to him. Sometimes a threat of going to these organizations is better than actually going.

You can contact the local real estate board, assuming your broker is a member. This may be a necessity if you have a multiple listing. Real estate boards usually function independently but are associated with the National Association of Realtors. You can find them by looking up "Real Estate Board" under your city listings in your phone directory. These groups tend to be very public relations–minded and often have grievance committees just to handle consumer complaints. Be prepared to state your case fully and to document it with evidence. These boards are often barraged with sour grapes complaints by buyers and sellers who didn't get what they wanted because they weren't really entitled to it. Also, the amount of work a broker should do on a listing is a very vague subject. The board will probably try to convince you that you've made a mistake. If you haven't, stand your ground. If you are persistent and loud, the board's next step will probably be to talk to your agent.

This puts your agent in the embarrassing spot of being judged by his or her own peers. Most agents would not like this to happen. Consequently, a threat to speak to the local board plus a follow-up phone call to the board may be sufficient. If it is not, however, and the board talks to your agent, you may be worse off than before. If the agent were now to give back your listing it would seem like admitting guilt.

Once the board talks to the agent and discovers your only complaint is that the broker is not working hard enough, a very subjective judgment on your part, particularly since you're not in the business (and you can expect this to be pointed out to you), nothing more to your advantage may happen here, although your broker may be quietly chastised for getting the board involved. Remember, however, if you scream loud enough, even though you may not have a leg to stand on, the broker may give your listing back just to avoid bad publicity. Now, however, you'll have trouble finding another broker to take it and put it on the multiple.

Finally, you can threaten to take your case to the real estate commissioner of your state (see appendix for addresses). This sounds better than it actually is. The real estate commission usually is concerned with law violations. If your broker hasn't really broken any law, there is little that the state can do. However, the threat of such action may get you the desired result.

Ultimately, it is best not to get a listing with a bad broker in the first place. If you're in it, though, and your attorney says you can't break it in court, threatening bad publicity is still your last, best bet. Rant and rave loud enough and any good broker will usually give you back your listing. (Of course, if you had a good broker, you wouldn't want your listing back, would you?)

5

Don't Confuse Your Personal Property with Your Real Property

In real estate all types of property can be divided into two groups. The land and everything connected to it, including improvements such as a house and even the air space above it, are considered *real property*. Everything else, including money, clothes, furniture, and television set, is normally considered *personal property*.

When you sell your home, you are normally selling only your real property. If any personal property is to go with the sale of the real property, it should be carefully itemized and noted on both the listing and the sales agreements. This seems simple enough, but it can present problems. Consider the story of Arlie, a seller I once knew.

Several months before he listed his house Arlie had gone to Mexico and bought a large Tiffany-style lamp. This he securely attached to the ceiling of his family room. Since there was no socket there, he installed the lamp right in the ceiling, doing the necessary rewiring himself. He was very fond of the lamp and intended to take it with him when he moved.

Arlie's house was duly sold. On moving day Arlie removed the Tiffany-style lamp. Since there was no ceiling socket, when Arlie took out the lamp he left a neat but rather ugly hole.

The buyers arrived and immediately noticed that the lamp was gone. They called Arlie and the agent, saying they bought the house only because of the lamp (a most unlikely story) and they insisted it be returned.

Did they get it back?

Yes. They were able to show that the lamp fit the three basic criteria of a *fixture,* a piece of personal property attached to real property in such a way that it became part of the real property. First, they showed that the *character* of the lamp was such that it required a permanent attachment to a ceiling. Secondly, they pointed to the hole and observed that the lamp had been *permanently affixed,* for its removal had damaged the real property (it had left a hole). And finally they pointed out that Arlie's *intent* must have been to make the lamp a part of the real property; otherwise he would have simply displayed it near the ceiling without drilling holes and rewiring, all done during the few months between the time he bought the lamp and sold his house.

Now consider the case of another seller. Jason was selling his two-story, older home in a fine residential section of the city. He had lived in the house himself for nearly thirty-five years. During this time he had built a very fine clothes line in the backyard. This clothes line was exceptional. It was made of 2-inch steel T-poles placed more than 20 feet apart and sunk 2 feet into the ground. It had wire lines that would support the heaviest blankets. Just before he listed his house, Jason carefully dug up the poles and laid them on the ground where they had previously stood. Then he carefully filled in the holes so that it was difficult to tell where the poles had been. Then he listed.

The buyer for Jason's house admired many things about the property, not the least of which was the steel clothes line in the back yard. She carefully noted it, thinking how useful it would be.

Imagine the buyer's surprise the day she took possession (after the sale had closed) when she found that the seller had removed the clothes line with his other personal effects. She called the broker and the seller and threatened to sue both unless her property, her *real* property, was returned.

Did she get the clothes line?

No. Jason was a smart seller. He knew that having the poles *in* the ground convincingly made them part of the real property. But by removing them before he listed, he changed them from real to personal property. Of course, he was being a bit sneaky by leaving them on top of the ground, but as he pointed out, he only did it so that any buyer could see how conveniently a clothes line would fit in the yard. The fixture had become personal property.

The thing to remember here is that a buyer will consider everything attached to a house as part of the real property unless you, the seller, describe it as personal property and exclude it from the sale. Here is a list of some of the things to watch out for:

1. *Lamps.* Before you list, remove any lamp that you wish to take with you. If removing it damages the property, *replace* it with a cheaper or different lamp. The lamp the buyers see with the house is the lamp they will expect to get.

2. *Built-in refrigerators, stoves, ovens, dishwashers, break-front cabinets, etc., that look permanent.* The buyer will assume these go with the house. If you intend to take them with you, you should give the buyer notice, or else you will have complaints and potentially a lawsuit. Although you may win, it will undoubtedly cost you time and money.

3. *Trees, bushes, shrubs.* If you intend to take with you any items planted in the yard, you should note that they are excluded from the sale.

4. *Television antennas.* If your antenna can be unplugged without damaging the real property, let the buyers know you are taking it; otherwise they will have an unpleasant surprise when they turn on their television. And they may take this up with you in the form of an angry phone call at 11 o'clock at night.

5. *Drapes, curtains, wall coverings of any sort.* The same precautions apply to these items.

Some sellers will show prospective buyers a list of personal property and offer to sell it to them separately from the sale of the house. They hope to get more money without actually jacking up the price. Don't do it! This plan almost always backfires in the following way:

When Louis sold his home in an arid section of the Southwest, he had three air conditioners installed in the windows of the master bedroom, the living room, and the family room. They were installed in such a way that they could be unplugged and removed without damaging the windows in any way. Louis offered to sell them to any buyer for $250 apiece.

When a buyer finally made an offer, it included a clause which made inclusion of the three air conditioners a part of the sale, without any additional compensation to Louis. The smart buyer was making the units in effect real property by including them in the sales agreement. Louis said, no, he wanted $750 for the units. The buyer said he would buy the house only if they were thrown in. Louis wanted to sell, and so he eventually conceded and let them go.

The best way to avoid any problems with personal property is to remove it before buyers see the house. What buyers don't see, they won't desire.

Protect your personal property during the listing period. When you list—particularly when you list on a multiple service—your broker will most likely ask your permission to put a lock box or similar device on your home. The purpose of the lock box (in which a key to your home is placed) is to allow the broker and other agents who are cooperating on the listing to show your home when you are not present.

Many homeowners are skeptical about such a service. They reason that their home will not be in perfect condition, all cleaned up, unless they know in advance when a buyer is coming by. They may also be somewhat hesitant to allow strange people to wander through their home, even in the presence of an agent.

While such fears may have some justification, they are usually outweighed by the agent's problems in selling your house. Agents rarely have more than a few minutes notice that a buyer wants to see a particular piece of property. The agent may receive a phone call from a buyer who saw the sign and wants to see the house right now. Or the agent may be showing another house and realize that this buyer would be perfect for yours.

Buyers won't wait a day or even half a day while you mop the kitchen floor, rake the leaves, and wash the windows. A buyer who is hot to buy wants to see the house immediately. And, if you're really sincere about selling, you should be willing to show your house on a moment's notice.

I always suggest using a lock box, although on very rare occasions there can be some risk involved. Recently, a case was widely reported in which a mother-daughter team operated a burglary racket relying on the lock box. The mother would telephone an agent and make an appointment to see a home. She would pretend not to like the property and ask the agent to show her several more. The agent would happily agree. Since it was the middle of the day, the owners of many of the homes would be away. The agent would enter these homes via the lock box and the burglary would be committed as follows: The mother would walk through the home keeping the agent's attention by asking lots of questions. The daughter would tag along behind, just out of sight, scooping whatever valuables she could find into a large handbag she brought along just for that purpose. After a half dozen houses or so, the agent would give up and they would part company. It would not be until hours later when the owner came home and noticed items were missing that a burglary was even suspected.

Although most of the time the agent probably was liable for the loss, the homeowner still suffered the grief and discomfort associated with such a theft. And, if heirlooms or other irreplaceable items were taken, the loss was permanent.

There are certain obvious things you can do to protect yourself. During the listing period (if your house is well priced, this should be short) make a supreme effort to have your house ready all the time. Second, if you have valuable items that are not insured or that cannot be replaced because of sentimental value, remove them from sight. And tell your agent about any precious art works or other such items. Usually agents will go out of their way to protect themselves by protecting your property.

An important thing to keep in mind is that buyers don't like to have sellers around when they look at a house. They like to wander around and pretend the house is already theirs. They like to get the feel of it. You stand a better chance of selling when you're not there than when you are.

6

Hazards in the Sales Agreement

The sales agreement goes by many names: deposit receipt, binder, purchase agreement, or preliminary contract. It is the first document that binds the seller to the buyer. It starts the final phase of selling a house called *closing*. What terms and conditions are written in the sales agreement will bind you through escrow until the deed is transferred to the buyers and you receive your money.

Since escrow is based on the sales agreement, it should be apparent that this agreement is the critical document, the key to the real estate transaction. If it is executed improperly, if it has terms or conditions that you cannot fulfill or that are not to your benefit, you could lose time and money, not to mention getting an ulcer in the process. Some of the hazards you are likely to run into are explained in this chapter along with clues to protecting yourself.

1. *Should an attorney look over the sales agreement?*

The answer here is a simple and unqualified yes. A sales agreement is the single most important document (outside of the deed itself) that you are likely to sign in a real estate transaction. To protect yourself, you should have an attorney examine the sales agreement *before* you sign.

A word must be said, however, about the differences in real estate practices in various parts of the country. In the East it is more common for a lawyer to examine a sales agreement before it is signed. A lawyer also usually examines the title report and prepares the important documents, such as the deed or second mortgage. This practice is so common, in some areas, that in Massachusetts, for example, it is apparently illegal for a broker to advise a buyer or seller against using a lawyer. Indeed, many attorneys are well versed in real estate and derive a significant portion of their business from real estate transactions.

Real estate practice on the West Coast and in other parts of the country, however, is considerably different. A lawyer rarely becomes involved in a transaction unless something goes awry and there are threats of a lawsuit. An agent commonly fills out the sales agreement, and a clerk in an escrow office prepares all the documents. Lawyers tend to be less familiar with the ins and outs of real estate transactions. On the East Coast if you didn't want to use the services of a lawyer, your action might be thought strange (if not foolhardy); a similar reaction on the West Coast might occur if you did insist on an attorney.

Agents and lawyers in recent years have sometimes quarreled over who should have authority to fill out documents such as the sales agreement. Because legal rights and obligations are involved, lawyers have often taken the position that, as officers of the court, they are in the best position to protect buyer and seller. Agents have often held that in order to get buyer and seller to sign, that is, to get a sale, they need to have some right to handle the sales agreement. The laws on the matter vary from area to area and are made up of common practice and precedent-setting cases. In the Colorado case of *Conway-Bogue Investment Co. v. Denver Bar Association,* the state supreme court questioned:

> Should the defendants, as licensed real estate brokers [none of whom were licensed attorneys] be enjoined from preparing in the regular course of their business the instruments enumerated above [common real estate forms], at the requests of their customers and only in connection with transactions involving real estate, loans on real estate or the leasing of real estate, which transactions are being handled by them?

The court's answer was in the negative.

Other courts have held that a real estate broker is customarily allowed only to *fill in the blanks* on a printed sales agreement form which is in common use in the area.

In actual practice brokers usually do fill in the blank spaces on a form. Usually the agent's lawyers have previously prepared the form that is used. Nonetheless, to ensure that their interests are protected, every seller and buyer would be wise to consult with an attorney before signing a sales agreement.

Note: According to the statute of frauds in every state, real estate sales contracts must be in writing to be enforceable.

2. *Is the deposit big enough?*

As the seller, you should want the buyer to put up as large a deposit as possible. If the buyer were to put up the entire down payment on your home, it would not be too much, for you. The deposit is the guarantee that the buyer will pursue the deal to its closing. Under no circumstances would I take a deposit of less than $500, and $1000 would be better. If a buyer is intending to purchase a $40,000 house, for example, it shouldn't be too much to ask the buyer to put up one-fortieth of the amount as a deposit.

There is also the matter of the form of the deposit. Cash, a cashier's check, or a bank draft is fine. A personal check is not as good, but I find it acceptable if drawn to the broker's account (see discussion under listings in Chapter 3). For me, a promissory note (a promise to pay an amount at a future date) is definitely out. If the buyer eventually refused to go through with the deal and refused to make payment on the promissory note, my only alternative would be to go to court—an expensive proposition, particularly for an amount under $1000.

The whole purpose of a deposit is to act as a kind of hostage on the buyer's good intention to perform. Just as in a war, no soldier would accept a piece of paper with the word *hostage* written on it in lieu of an actual person, neither would I as the seller accept a note in place of cash.

It should be pointed out that some sellers insist on the deposit check being made out to their name. This may be their right, but it has certain disadvantages for the buyer. If the check goes to the seller, who cashes it, and the deal falls through with no blame to the buyer, the buyer might have considerable trouble getting the deposit back. On the other hand, there should be no problem getting it back from an agent. Agents are required by law in more than forty states to maintain special trust funds for holding deposits. It is usually a crime for them to commingle trust money with their own money. Money deposited into such a trust fund is usually secure because the agent stands to lose his or her license if it is improperly handled. Letting the buyer draw the deposit check to the broker's trust account is a good idea because it keeps the buyer from becoming suspicious of the seller's motives—such suspicions can lead to the loss of an otherwise sound deal.

Finally, regardless of what the listing agreement said, the sales agreement should spell out what is to happen to the deposit money in the event the buyer reneges on the deal. Usually there is a paragraph stating that if the buyer fails to purchase as stipulated, the deposit is forfeited. In such a situation, the seller usually has three options: (1) Sue the buyer for *specific performance,* that is, force the buyer to complete the purchase. (2) Resell the property and then sue the buyer for any loss in difference in price between the first and second sales. (3) Keep the deposit as liquidated damages. The agreement also usually specifies that in the last event, seller and broker will split the deposit (as long as the broker doesn't receive more than the commission amount).

3. *Is the buyer properly identified?*

In some sales agreements the buyer's name (usually called the *vendee*) is left blank. The broker can write it in at a later date. Or the buyer's name might be entered as "John Doe." This usually means that before the sale closes, the sales agreement will be assigned to another party.

Beware of such blank or undisclosed buyers. The agent may actually be buying the home and not want you, the seller, to know. This might mean you are selling too low and the agent can resell and make a quick profit. An agent who buys your property is normally required to make a full disclosure of that fact.

There is another, similar reason for not identifying the buyer. The actual purchaser may be planning to quickly resell your house for a profit. This buyer may not be planning to put up any money at all! Consider the case of Tillie and Sam:

Tillie and Sam made a living out of "double escrowing." They would find a house that was underpriced and then make a ridiculously low offer. Every so often a seller, desperate to get out, would accept. Tillie and Sam would use a different method of buying "blank." They would write their names in the deposit receipt and immediately behind them write "or to whomever they assign." Such a note of assignment probably wasn't necessary, but Tillie and Sam wanted to be careful. They gave a promissory note as a down payment and insisted on a ninety-day escrow. Then they set out to find a legitimate buyer. They would even show the house (the seller often unaware of whom they were bringing by). Tillie and Sam managed a large apartment building, so they would often have one of their tenants already lined up as a buyer.

When a legitimate buyer was found, Tillie and Sam would sign a separate sales agreement with them and open a second escrow. Then they would assign their first sales agreement to the new buyer, who would put a cash deposit and down payment into escrow. When the legitimate buyer had fulfilled all the requirements of the second escrow, and the sellers had fulfilled their requirements in the first escrow, Tillie and Sam would close both escrows simultaneously. The title to the property would pass from the seller to the legitimate buyer. The money would pass from the legitimate buyer (via down payment and new mortgage) to the seller. But since Tillie and Sam sold for a higher amount than they bought, the legitimate buyer was paying more than the legitimate seller was getting. Tillie and Sam would pocket the difference, often a sizable amount. In one instance, Tillie and Sam bought a home for $31,500 and sold it by means of a double escrow for $38,000. The legitimate buyer got the house, the seller got $31,500, and Tillie and Sam got the difference, $6500.

The beauty of this scheme is that our real estate hucksters never had to put up a single dime. The legitimate buyer always put up the down payment and arranged for the loan. The deposit was a promissory note. If, for some reason, Tillie and Sam couldn't find a buyer within the ninety days, they simply forfeited their deposit. But since their deposit was a piece of paper with "promise to pay" written on it, in essence they forfeited nothing. They refused to pay, and as far as I know only one seller ever took them to court to collect.

Needless to say, such tactics are almost always harmful to a seller, who usually gets much less than the property warrants. Many states have even made the practice of double escrowing illegal unless the seller is made fully aware of what's happening.

Of course, if you are getting all cash, are not taking back a second from the buyer, and are satisfied with the sales price, you may not care who is assigned the sales agreement. On the other hand, if the buyer is giving you a second as part of the sales price, you will want to be very careful who buys. You will want to be sure the buyer can actually pay you the money.

There are several common ways to avoid such problems. One way is to have the buyer fully identified, including address. Probably the best way is to have a clause inserted which specifies that the sales agreement is not assignable.

4. *Is the price accurate?*

Somewhere on the sales agreement, usually close to the top, should be listed the full purchase price. This is the total amount of money the buyer is putting up for the real property (although a separate sum of money may be paid either in or out of escrow for personal property—see Chapter 5). It stands to reason that you should check this item first. Make sure it's accurate. Severely question any suggestion from the agent that adding up all the terms of the agreement will actually give you more than this amount. Although this is possible through prorations and impound accounts (see Chapter 11), the down payment, including deposit, plus all the mortgages should equal the price.

Also, be very careful of "ballooning." See Chapter 9 for a detailed explanation of this practice.

5. *Are the buyer and the house qualified?*

Even if legitimate buyers put up a legitimate deposit, they may not be able to purchase your home unless they can qualify for a substantial loan (unless, of course, it's an all-cash deal). Usually sales agreements allow buyers a certain amount of time to get a mortgage commitment from a lending institution, often two weeks. But during those two weeks, your house will in effect be off the market. If the buyers never really had any chance to qualify, you've wasted precious time. Therefore, you should receive some basic credit information about the buyers before you sign the deposit receipt.

While a complete discussion of real estate financing and buyer qualifying would itself probably fill a book this size, there is certain basic information you should know to help you decide whether a buyer can get a loan.

A. Almost all lending institutions require that a borrower of a real estate loan be making in gross income a minimum of four times the monthly payment, less any long-term expenses such as a car payment. If the payments are going to be $400 a month including taxes, principal, and interest on the loan, the buyer should be making $1600 a month before taxes. In the past many lending institutions would count only a husband's salary. Today, many will count both spouses' incomes as long as the wife draws a salary from a full-time profession (as a secretary, teacher, or salesperson, for example) and not from temporary or part-time work (such as baby sitting).

B. Most lending institutions will not approve a buyer who cannot show good credit. This means the buyer must have borrowed money in the recent past (via bank loans, credit cards, personal loans, etc.) and paid it back when due. Even one repossession or several late payment notes can cause a rejection of the mortgage.

C. A buyer applying for a loan which is insured by the Federal Housing Administration must intend to live in the house (and not rent it out). A buyer applying for a loan guaranteed by Veteran's Administration must have been on active duty in the military service during specific prescribed dates. (See Chapter 18.)

D. The buyer must show, in addition to income, that he or she has worked steadily for a minimum of the past three years, preferably at the same job. If the buyer held different jobs, each job should have been at an increased salary.

E. The buyer must show that he or she has sufficient money in the bank or in cash to make the down payment without resorting to additional borrowing.

This information is of a highly confidential nature. However, you should have no qualms about asking a buyer for it. You need to know before you tie up your house. The buyer will have to provide it in any event to get the desired loan, and a good agent will have found out this information before taking a deposit. An agent who brings in a sales agreement without knowing the above information hasn't properly qualified the buyer, and your sale could be in jeopardy. It is wasting everyone's time to sign a sales agreement only to find out that the buyer can't possibly qualify for a needed loan.

The second part of question 5 concerns your house, that is, does your house qualify for the desired loan? Often lending institutions will offer to loan 80 percent of the sales price, up to a maximum amount on a home. While this was formerly a satisfactory means of obtaining needed financing, problems have arisen recently. In the past few years, prices on homes have increased dramatically, but lending institutions have not always kept up. For example, suppose you are selling a house for $65,000 and discover that the lender will loan only 80 percent on a maximum sales price of $60,000. To make the sale, the buyer will have to come up with an additional $5000 in cash. If the buyer doesn't have the money and you don't lower the price, the sale could go out the window.

To avoid such situations, it is best, if possible, to find out beforehand whether your home is within the maximum lending amount of the lending institutions. If not, you will want to seek out the buyer with more cash and not waste time on deals that will fall through.

If the FHA, the VA, or a private mortgage insurer (PMI) is insuring the loan on your house there may be additional qualifications. The FHA requires that each home on which it insures a loan be appraised by an FHA appraiser. The FHA will not insure any loan on an amount over what its appraiser values the home. An FHA appraisal can take anywhere from two weeks to three months depending on the FHA's workload. If you sell on an FHA-insured loan it is best to get an appraisal well in advance of listing. Usually any bank will do this for you for a $50 fee. If you haven't got an FHA appraisal and the buyer wants to go that way, be careful; your house could be tied up for a lengthy period awaiting a valuation and then not sell if the appraisal comes in too low.

VA sales present a similar problem. In order to get a VA-approved loan, your house must be appraised by the VA. A certificate of reasonable value or CRV is then issued. This is the price a veteran may pay for your home. If your price is higher, the buyer must sign a form indicating that he or she is aware of this and then must make up the difference in cash that has not been borrowed. (See Chapter 2 for suggestions on getting a VA or FHA appraisal.)

A PMI loan works like a combination of VA and FHA loans. The difference is that a private insurance company instead of the government guarantees the loan. In a VA loan, the government guarantees the mortgage up to a maximum of $17,500. (If the loan were for $50,000, the VA, in theory, would pay off up to $17,500 and the lender would be stuck for the balance.) The FHA insures the full amount of the loan against loss. A PMI insures the top 20 to 25 percent, depending on how much insurance the lender wants. In the event of a default, for example, of a $50,000 loan the insurer would pay off $10,000 if the PMI was for 20 percent, and $12,500 if the PMI was for 25 percent.

The PMI insurer normally accepts the lender's appraisal, so there is no time lost waiting to get the house evaluated. However, only top-quality homes qualify for PMI loans. These are houses in the best neighborhoods that normally have at least three bedrooms and two baths and also have no detracting features. Probably less than half the homes in existence today would qualify for this type of loan. (A PMI loan is occasionally called an MGIC loan for the company which first started issuing them, Mortgage Guarantee Insurance Company.)

6. *Is the buyer's financing realistic?*

If a sales agreement proposes that a buyer obtain a new FHA loan and you've already discovered by means of an FHA appraisal that your house as it is does not qualify, you would reasonably not want to sign. There are, however, other less obvious conditions which might make the buyer's offer unrealistic and signing would again waste your time.

An inexperienced agent might bring in a buyer who wants to assume your current conventional mortgage. (A conventional mortgage is any mortgage other than a government-insured FHA or VA mortgage.) Prior to 1974, many lending institutions would allow assumption of existing loans with payment of a penalty fee. Basically this meant that the buyer would take over responsibility for repayment of your loan at the old interest rate. However, virtually all lending institutions have stopped this practice. Today almost all conventional mortgages for single-family homes contain an acceleration clause which allows the lender to accelerate the payments, that is, make the loan come due upon transfer of title. This means that a buyer probably cannot assume your existing financing. The lender will require a complete new credit report and will issue a new mortgage with a new up-to-date interest rate. If a buyer comes in with an offer and the sales agreement indicates the purchase depends on the buyer taking over your low-interest-rate conventional loan, you'd probably be better off forgetting the deal.

There are two exceptions. The first depends on the outside chance that your existing mortgage does not have an acceleration clause. If you bought the home within the last twenty years this is extremely unlikely, but you can check your mortgage papers. Usually the phrase "accelerate the payments in the event of transfer of title" indicates the clause. Secondly, if you have a VA- or FHA-insured loan, any buyer can assume it without any qualifying whatsoever, *at the old interest rate!* But beware, for if the buyer assumes such a loan, you, the seller, may not be relieved of liability. Should the new buyer fail to make the payments, the government may come after you to make them up.

It is possible to get a total release of indebtedness from such a mortgage. You must write your lender and/or the FHA or VA for permission. Usually the buyer must qualify as though applying for a brand new mortgage. The advantage, of course, is that the old interest rate may be retained.

7. *Will you be required to fix up your house as part of the sale?*

FHA and occasionally VA loans may require that the home being sold be brought up to local, state, or federal minimum health and safety codes before a loan will be granted. This could include installing a new water heater, repairing or installing a new roof, buying a new floor, repairing or altering windows, changing wiring, removing all old lead-based paint and repainting with nontoxic paint, or installing new plumbing. As you can see, this sort of repair work could be costly. If you agreed to allow a buyer to obtain a new FHA loan, you would probably be responsible for the entire cost of fixing the house—from a few dollars to several thousands of dollars. To protect themselves, in a situation where the FHA appraisal is not in and no one yet knows how much repair work may be required, many sellers include a limiting clause in their sales agreement. This usually reads something to the effect that the sale is subject to the seller not having to pay more than a certain amount to bring the home up to FHA minimum standards. This allows the seller to back out of the deal if the repair bill is abnormally high. Or to negotiate with the buyer and the broker about who is going to pay it.

8. *Are the points and other closing costs limited?*

In addition to the agent's commission, the seller normally has such other costs as:

Loan points (a point is 1 percent of the total loan amount)

Prorations of taxes, insurance, interest, rents, etc.

Title insurance fees

Escrow fees

Prepayment penalty on current loan

Outstanding liens

Fees for structural reports, surveys, etc.

Recording fees

Document preparation fees

Loan preparation fees

Attorney's fees

Appraisal fees

Title search fees

Other costs incurred in the sale

(An explanation of these costs as well as guidelines for their normal size is given in Chapters 11 and 24.)

As the reader may guess from the long list or may know from actual experience, closing costs can be very high, often more than the commission itself. One cost that might be saved, however, by proper care during the preparation of the sales agreement is the *prepayment penalty*. Very often lenders will waive this penalty on your old mortgage if the buyer agrees to take out a new mortgage from the same lender.

Wise sellers, particularly those who have sold before and have been stung by high closing costs, often resort to an effective means of limiting the amount they must pay. To work, however, this limiting must normally be considered in advance and carried out in the sales agreement. Usually a clause is inserted in the agreement which states that the purchase is subject to the seller's total closing costs including prorations and all other expenses not exceeding a certain amount. Some sellers, hoping to gain a profit on this, have a clause inserted which reads that they are not to pay *any* closing costs or that the buyer is to pay *all* costs. (FHA loans limit the buyer to paying no more than 1 point plus other closing costs.)

The immediate effect of such a clause is to limit the seller's costs. It, however, has other effects which might cause a deal to sour. Regardless of whether or not the seller pays them, the costs are there. If the seller doesn't pay, there are normally only two other parties to pay—the buyer or the agent. Most buyers will refuse to sign a contract with such a clause in it. They will insist that each party pay its own normal costs or even that the seller pay the buyer's costs. The limitation on closing costs now becomes a pawn in the bargaining over the sale of the property (see Chapter 4 on the art of price bargaining).

If both buyer and seller are adamant, occasionally a broker, to make the deal, will pay part of the closing costs out of the commission. This, however, is the option of the broker. If the broker chooses not to lose part of the commission, and neither buyer nor seller will pay these costs, there simply won't be enough money to go around and the deal will fall through.

Inserting a limiting clause in the deposit receipt can save the seller a considerable amount of money. The danger, of course, is that the sale may be lost in the process.

9. *Are the second mortgage terms spelled out?*

In many deals, the seller will take back a second mortgage. If this is going to happen in your case, it should be spelled out in the sales agreement. At minimum the agreement should include the following:

The total amount of the second mortgage

To whom it is to be paid

The exact interest rate

The full term (when it comes due and payable)

How it is to be repaid (monthly, semiannually, annually)

The amount to be repaid in each installment

Whether or not the above amount includes interest

Where it is to be repaid

This may seem like a lot to spell out, but an agent can usually fit it all into one or two lines. For a more thorough explanation of seconds see Chapter 8.

After the sales agreement is signed and before escrow closes, it will be necessary to have a note, deed of trust, mortgage paper, and/or other instruments made out to formalize the second mortgage. Be sure that this is done by a competent lawyer as mistakes here might invalidate the loan. As we have noted, on the West Coast this is often done by the escrow company's lawyers.

10. *Does the buyer have unrealistic contingency or subject-to clauses?*

Occasionally a buyer will make an offer that will have a clause in it containing the words *subject to,* for example, "purchase subject to the buyers selling their present residence." The words *subject to* mean that the sale is contingent upon whatever follows, in this case upon the sale of another house. If the buyers do not sell their current home, you have no deal.

Sometimes agents will urge sellers to accept this sort of offer, arguing that a bird in the hand is worth two in the bush. They may claim that any buyer is better than no buyer at all, even one who must sell his or her house before yours can be purchased. Don't be misled. Some buyers can be worse than no buyers. If you agree to this sort of contingency clause, you now have to worry about the sale of two homes instead of one—yours and the buyers'. And while your buyers are trying to sell their house, yours is off the market, preventing potentially better buyers from seeing it. I turn down such contingency clauses with one exception. *If* the buyer has already sold his or her house, and *if* the buyer's buyer has already qualified for a new loan, and *if* no problems are apparent in that escrow, I will sign. It often happens that buyers will sell their home and while the sale is in escrow go looking for a new one. They may even be holding up the close of escrow until another house is found. These are good buyers, and a clause allowing the sale of my home to be contingent on the sale of theirs is perfectly reasonable.

Buyers may insert other contingency clauses. A buyer may make the purchase subject to obtaining financing. Be sure the financing applied for is reasonable and the buyer can qualify. And then allow the buyer only a certain time to get the loan, say two weeks, so that your house is not off the market unreasonably long for a bad buyer.

A buyer may include a contingency clause making the property subject to a third party's approval of the deal. A husband wants to tie up your house until his wife, who is coming in on the train from across the country, can see it. Or a couple want their attorney or business manager to approve the house. If the buyer is solid, this may be a perfectly reasonable request, one which I would be willing to grant. There is nothing wrong with giving a solid buyer twenty-four hours to get a third party's approval as long as there are no other hot prospects (but under no circumstances would I allow them more than three days). However, I would make it clear that while this buyer is getting approval, I, the seller, will be willing to accept other offers contingent upon this first one falling through.

A buyer may request a contingency clause while a termite inspection or soil report or structural report is made. If your property is in an area of termite infestation, ground slippage, or earthquakes, such a request may be normal. As long as you're fairly sure your house will pass such an investigation, there should be no reason not to sign with such a clause, but again insist on a time limit, whatever is reasonable for having such a report made (usually not more than two weeks). If you know your house won't pass, don't waste time. Find a buyer who'll purchase as is.

Buyers may insist on other contingency clauses. Common sense here is the best bet. If the buyer seems solid and the request reasonable, I would be hard put not to go along, always of course, inserting a time limitation.

11. *Does the sales agreement have a time-is-the-essence clause?*

This is a clause which makes the timing of the contract an essential element. If it is included, then all the items in the contract which stipulate a certain time, such as the limiting clauses discussed above, will normally be understood to be specific and not extendable unless specifically authorized. If, however, no such clause is contained in the contract, the buyer might extend any of the times stated and you, as the seller, might have to go along, even in a court of law. Without such a clause, it might be interpreted that a two-week limitation, for example, was just a ballpark guess and that a reasonable extension was within the intent of the agreement. If time is not made essential in the sales agreement, all the limiting clauses you may insert may be meaningless.

Often sales agreements will include a *time-is-the-essence* clause and attach it to another clause which states that the broker has discretion to extend the time of performance of any item for a period not to exceed thirty days. This usually means that the broker may extend any limiting clause you may insert for up to thirty days in order to allow the buyer time to comply. Many agents feel this is essential in order to allow sales to be completed. In general it allows as much protection to the seller as to the buyer and so is usually a beneficial part of the agreement. However, if I want to be sure that a time-limiting clause I have inserted is upheld, I strike out the broker's extension privilege.

12. *Do you have to give a termite clearance?*

In certain areas of the country termite infestation is a severe problem and some lenders (particularly on FHA- and VA-insured loans) require proof that your home is free of them. The form of this proof is a report or *termite clearance* from a pest inspector. (For a further explanation see Chapter 10.)

In most areas of infestation, there will usually be some termite damage. Getting a clearance can involve replacing a single board or covering the house with a tent and fumigating it. The cost also can vary greatly. Normally it is up to the seller to pay for repair of any termite damage as well as for any costs involved in eliminating this pest. The buyer usually has to pay for any preventive work required.

Because at the time a sales agreement is signed the seller may not know how much damage, if any, has been done and what the cost will be, some sellers insert a clause limiting the amount they will pay to a set maximum. If the cost is higher than this amount, this contingency clause will allow them to back out of the deal and find a purchaser and lender who won't require termite work to be done.

13. *Do you have to warrant the appliances?*

The old rule in selling a house used to be *caveat emptor,* meaning "let the buyer beware." This rule has been modified in recent years by consumer awareness, and the change has been felt strongly in real estate in the area of home appliances.

In many parts of the country the seller must leave a sum of money, often $200 or more, in escrow for two weeks after the close to pay for any appliances the buyer finds are not in working order. Many buyers will want inserted in the sales agreement a clause that states the seller will warrant, or guarantee, the workability of all appliances in the home, including the water heater.

To my mind, this is totally unfair to the seller. It seems ridiculous to me, for example, that a seller, who has lived with a broken dishwasher for three years should have to repair it for a buyer, even when this seller tells the buyer before the sale that the dishwasher is not working. Purchasing a used home should be like purchasing a used car. Except for items that effect health or safety, there is no reason the seller should warrant the car or the house. The buyer who wants a guarantee on the appliances should buy a *new* house.

To counter this trend, sellers may have two alternatives. In areas where it is permissible, a seller may insert a clause in the sales agreement specifically insisting that the buyer take all the appliances on an as is basis. In other areas, certain real estate offices, usually the larger ones, will have appliance warranty insurance that the seller can purchase. Often agents from these offices will insist that the seller obtain the warranty insurance as a condition for taking the listing. (The reason is that the warranty insurance company usually insists that the agent offer the insurance on all houses handled.) Since this insurance can often cost in excess of $200, the seller might reconsider using the services of such an agent. This $200 will protect against having to repair any appliances that become inoperable often for as long as a year after the sale; however, the insurance will add another cost to the closing. The seller should weigh any possible advantages against immediate costs, bearing in mind that having a water heater repaired by a plumber can easily cost $200, and a furnace as much as $1000.

The reason some brokers push warranty insurance is that if an appliance breaks down after a sale, the buyer often goes after the broker to fix it, before going to the seller. To keep public opinion favorable and to avoid lawsuits, brokers often have to install many water heaters and other appliances at their own expense over the course of years. It is understandable that they would prefer that sellers take out insurance that will automatically cover such costs.

14. *Is personal property listed separately and is payment for it specified?*

Personal property usually includes such items as drapes, lamps, refrigerators, etc. (For a complete discussion of personal versus real property, see Chapter 5.) These can be made part of the sales agreement by inserting a clause which includes them in the sale. Or they can be sold separately, outside of escrow, for a sum of money and a bill of sale.

There's a big advantage for the buyer in including the sale of personal property in the sales agreement. To take an example, suppose you list and sell your house for $40,000 and the buyer agrees to buy your refrigerator for an additional $300. If the sale is written up for $40,300 and the buyer gets an 80 percent loan, the lender will pay 80 percent of the $300 cost. It will cost the buyer only $60 out of pocket to buy the refrigerator.

There is a disadvantage for you, the seller, however. If the lending institution sees your house listed for $40,000 and notices that you are selling for $300 higher, it will want an explanation. If the lender discovers that the extra amount is for a refrigerator, it may limit the amount of the loan to 80 percent of 40,000 and insist the buyer take out a personal loan or pay cash for the personal property. This can slow down your sale, and you as the seller may be wise to avoid this problem by insisting on the money for the refrigerator being paid out of escrow.

If you are selling for less than you listed, the lender is less likely to question the personal property; nonetheless, it is best to mention it in the sales agreement.

However you handle it, the buyer will usually want a bill of sale for personal property.

15. *Are you exempted from clearing restrictions and covenants from title?*

Restrictions and covenants are often made part of the title when homes are first built. They may include such items as limiting the size of homes to be built in the tract to no less than 1200 square feet or to no more than two stories. These are passed along in the title from owner to owner and normally cannot be removed except by court action. Restrictions on the basis of nationality or color are almost universally void (see Chapter 26 on open housing law).

Most sales agreements require the seller to give clear title. As you can imagine, if you weren't exempted from clearing restrictions and covenants of record, it would be virtually impossible for you to meet this requirement. Most sales agreements make such exemptions, but it won't hurt to check it out, just to make sure the person who prepared the document didn't leave out the exemption.

16. *Are you aware of all existing liens that must be paid off?*

A lien can be any money item that effects the title. The seller normally agrees to clear all liens from the property in order to give the buyer good title.

A mortgage is a lien, and as the seller you will generally know what mortgage you have on the property. If the buyer is getting a new loan, you will have to pay off the old one. You probably have a good idea how much this will cost you, and since you're going to have to pay it regardless, you may not want to clutter up the sales with any clauses pertaining to it.

However, there are other types of liens, for example, special assessments. If the city put in a new street in front of your house, you may be assessed to pay for it. This assessment usually takes one of two forms: you pay so much a month until the assessment is paid off or you pay the entire amount when you sell your property.

Such an assessment on your property can take a big chunk out of your profit. It would be wise for you to ascertain this before you sign a sales agreement. You may want to insist that the buyer pay part of this cost.

There are other liens that can cost you money at closing, particularly "hidden" liens.

If you borrowed money on a credit card or from a department store, for example, and didn't pay your bill, the financing company may have gone to court and secured a judgment against you. In theory, you would have been notified of any such court action by means of a summons. However, in actual practice, many notices are improperly served, and thus you might never receive yours.

A recorded judgment against you will affect property you own. When you sell your house, you will have to pay off the debt. There is really no way to protect yourself against execution of such a lien; you will undoubtedly have to pay in order to close the escrow.

Another similar lien is a mechanic's lien. This usually is recorded by a person who has performed work on your house, such as a plumber or carpenter. If you didn't pay this person or the payment was disputed, the lien could be on your property. Again, you will either have to settle with the worker or pay the lien out of escrow to close the deal.

17. *Is a date set for close of escrow?*

Your sales agreement should include a date for closing the escrow. This can be any time mutually agreed upon by buyer and seller. If you are anxious to get your money and move, you will want a short escrow.

If you have to find another house, you may desire a long one. Either way, you should specify how much time is allowed before escrow closes. Thirty to sixty days is common.

Unless your contract specifies that time is the essence, the end of escrow may be extended a reasonable period of time.

18. *Are you allowed enough time to vacate the house?*

Sales agreements normally specify that the buyer will take possession at close of escrow. This means that you must be out of the property by the end of the day escrow closes. If you aren't out, you can probably be evicted like a tenant who refused to pay rent.

If you feel you may need additional time, you should insist on a long escrow. If you think you might need time after escrow closes, you should specify in the sales agreement that you will be allowed to remain in possession of the property for a specified period of time after escrow closes. Since most buyers won't accept such an arrangement, it is common (and only fair) to sweeten the pot by offering to pay a reasonable rent for the extra time you occupy the house.

Great attention should be paid to possession. If you've agreed to move out by a certain date and do not move on time, a buyer who has been planning to move in may have to pay extra storage charges for belongings, pay for a motel, and pay additional amounts for meals eaten out, not to mention incidentals such as baby sitting and loss of time from regular work. An angry buyer could sue you for this loss.

19. *Is the commission to be paid only on the close of escrow?*

Even though you may have agreed to pay a commission to your agent in the listing agreement, you should see to it that the exact commission amount is written into the sales agreement (not just a rate). Since you will know the sales price, this should be easy to compute, and don't worry, most agents will race you to the spot where this figure is to go. Just be sure their arithmetic is accurate. You wouldn't want to pay more because an agent couldn't multiply.

It is also important that the sales agreement specify that the commission is to be paid only upon close of escrow; otherwise you could be liable for a commission to the broker even if the deal fell through!

20. *Is there anything about the sales agreement that doesn't make sense or that you don't understand?*

If there is, ask for a thorough explanation from your agent. Listen carefully to what the agent says and ask questions. If there is still something you don't understand or that doesn't make sense, don't sign. Consult your attorney (if you haven't already consulted one) and real estate counselor (often people will have a broker friend they know and trust)

CHECKLIST OF HAZARDS IN THE SALES AGREEMENT

1. Have you had an attorney check over the sales agreement?
2. Has the buyer put up a large enough deposit?
3. Has your property been properly identified on the agreement?
4. Is the price written in accurately?
5. Are the buyer and house qualified?
6. Is the buyer's proposed financing realistic?
7. Are you required to do extensive repairs on the house as part of the sales agreement? Couldn't you get just as good a deal selling as is to someone else?
8. Are your points and closing costs limited?
9. Are the terms of the second mortgage spelled out?
10. Has the buyer flooded the sales agreement with unnecessary subject-to clauses, making it impossible for you to enforce in the event the buyer decides to back out of the deal?
11. Does the agreement have a time-is-the-essence clause?
12. Will a termite clearance cost you too much money?
13. Do you have to warrant the appliances? Will this cost you extra money?
14. Have you distinguished your personal property from your real property?
15. Are you exempted from clearing restrictions and covenants on your title?
16. Are there any hidden liens on your property that could cost you extra money?
17. Is a specific date set for the close of escrow?
18. Have you allowed yourself enough time to vacate the house?
19. Does the agreement specify that you will pay a commission only upon the close of escrow?
20. Do you fully understand *all* parts of the sales agreement? Did you consult an attorney and/or broker about any parts you don't understand?

immediately and get an explanation that you can understand and that does make sense.

The agent may argue against this, saying that the buyer gave only one day for you to sign the sales agreement and that only a few hours are left. It won't take that long to get an expert opinion, and if it does, a sincere buyer will usually allow you a little extra time, if the agent explains why you need it. You may have a little argument to get your way here, but doing so may save you a headache, money, and wasted time. The clause that's giving you trouble may in fact be written against your interests. Or your broker may not have properly filled out the blanks in a sales agreement. Or your agent may simply not know how to explain something that is perfectly normal.

Don't take any chances. If you're not sure, find out. Remember, the more you know, the better off you are.

7

The Art of Price Bargaining

When your agent brings you a sales agreement, you may think of it as a time for rejoicing. However, unless the offer is for the exact price and terms you wanted, don't rejoice, at least not yet. The hardest part of selling your house remains—the bargaining.

It's been my observation that some individuals swing into price bargaining with a great deal of exuberance and enjoyment while others shun the whole process. I have been asked, "Why is the buyer making an offer? He knows my price. Why doesn't he either meet it or buy another house?"

This type of seller often has the hardest time when it comes to price bargaining. Such a seller is to a large degree a victim of the Western European and particularly American modern way of life. Up until the past fifty years in this country and even today in most of the world, bargaining over price is an accepted and dignified method of purchasing any item. I can still remember the time I was in a large supermarket on the West Coast when a husband and wife, apparently recent arrivals from the Middle East, attempted to haggle with a clerk over the price of a jar of mayonnaise. The clerk was stupefied when the man offered him 30 cents less than the marked price. The manager quickly arrived, and the man offered him 25 cents less than the marked price. The manager explained that the price marked was the actual price and that the man could take it or leave it. The man offered 10 cents below the price.

The manager, the clerk, and most of the other customers observing became embarrassed. One of the customers began explaining that in this country one did not haggle over price. The man offered 5 cents below the marked price and said it was his last offer. The manager refused.

The foreigner put the mayonnaise back and began walking away. I went over, stopped him, and asked why he didn't pay the full price if he wanted the mayonnaise? Surely the nickel separating the offer and the price couldn't make that much difference to him? The man looked at me strangely, then replied, "I could never pay full price—it just isn't done."

While we Americans may have "progressed" to the point where we never haggle with the grocer over the price of mayonnaise, we behave like the rest of the world when it comes to buying big items such as cars or houses. Haggling or bargaining is the name of the game. I have never yet met a buyer who didn't want to offer a seller something less than the asking price, even if the asking price was already ridiculously low. As the seller, you had better be prepared to deal with offers that come in at considerably less than you are asking. And unless you're an investor in real estate and can offer unusual terms or a unique property, you had also better be prepared to accept something less than your asking price and terms, even if only a token amount. (See Chapter 2 on appraising.) Occasionally a buyer will fall in love with a house and pay full price, but that is the exception, not the rule. Most buyers will feel they are getting ripped off unless they bring the seller down at least a little.

The real question, then, is how little can you the seller come down and still make the deal? This is where art enters price bargaining.

It is important at this stage to realize that price bargaining includes both price and terms. For example, a buyer may offer to pay full price, but insist that you the seller pay all closing costs. Since the buyer's costs may run as much as $1000 to $1500 on the deal, this buyer is actually offering to pay that much less for your home. (Usually the reason buyers want sellers to pay their closing costs is that these costs are cash out of pocket while 80 percent or more of the purchase price will be paid by a new loan on the property.) Or a buyer may offer full price and insist that the home be financed by an FHA-insured loan. Since more than likely there will be several points to pay on this loan (5 points on a $30,000 loan is $1500) and since the buyer cannot pay more than 1 point on an FHA loan, again you are being offered less. (Much less if it turns out your house doesn't meet FHA minimum standards and you have to pay to fix it up.)

Finally, you might get an offer in which the price is dramatically lower than what you are asking, but the buyers hope to induce you to sign by offering "all cash." All cash here probably means that these buyers will put down 20 percent and arrange for an 80 percent loan by themselves.

When an offer finally does come in and it is lower in either price or terms than you were asking, what should you do? Should you turn to your agent and ask for advice?

Yes and no. Most honest agents will not want you to get ripped off, that is, to get, for example, $25,000 for a house easily worth $40,000. But if the offer is anywhere within reason, even if it's 6 or 7 percent below what your house might be expected to bring, an honest agent may encourage you to sign. The reason is that your interests at this stage of the deal are different from those of the agent.

When you sign a listing, both you and the agent have a single goal: to find a buyer. But once a buyer has been found, your goals separate. You now want the best price and terms; however, the agent wants a sale. No sale, no commission. It is this divergence of interests that makes it necessary for the seller to take with a grain of salt the reasons an agent gives for accepting a low offer.

Consider the case of Gail, a salesperson we met in Chapter 1. Gail's seller, who eventually complained to me, was a middle-aged divorcée, Mrs. Nelson. She had her paid-off home listed with Gail for nearly five months, was asking $35,000, and hadn't received any offers. The listing was about to expire.

Gail began showing the house to buyers and "begging" for any offer. Eventually a buyer who was not particularly in love with the propery, but figured it wouldn't be a bad investment if the price was good, made an offer of $28,000. Gail presented the offer and tried to get Mrs. Nelson to sign. She said there was no point in making a counteroffer (offering to sell for less than asked, but more than offered) because the buyer wouldn't budge. When Mrs. Nelson, outraged at the low price, refused, Gail said she understood, but that Mrs. Nelson was making a serious mistake.

Within a week, Gail had her brother and sister-in-law make an offer of $25,500. They, of course, had no intention of buying, but for a fee were helping Gail out. If, by chance, Mrs. Nelson did sign, Gail knew the price was so low that she could resell to a legitimate buyer before escrow closed and split the profit with her brother and sister-in-law.

When Mrs. Nelson again refused to sign, commenting dejectedly that this offer was worse than the first, Gail reminded her that she had said it would be a mistake to refuse the first offer. Again she insisted there was no point in countering (as there really wasn't in this case). Mrs. Nelson was shaken. She pleaded with Gail to get her house sold for a fair price.

Now the seller was set up: two offers, the second lower than the first, in more than five months of waiting. Gail moved in for the kill. She contacted the buyer who had made the first offer and suggested that if the offer was made again, the seller now might sign. It happened that this buyer was still in the market for investment property. (If he wasn't, I have every confidence that Gail could have found another to take his place.) This time, however, Gail asked the buyer whether, in order to help convince the seller, he would consider a slight inconvenience, a $1500 all-cash deposit.

Gail called Mrs. Nelson and said that she had a good offer. She wouldn't say how much it was over the phone. When Gail arrived, she reiterated that it was a good offer and then handed Mrs. Nelson fifteen $100 bills and asked her to count them to be sure the deposit money was all there. While Mrs. Nelson happily counted, Gail told her the offer was again $28,000 from the first buyer. She said she knew that Mrs. Nelson had made a mistake the first time and that the second low offer was the proof. Gail said she had gone back to the first buyer and pleaded with him to try one more time. This was Mrs. Nelson's last chance. She said she felt it was her duty to see to it that Mrs. Nelson didn't make the same mistake twice and she was going to sit there until Mrs. Nelson signed, even if it took all night.

Mrs. Nelson eventually signed.

The sad truth is that although Mrs. Nelson's house probably was over-priced, dropping the listing price $1000 or $2000 probably would have attracted a good buyer in a short time—and saved Mrs. Nelson a considerable amount of money.

Fortunately, as far as I know, Gail is no longer in the real estate business. She was obviously the exception, totally unscrupulous and dishonest, and the vast majority of agents would not do what she did. Her example, however, does serve to illustrate a few of the problems a seller can get into by listening too closely to the agent.

Another broker's tactic to be aware of is that of not presenting more than one offer at a time.

Harry, one broker who used this technique, had a knack for listing properties that sold very quickly. He would get two or even three offers on the same day on a house he had listed. One offer might be from a buyer he had personally found; others might be from buyers other brokers had brought in. When the first offer arrived, Harry would call the sellers. Often he couldn't present the offer until the evening, when both husband and wife were home. Sometimes another offer would have come in by noon and another by dinner time.

When Harry arrived at the sellers', he would dutifully present the offer he had personally taken from a buyer and try to get the seller to sign it. He wouldn't even mention that he had other offers, some of which might be higher, until the seller had totally rejected the first offer, including going through several counteroffers. Harry, of course, had a selfish reason. He would get the whole commission if the seller accepted an offer from a buyer Harry had personally found. If the seller accepted an offer from another broker, Harry would have to give half the commission away.

If the seller accepted Harry's buyer's offer, Harry would never mention the other offers at all. He would just return them to the other brokers, saying the buyer had accepted a previous offer. Only if the sellers flatly rejected Harry's buyer's offer would he then present the other offers.

Naturally, the other brokers knew what was going on and didn't like it, but it was difficult for them to catch Harry in the act.

If the sellers had known what was happening, they would have liked it even less. If one of those other offers had a better price or terms, the sellers may have lost a considerable amount of money.

As a rule, it is always a good idea to ask your agent if any other offers have been made on your property at the time the agent presents an offer for your consideration. The agent is obligated to present *all* offers to the seller as they arrive, even if they arrive simultaneously. Arguments that the sellers can't figure out more than one offer at a time or that they will become confused have no bearing on the issue. If I asked an agent whether he or she were presenting all offers and that agent had another offer and then lied about it, I would be more than mad. If I subsequently discovered that a second, higher offer had been made, I would high-tail it to my attorney's office and get the difference between the first and second offer from that agent's hide. In such situations, occasionally the second broker will call the sellers to verify that they actually saw the second offer or that they accepted the first offer at least one day before the second one arrived. Such a call is your clue to take action.

When bargaining, common sense and a knack for judging people are your best bets for getting your price. In addition, I have found five rules which help protect me when it comes time to decide on an offer. These rules, however, are only guides; they may not apply to any transaction you are involved in.

1. *I never accept a first offer that is 10 percent or more below my asking price, even if it is close enough to what I want so that I could make the deal.* If the house is properly appraised, it should bring very close to the asking price, given enough time. (An exception arises when I have to get rid of the property very quickly. Then, any reasonable offer will have to do.) In many cases buyers are testing out the seller by beginning with a low offer. Agents have a tendency to insist that the seller sign, threatening that *this* buyer is not testing; *this* buyer won't offer a penny more; *this* buyer will back out of the deal if the seller doesn't agree to exactly what is offered.

Their actions are often based on self-interest. The quickest and safest way for them to get a commission at this stage of the deal is to get a seller to sign. They have no way of knowing whether the buyer will accept a counteroffer until they actually present it, and they simply don't want to take the chance of rejection or spend the time in negotiations.

2. *I always counteroffer any offer I don't accept.* When the price offered is more than 10 percent below the asking price, I usually make a token counteroffer, perhaps $100 to $250 below the asking price, just enough to allow the buyers to come back with a more sincere offer if they should so desire. Good listing agents will present every legitimate offer from a buyer to the seller, and almost every agent will carry back a counteroffer to the buyer, regardless of how loudly they protest. Remember that a counteroffer is a *new* offer; it *rejects* the original offer of the buyer and therefore must be submitted only after careful consideration.

3. *When an offer is within 10 percent of the selling price, I always counter with my lowest possible price, holding back just a few hundred dollars with which to seal the bargain.* If I was selling my house for $40,000 and someone offered $37,000, I would *not* make a token counteroffer of a few hundred dollars below $40,000. If I was prepared to accept a minimum of $38,500 I would now offer this price, plus $200. (The reason for the $200 will become obvious very soon.) Many sellers feel they should hold back a large amount regardless of what the buyer offers. They feel that the ultimate price will arrive only after many concessions on both sides, and they hope that perhaps they can ultimately save a few hundred dollars.

Quite the contrary. A buyer who sees the seller reducing the price in large increments is likely to think this seller is wishy-washy and doesn't have any real bottom price. At best a buyer in this situation may stick with the original offer and refuse to budge. At worst such a buyer may think that even the original offer was too high and try to back out of the deal.

Remember, the buyer doesn't deal directly with you, the seller. The buyer sees only the agent and can only rely on the agent's judgment of whether you are a hard-nosed character or an easy mark. No matter how hard the agent argues that an offer is your last price, what is a buyer going to think if in three offers you've lowered your price three times?

4. *Once I've made my lowest offer, I stick to it.* In our example, a buyer who likes to bargain might counter my $38,700 offer ($38,500 plus $200) with an offer of, perhaps, $37,500—$500 more than the original offer and $1220 less than my counteroffer. I will refuse to accept it. I will send back my original counteroffer, $38,700. I instruct my agent to present it again to the buyer and tell the buyer to take it or leave it.

What I risk here is losing the buyer and the sale. What I stand to gain is my price. It has been my experience that in the vast majority of cases, a sincere buyer will now realize that this is my rock bottom offer, particularly if I have conveyed that feeling to the agent and the agent says to the buyer something like, "That guy is really tough. He won't come down another penny. I talked till I'm blue in the face, and this is his absolute bottom offer." The difference of a few thousand dollars to a buyer is usually not that great. Most buyers are coming up with 20 percent or less in cash and 80 percent in the form of a loan. The $1200 difference between my last position and the buyer's offer in our example is only about $240 in cash to the buyer. In monthly payments for the remaining $960 it is only about $9 a month at 10 percent interest on a thirty-year loan. I have seen cases where the agent, in order to make a deal, has thrown in the $240 cash required from the commission. The buyer has nearly always come up to my price. If the buyer should counter at a higher price, but still short of my last offer, I will again refuse.

5. *To save a sale, I will come down $200.* Once the buyer realizes I have given my lowest offer, he or she may be ready to accept it, except for the matter of ego. The bargaining may have started at six in the evening and it may now be three o'clock in the morning. To now agree to buy for $38,700 (my only counteroffer) may mean the buyer will have to admit wasting the last five or six hours bargaining. Personal pride may prevent the buyer from agreeing to the full amount. The buyer may prefer to lose the deal, even after having come so far, simply because it has become a matter of "principle" to get my price down. If this buyer now offers, for example, $38,500 as the last and final offer (a token reduction in my price), I will accept it. I have no desire to strip someone of pride or self-image, particularly when I was ready to accept this amount all along.

These five rules certainly won't apply in all deals, but they do present the psychology that is behind the maneuvering of price bargaining and should give you some guides by which to protect yourself from buyer and agent "pros." Remember, the goal is to get *both* your price and the deal.

8

The Deadly Second

A *second* is short for a second mortgage or a second deed of trust. As the seller, you may be asked to accept this in lieu of a full cash down payment in order to sell your home, even if you've specifically rejected the idea in your listing agreement.

A second mortgage is simply a real estate loan that is second in order to a first mortgage. The order of loans is very important. In the event of a foreclosure, the first loan is the first to be paid off from a forced sale of the property. Then, if there is any money, the second and subsequent loans are paid.

Second loans have certain advantages, mainly that you get part of your sales price paid to you *with interest*. There may also be a tax advantage. If you are going to receive a large portion of the sales price of your home as a taxable profit and are not going to defer this by buying another residence within one year (or eighteen months if building a new home), you might want to take advantage of the 30 percent limit. Briefly, this allows you to amortize (or pay over an extended period of time) the tax on part of your profit as long as you receive less than 30 percent in cash at the time of the sale. It may be that taking a second will allow you to pay a lower tax. If you are in this situation, you should check with your accountant and/or tax lawyer.

The disadvantage of a second is that the borrower might not make the payments and you could lose your money.

Should you take back a second in order to make a deal? It depends on your situation. Should you decide to, here are several things to watch out:

1. *Be sure the buyer/borrower is credit worthy.* Lending institutions require a credit report and lengthy loan application. Ask to see copies of these and judge for yourself whether you would lend money to this individual. If buyer is assuming an existing VA or FHA loan and no credit report or loan application is being made, ask your agent to supply you with one. If the agent hesitates, insist on this as a condition for giving a second.

2. *Be sure the interest rate isn't usurious.* Most states establish the maximum amount of interest that can be charged on a loan. (Check the appendix for your state's limit.) It is not legal for you as an individual to charge a higher rate. Doing so may invalidate the loan. (It is interesting to note that in California most banks, savings and loan associations, and other large lenders are exempt from usury laws!)

3. *Be sure to place a request for notice of default on the first loan both with the county recorder's office and with the lender of the first mortgage.* This is to protect you in case the borrower makes payments on the second, but not on the first. In this situation, the holder of the first could foreclose and sell the property without your even knowing about it until it was too late to take appropriate action. The request ensures that the lender of the first mortgage will notify you if the borrower isn't making payments. You may have to demand that this be written into the first as a condition of the sale.

4. *Be sure your mortgage note includes a clause that allows you to foreclose in the event the borrower does not make the payments on the first loan.* Your lawyer should check this over to make sure it is done correctly. This allows you to take over the first. Usually such clauses provide that you may make the payments on the first loan to keep it current and add this amount, plus interest, onto the second while you foreclose. This is necessary to allow you to sell the property, thereby helping to assure that you get your money out. If the first loan is allowed to foreclose, that lender is not going to care a bit about your interest. That lender will sell the property for just the amount of the first loan, and you could get nothing.

5. *If you are forced to take a second against your wishes and plan to sell it for cash, be sure you wait at least six months before you sell.* This will allow the second to "age"; it will give the borrower time to make several monthly payments to show that he or she really intends to pay back the sum.

Second sales are almost always discounted. If you sell immediately, you will probably only get 60 cents back on the dollar ($600 for each $1000 of the loan). If you wait six months, you probably can get as much as 80 cents on the dollar ($800 for each $1000 of the loan).

6. *If you plan to sell your second, be sure you're getting a big enough mortgage.* Remember, a $5000 second doesn't translate into $5000 when sold. Even at 80 percent you only get $4000. (Of course, if you hold it for the full term you should eventually get the full amount.) If you want to get $5000 cash back, assuming an 80 percent sale, the second should be for $6250.

9

Be Careful of Ballooning

Ballooning or kiting, as it is sometimes called, has been a much too common practice among unscrupulous real estate agents. Ballooning usually occurs when unqualified buyers try to purchase a home that is too expensive for them. Let us say that a Mr. and Mrs. Green are brought to your home and fall in love with it. Your agent winks to you indicating these are serious buyers. A few hours later the broker calls saying she has an offer.

When the broker arrives, you find the offer is exactly what you want —the exact price and terms you hoped for. And the agent has a bona fide $500 deposit. Naturally, you are ready to sign. But before you do, the agent pulls out a second sales agreement. It is for a price $5000 higher than the other document. Her explanation goes something like this:

"Mr. and Mrs. Green are in love with your house. But unfortunately they don't have enough money for the down payment. Your selling price of $40,000 will entitle them to an 80 percent loan of $32,000 from a lending institution. The problem is they have only $4000 to put down and you don't want to take back a second. They are $4000 short. Here's the solution. We'll have a second sales agreement for $45,000. This will entitle them to an 80 percent loan of $36,000 or enough money to make the deal. You and the buyers will honor the $40,000 agreement and we'll show the $45,000 to the lender in order to get the loan. This way all parties get what they want; your house is sold, the buyers can make the sale, the lender can make a loan. And nobody gets hurt, right?"

Wrong!

Ballooning the price hurts the lender. Loans are made on the basis of a percentage of sales price for a specific reason: to provide a margin of safety. A lender who makes an 80 percent loan wants (or may be required by federal or state law) to maintain a 20 percent margin. This is so that in the event of a foreclosure, the lender won't be hurt if it is necessary to sell the property to satisfy the loan. Lending institutions must have such protection in order for them to make real estate loans plentiful and relatively simple to get.

I'm not suggesting, of course, that any seller be altruistic and give up a deal just so that a huge and impersonal lending institution won't get hurt. There's a much more direct and personal reason—ballooning is usually illegal. If you go along with the double sales agreement, you may be participating in a crime, and your signature on two conflicting documents is proof of your participation. If you are dealing with a state-chartered lender, you could be in violation of state and local civil and criminal codes, and if the lender is federally chartered, the offense could be a federal one. Federal law prohibits making a false statement in applying for a government-insured FHA loan.

Furthermore, lenders are always on guard against ballooned deals. Very often they receive copies of multiple listings or use other sources to verify your asking price. If they find out you've sold for more than you asked (as is often the case in a ballooned deal), they'll become very suspicious and investigate further. If they turn up ballooning, they'll at the very least reject the loan.

There should be no reason for ballooning. It is possible today for highly qualified buyers to get up to a 95 percent loan on most pieces of property by means of private mortgage insurance. (See Chapter 6 for a description of PMI loans.) If your agent proposes ballooning, suggest that the buyer try for a PMI, available at most banks. Or you might reconsider taking back a second. But, even if your agent says, "It's done all the time," under no circumstances should you allow yourself to be drawn into a ballooned contract.

10

Tricks of the Termite Inspector

Many lenders require a termite clearance or a termite report as a condition for lending money on a home, and it's required on all FHA loans. Some areas of the country have local laws which require a termite report before a sale can be concluded. Many wise buyers also insist on a termite clearance as a condition of sale. If you discover that you must get a termite report on your property, you should be prepared to pay some money. The report itself will probably cost anywhere from $25 to $50. (Local custom determines whether the buyer or seller pays this fee.) And the cost of repairing any damage found as well as eliminating any pests that may be living in your house can range from a few dollars to a thousand or more.

A termite report is sometimes mistakenly considered a true clearance. Almost never will an inspector give a blanket clearance. Usually the report reads "no visible evidence" of termites or other pests or has some other limiting clause. The reason is simply that short of tearing a house down board by board, there is no way anyone can know with certainty that no termites are present. An honest termite inspector will usually examine the attic, the roof, the outside walls of the house, the basement or crawl space beneath a house (if there is one), and the interior. If no termites are seen and if no wood is rotting and no water leaking (items also usually covered by the report), then a *limited* termite clearance, as explained above, is given.

It has been my experience, however, that even if no termites are found, some repair work often will be required. Since getting the termite clearance is contingent upon doing the work and getting the loan is often contingent upon getting the clearance, the seller often has to pay. The question, then, is how to pay the least amount.

If your house is found to have termites, you might as well figure you're going to have to pay an expert to get rid of them. Shop around for the best price. If, however, no living termites are found, but there is wood damage from water, dry rot, or termites and repair work is required, you usually have an option of paying the exterminator to do the required repair or doing it yourself. Such repair work may consist of nothing more than removing a few beams in the attic which have been weakened by old termite tunnels, even though the pests are long gone, or changing certain wood supports around a shower or tub which may have rotted away and must be replaced. On the other hand, an inspector may find that the protective metal shielding in a shower has rusted out, allowing water that penetrates the tiles to seep into surrounding wood and perhaps accumulate under the house. Tearing out a shower and replacing the tile, shielding, etc., is a job for a professional.

The problem is that the termite inspector's company is usually the one that does the repair work. Consequently, the seller who must pay is always wondering whether the job is really necessary or whether the inspector is just exaggerating or finding fault where there is none to get more work. Because you need the clearance, the inspector has you over a barrel.

What do you do?

If the termite inspector requires that under $50 of repair work be done (in addition to the inspection fee), I let him do it. The reason is that if I do it myself, or hire someone to do it, the inspector will have to come out and check it over to see if it was done correctly. The charge for this second visit can be $15 to $25. If I've done it incorrectly, and only the inspector can say, it has to be redone and reinspected at a cost of another $15 or $25. On the other hand, if the inspector's company does the work, there is usually no reinspection fee.

It's a different story, however, if the costs are over $50. The inspector's company may want $150 to replace several attic beams. I can do it on a weekend, if I don't mind some hard work and am handy, and save more than half of that fee even with two reinspections.

And then there's the case of the leaking water. Marion had this experience when she asked for a termite clearance:

When the termite inspector came, he said he had to check Marion's shower to make sure it wasn't causing damage to wood surrounding it. He temporarily sealed the door of her shower and filled it with more than a foot of water. Then he went under the house.

Water was pouring down through the wood from the direction of the shower. Marion was told that the protective metal sheeting on the shower had rusted away and must be replaced. This, of course, required installing a new shower—cost, $450. Marion hadn't had a problem with the shower in fifteen years and felt there must be a better way. The next day she called for another inspection from a different exterminator. This inspector, Mrs. Dawes, found that the ground under the house and many supporting timbers were already wet. She said they would have to be replaced to avoid mildew and fungus damage in addition to fixing the shower—cost: $800. When Marion protested that the reason the ground under the house was wet was that the first inspector had poured gallons of water in from the plugged-up shower, Mrs. Dawes turned a deaf ear. The water was there, and the situation had to be properly corrected.

Our seller took this last bit of instruction to heart. She had a long escrow and the weather was warm, so she waited, almost two weeks. Then she called a third company for an inspection. The inspector from this company, Mr. Perrymount, dutifully filled up the shower. Now, however, it didn't leak. Apparently the water from the first two fillings had swollen up the surrounding boards to such a degree that they did not let additional water pass. When Mr. Perrymount inspected under the house, he found it dry. Although the boards surrounding the shower had swollen and retained moisture, the ground and timbers under the house, exposed to air, had dried out. Mr. Perrymount found no evidence of any problem. He gave the seller a termite clearance. Cost? $25 (plus $50 for the two previous inspections).

The moral? If you don't like the inspector's findings or the price for repairs, shop elsewhere. Giving a house an inspection is a very subjective process, particularly if no signs of active infestation are evident. I have seen cases involving termite-ridden floors where one inspector insisted that certain repair work be done, while another said there was no problem with the existing condition at all.

Custom varies from one locale to another, but in general, the seller pays for the repair work while the buyer pays for any preventive work. Preventive work is sometimes optional.

Several states now require that copies of termite reports or clearances be sent to the state capital, where they are kept on file for a period of years. Should anyone feel that there has been any improper conduct on the part of inspectors, these files are usually open for public examination.

One final word of caution about termite clearances. Usually they contain a time-limiting clause. This may read that the clearance is valid only on the day the inspection was made or for a certain period of time from the date of the inspection, usually no longer than thirty days. The reason for this is simply that an inspector could see a home on Monday and find no termites, yet by Friday a colony of flying termites could have nested in the roof and begun devouring the wood. (There are many varieties of termites: those that live in the ground and come up to eat wood; those that live in wood; those that during a certain cycle of their lives fly to new nesting grounds like ants or bees.) It is probably wise, therefore, to wait until your house is in escrow before requesting a termite report.

11

How to Avoid Escrow Problems

An escrow is the most common and usually the preferred method of closing a real estate transaction.

Unlike selling a car or a piece of furniture, when you sell a house you must offer proof that you can deliver a clear title, that is, that you actually own the property and have no outstanding liens (taxes due, mortgages not reported, etc.) or encumbrances that affect your ability to sell. Unless the deal is strictly for cash the buyer must apply for and obtain a loan. Clearing title and obtaining a loan takes time. Furthermore, there is the problem of trust. How can the parties trust each other to fulfill their obligations?

In certain parts of the country, particularly along the East Coast, a strange combination of trust and legal advice are sometimes necessary to close a deal. The buyer and the seller each hire an attorney, and then the attorneys see to it that their clients fulfill their obligations to the transaction. There is some consultation between the lawyers and then, at closing, there is often an exchange, examination, and signing of documents. This is a traditional method that has been used for many years, and that it is still used attests to its workability.

A more common method of closing a real estate transaction that is used in the West and with more and more frequency in the East and South is the *formal escrow*. In the formal escrow an independent third party is established to handle all funds and follow the course of title clearing.

Technically an escrow is started when a seller *delivers* to a third party —the escrow holder, escrow agent, escrow officer, or escrowee—a deed with instructions to deliver the deed to the buyer only upon the performance of certain conditions, such as receiving all the monies required for the deal.

The escrow holder can be either a state-registered corporation or an attorney who acts for both buyer and seller and specializes in this sort of work. Escrow is opened by presenting the sales agreement to the escrow officer. The escrow officer draws up a set of *escrow instructions*. These are formal documents that empower the escrow officer to perform the sale, if properly signed by all parties. They are normally irrevocable. Such things as getting the loan and clearing the title are called *fulfilling the escrow instructions*. *Closing escrow* is simultaneously recording the mortgage and the deed in the buyer's name and giving the seller his or her money.

WHO OWNS THE ESCROW?

In general, the escrow officer is a limited agent for both buyer and seller until the escrow closes. Then the officer is trustee for all the monies until they are disbursed. On the surface this seems simple enough. In actual practice, however, the escrow officer has a bit more power than this limited role would indicate.

If two agents from different offices are involved in the sale of your home, a small argument will undoubtedly ensue over which escrow service to use. Each agent will want to use a different escrow service. If all services are alike, why should they squabble?

There are two reasons. First, the escrow officer or company may pay a fee to the agent who brings in a deal. Depending on the area, this may or may not be aboveboard. In any event, since escrow charges normally total only a few hundred dollars, this fee, if it exists, is not large.

The second, and more important, reason is that the agents know the importance of getting an escrow officer friendly to them. They are squabbling over who will *control* the escrow.

If the escrow officer is an independent third party, what is the importance of a "friendly" escrow officer?

It is because of the many things that can go right or wrong during the closing of a deal and the influence the escrow officer has on these. First, the escrow officer draws up a set of instructions. These are supposed to follow exactly the instructions on the sales agreement. (Since buyer and seller must each do different things to close the deal, instructions for each are normally different.) In theory if the sales agreement is unclear, the officer should not proceed until the matter in question is cleared up, possibly by a new agreement between buyer and seller. In practice, however, if the sales agreement is not clear on a certain point, an escrow officer could interpret that point to favor one party or another. An officer friendly to one agent could be more inclined to interpret it to that side's benefit.

Once buyer and seller sign their separate escrow instructions, they become as binding as the sales agreement, possibly more so. In fact, these instructions are often referred to as the *formal sales agreement.* If the instructions are wrong, and you discover this after you've signed, and the escrow officer won't or can't change them, hurry to an independent attorney.

The escrow officer also controls the speed of closing. This can sometimes be critical in completing a sale. Let us suppose that you've sold your home and set the fifteenth of January as the date for closing escrow. The buyers are securing a new loan and they learn that the scuttlebutt is that on the twientieth of the month, loan rates will drop ½ percent. Instead of a 9 percent loan, if they wait an extra five days, they might get an 8½ percent loan. They naturally want to delay the close of escrow. But you, the seller, are committed to buying another house. You've got to move on the fifteenth. You tell the buyers escrow is going to close on the appointed day come hell or high water.

Who's in the right? You are, of course. Does it close on the fifteenth? Not if the buyers or their agent controls escrow. Even though all the necessary papers from the loan company have been submitted, even though the money has been funded, even though your title has been cleared and you're ready to sign, a critical document somehow gets lost. A letter from the lender explaining dispersal of funds can't be found. A new one has to be sent. This takes three days. Then the escrow officer has to retype the closing instructions which show the amounts of money to be paid and received and which both you and the buyer have to sign. But it takes the escrow officer two more days to draw up and type these documents. You fuss; you fume. Was it an accident? Was it avoidable? Who can say? You lose five days and the buyer gets an 8½ percent loan.

Finally, you want to be sure that your escrow officer knows what he or she is doing. It is not enough that the escrow company be bonded and that it will cover any improperly handled escrow work resulting in a loss of money. You don't want the headache of lawsuits or rescinded deals. You want to know the work is done correctly the first time.

If you find that your agent is squabbling with another agent over who's going to control escrow, make sure your agent wins. The way you do this is quite simple. You say that you won't sign the sales agreement unless you can choose the escrow company or officer. You make it a condition of sale. All the smart buyers and sellers do.

An even wiser move, however, is to open the escrow yourself. This might even save you some money. In the East or Midwest, where attorneys sometimes handle escrow, it might be wise for you, before a sale is made, to contact an escrow attorney whom you know or who is recommended by friends and ask this person to handle your escrow. Then when a sale is made, you can be very concrete. You simply insist that such-and-such attorney will handle the escrow.

In other parts of the country, particularly the West Coast, escrow companies are used. In the northern areas these are often owned and operated by title companies. In southern California, particularly in the Los Angeles area, they are often small independent companies occasionally affiliated with real estate agencies. If you have trouble deciding which company to use, you might consider using a bank's escrow service. Many of the larger banks are now offering to handle escrows, often at very competitive rates.

ACCURATE INSTRUCTIONS AND THE FLOATING DEPOSIT

It is, of course, extremely important that the escrow instructions be accurate. If an attorney isn't already handling the escrow, it would be wise to have one look them over.

One item that tends to get overlooked in the escrow instructions is the matter of disposing of the deposit in the event the deal doesn't go through. The instructions are usually explicit in making the deposit a part of the down payment when the deal does go through. But occasionally a deal won't close. What happens to that deposit? If the instructions haven't specified, the deposit may remain in the inactive escrow for up to a year and then may be forwarded to the state for disposition. Unless the disposition of the money is spelled out in the instructions that both buyer and seller have signed, the escrow officer will hesitate to give the money to either party. (For this reason, many agents will not give the deposit to escrow until just before the deal closes.)

As the seller, I always make it a point to have included in the escrow instructions that I sign and that the buyer signs the statement that the full deposit is automatically to be paid to the seller no later than thirty days after the date set for close of escrow unless the buyer has fulfilled all his or her escrow instructions. In that event, the money is to be returned to the buyer (if the deal falls through). Since the deposit is the seller's money, neither the escrow officer, nor the agent, nor the buyer should mind.

YOUR AGENT'S ESCROW RESPONSIBILITY

The important thing to get straight about escrow holders is that they are passive, not active. They don't really do anything except type instructions and documents (and occasionally lose papers). If you need a termite clearance, the escrow officer won't get it for you. If you specified in the sales agreement that the buyer has to secure a financing commitment within two weeks, the escrow officer won't know whether the buyer is working at it, even if the commitment has been given (unless the lender sends the escrow holder a formal letter). If you were divorced and it turns out you can't give clear title unless your former spouse signs a quitclaim deed or other release, the escrow officer won't find your spouse or talk him or her into signing (although the escrow officer will usually provide you with the proper forms). A good agent will do these things and will find out the proper information and keep you informed. If, however, you've got a lazy agent, it is your responsibility to fulfill all your escrow requirements and to see to it that the buyers are fulfilling theirs. If your agent won't act even after you've cajoled and threatened, you've got to do the work yourself, if you want a sale. Remember, your sales agreement probably specified that time is the essence, and if somebody (meaning you) doesn't get moving and do the legwork, time will run out.

Every deal is different, and every seller will be required to fulfill some different needs. You should check with your escrow officer to find out what documents and actions you need to take to close escrow.

Generally, the seller should provide one or more of these:

1. Your copy of the sales agreement for examination

2. Certificate from your mortgage company showing amount and interest paid

3. Your old deed or evidence of title

4. A receipt for water, tax, or assessment bills

5. Your current fire insurance policy

6. Bill of sale for personal property

7. Satisfaction of payment for mortgages, liens, or judgments affecting title

8. Names of tenants and rental information

9. Any assignment of leases

PREPAYMENT PENALTY

Many times when you pay off a mortgage in advance of the date it is due, the lender will charge you a prepayment penalty. This penalty will show up on your escrow closing papers as an additional cost and can be a fairly substantial sum of money. Usually prepayment penalties are 1 to 2 percent of the remaining balance of the mortgage or, alternatively, six months' interest. If your mortgage balance is $30,000 and the prepayment penalty is 2 percent, the cost to you to pay off that loan early would be $600.

There are a number of things you can do to protect yourself against prepayment penalties. First, you should check to see what, if any, payment for early payoff exists on your mortgage. Provision for this penalty, if it exists, will be written right in your note or mortgage papers. Second, you should find out if your lending institution will waive the penalty in your case. If you have a government-insured FHA or VA loan, these penalties are now automatically waived by a recent federal law covering prepayments. If you have a conventional loan, the lending institution will often waive the penalty if you can get the buyers to obtain their financing at the same lender that you had. For example, say you borrowed money to buy your home from XYZ savings and loan. Now, three years later, you want to sell your property. If you can get your buyers to get their new loan on your property from the same XYZ lender, that lender may very likely, as a bonus to you for keeping the mortgage with them, not charge the normal prepayment penalty. The time to take care of this is before signing the sales agreement. Make sure your buyer knows you expect that new mortgage to come from the old lender. You might even make it one of the conditions of sale.

Some conventional lenders may also waive the penalty if you've had the loan for a long time, usually over twelve years; however, this is increasingly rare in today's market.

If the prepayment penalty is written into your mortgage and the lender insists on it, you cannot simply refuse to pay. If you refuse, the lender will not allow the mortgage to be cleared from the title to your property, and you will not be able to give clear title to your buyer.

Prepayment penalties serve several purposes for the lender. If you were to ask a lending institution why such a penalty is imposed, the answer would probably be that the penalty is needed to offset the loss of interest to the lender between the time the mortgage money is taken off your property and a new mortgage is given to someone else. This is particularly applicable when the borrower pays off a loan in the first year or two.

There is another reason, however, that lenders rarely mention, primarily because it is punitive. The purpose here is to punish borrowers who want to get a new loan to reduce the interest rate they are paying. For example, say that you currently have a fixed-rate mortgage at 10 percent annual interest. You got the loan several years ago and now learn the interest being charged to new borrowers is 8 percent. You decide to turn in your old high-interest loan for a new low-interest one from the same lender. But you might think twice about doing this, and you might not do it at all, if the lender charges you a 2 percent penalty to pay off the old loan.

The punitive nature of prepayment penalties is demonstrated by the fact that almost all lending institutions will waive the penalty if you obtain a new loan at a higher interest rate. For example, say you wish to add on to your home and you decide to get a new loan from the same lender. If your current interest rate is 8 percent and the interest rate on new loans is 10 percent, it is very likely that your lender will waive the prepayment penalty when you refinance.

THE DEAL THAT DOESN'T CLOSE

Sometimes in spite of everyone's best efforts (or because of them) a deal that has already gone to escrow won't close. If it turns out that the buyer's at fault and you feel justified in keeping the deposit as forfeited, you by all means should. If you've provided for this as noted above, you should have no problem.

There are other matters, however, regarding the escrow that doesn't close. Someone has to tell the escrow officer. You might want to do this in order to get back any document such as a deed or insurance policy you've left with escrow and to get your deposit. It is at this time that the escrow officer will inform you that a certain escrow fee is due, whether or not escrow closes. (Escrow companies often overlook this fee for brokers who bring them deals on a regular basis—it is a kind of left-handed payment for bringing them business.) The escrow officer may say that all or part of the escrow fee is due and you, the seller, must pay. Since the escrow officer is probably holding the deposit, he or she has you over a barrel. Now is the time to be extremely courteous. You might offer to strike a bargain. If the escrow officer will overlook the fee this time, you will bring the company your business on the next deal. After all, your house is on the market and you do expect to sell it soon. If the escrow officer appears somewhat skeptical about this proposition, you might volunteer to let the escrow officer hold onto this deposit and the documents until you get another buyer. This offer will usually be accepted, and you probably don't have anything to lose. Just be sure that when your house does sell you take the deal back to the same escrow company. If you don't, the worst that's likely to happen is that you'll end up paying the escrow fee.

12

Fraud, Recision, Taxes, and Other Deadly Snares

A few words should be written about some of the more serious problems that a party to a real estate transaction can get into. However, before beginning, the reader should take note that this section should not be construed as providing legal or tax advice. The reader should not rely on any legal or tax material in this book. The examples that follow, whether real or imaginary, are given solely to illustrate some of the problems that others have gotten into in real estate and do not cover all possible situations. Since every individual's legal and tax situation is different, the reader should consult an attorney about any legal matters.

Real estate brokers quickly learn that they are likely to get into trouble if sellers misrepresent something to them and they pass that misrepresentation on to the buyers. As agents, they are in a position to know what is truthful and what isn't. If the sellers say the taxes on their house are $300 a year and all the other houses in the area are paying $1,000 a year, it's up to the broker to get a copy of the sellers' tax bill or other proof before representing to a possible buyer that the taxes on the property are actually $300 a year. An agent who doesn't follow through in this matter could be said to be *negligent.* In the event a buyer bought and later sued to get out of the contract, saying the purchase was based on the taxes being $300, the agent might have to pay the costs.

Many sellers, knowing of the agent's responsibility, take it upon themselves to fool their broker. They are like the patient who goes to a specialist, and when the specialist says, "What's wrong with you?" answers, "You're the doctor; you tell me."

The seller might get away with a minor misrepresentation, one that the agent can check, even if a deal soured and the whole thing became embroiled in litigation. However, it might be the seller's withholding of essential information that caused the deal to go sour in the first place.

A seller should answer truthfully all questions the broker asks about the property. If the broker forgets to ask something critical, the seller should offer this piece of information. This is particularly true for sellers who have added onto their homes in violation of local building codes and zoning regulations. The seller who deliberately misrepresents something to the broker which the agent cannot reasonably verify may end up being the subject of a buyer's ire.

Every broker knows of a case where this has happened. The one most familiar to me involved a certain seller, Mr. Nept, who indicated that all the plumbing in his house was in working order. Since the area where the property was located was subject to freezing weather, the agent tried out the faucet in the sink and flushed the toilet in the bathroom. Everything seemed to be fine.

Eventually the agent brought a buyer by who was interested. When the buyer asked about the plumbing, the agent said that it worked fine.

A sales agreement was signed and eventually the deal closed. Imagine the buyer's surprise to find, upon moving in, that the house had no running water. A few calls to the agent and then to the seller revealed that during a freezing spell, just prior to listing, the pipe running from the water meter at the street to the house had frozen and ruptured along its entire length from the pressure of the expanding ice.

The water company had shut off the water at the meter, and the seller had closed the valve at the house. Then Mr. Nept had made an arrangement with a neighbor to connect a hose between the outside water faucets of their homes. Because of fear that freezing water might rupture the hose, they had wrapped it in fiberglass and covered it with ornamental rocks from Mr. Nept's garden. Since the houses were only 20 feet apart, this wasn't much of a job. This arrangement also explained why the agent hadn't seen the hose when he inspected the property. When the house sold and the seller moved, the neighbor turned off the water.

Naturally, the buyer was furious. When the agent told the seller he'd have to install a new water pipe from his house to the street, a job that would cost almost $500, the seller replied, "Caveat emptor," let the buyer beware. He said he had never told the buyer the plumbing was good; the agent had said that, and if anyone should pay, the agent should.

The seller was wrong. In this case the agent wasn't negligent. He had tried the water and found it working. The seller had lied, and his covering up the hose was construed as an attempt to conceal his misrepresentation. He had to pay for a new water line.

The old *caveat emptor* doctrine is going by the boards more and more these days. In general, sellers are duty bound to disclose any defects that may make their property dangerous to the life or property of a buyer who is unaware of them. This includes all manner of things, especially faulty wiring, faulty plumbing, and structural damage. Sellers should also correct a misrepresentation upon later learning it has occurred, and they should even avoid stating an opinion. Some courts have held that an individual who intentionally misstates his or her opinion is guilty of fraud.

Interestingly enough, misrepresenting an existing local or state law is seldom considered a sufficient cause for rescinding a deal. A law is considered common knowledge, available to all.

Recision of contract basically means that the contract is annulled or set aside. In the case of a sales agreement, both parties would have to put themselves as they were before the agreement was signed. Usually a recision takes place as a result of a court order or the threat of taking the matter to court. For example, the buyers could go to court claiming that the purchase was made on the basis of a misrepresentation and ask that the sales agreement be rescinded, that is, that the buyers get back their money and the sellers keep their house. The court may or may not go along with this request.

Recision of contract usually stems from fraud or misrepresentation by a party to the contract. (Fraud usually implies intent to mislead; intent is not always an essential element of misrepresentation.) It could be because the sellers or their agent lied. Even if the sellers acted honestly and in perfectly good faith, the buyers could ask that a contract be rescinded because of fraud or misrepresentation on the part of the broker. Thus it is extremely important that a seller engage an honest and competent broker at the beginning.

Specific performance of a contract basically means that a person must comply with what he or she has agreed to do. Either party can sue for specific performance. For example, if a buyer puts up a deposit and a sales contract is entered into by both buyer and seller, and then the buyer backs out of the deal without any escape clauses in the agreement, the seller might sue, asking that the buyer be forced to go through with the sale. Similarly, if the seller decided at the last moment to back out of the deal, a buyer might sue for specific performance, asking that the court order the seller to sell his or her house.

Specific performance suits and recision rarely occur in residential real estate transactions. Part of the reason is that it's usually much easier to find another house or another buyer than to go through the bother and expense of a court action. Occasionally, however, a buyer or seller is sufficiently angered by a deal to go to court over it.

Another reason for the general lack of suits is that the sales contract usually depends on the goodwill of all parties in order for it to be enforceable.

It often comes as a great surprise when a seller (or buyer) takes a sales agreement to an attorney asking for a suit and hears that the chances of winning are remote because the contract is so easily broken. This is the reason that you should have an attorney look over the sales agreement before you sign. It is often the case that those funny little sentences the agent has scribbled in have made the agreement practically unenforceable.

In the great majority of cases honest buyers and sellers deal with honest and competent brokers. Trust is the essential element of any agreement, and nowhere does it work better than in real estate. More than a million houses are sold every year by individual sellers, and only the exceptional deal gets into serious trouble. The point, of course, is not to be that exception.

Should you ever get involved in a legal fight over fraud or misrepresentation with an agent and win, it could be of considerable importance to be aware of state recovery funds. Many states have special funds to cover agents. (See the appendix to find out whether your state has such a fund.) Usually these funds provide that if you win a lawsuit for fraud with an agent and that agent does not have sufficient funds to satisfy a judgment, you may be paid up to certain limits from the state fund.

A final word should be said about taxes. Any time you sell real estate, your tax liability must be considered. If you sell for a profit, as most people do today, taxes on that profit must be paid. However, it is possible to take certain precautions to see that these taxes are paid at the lowest possible rate.

It is usually possible to defer your payment of any tax on real estate if the house you sell is your legal residence *and* if you buy a new legal residence within one year either before or after the sale of your old residence (eighteen months if you are building a new residence) *and* the cost of the new residence equals or exceeds the selling price of the old one. If your new residence is not as costly as your old, you may defer a part of the price.

It should be noted that you are only liable for tax on your gain. For example, if you bought a house ten years ago for $20,000 and you subsequently added a swimming pool for $7000 and other improvements for $3000, your tax base would be $30,000. If you subsequently sold for $50,000 but had to pay $5000 closing costs including commission, your actual sales price for tax purposes would be $45,000. The amount of money you would have to pay taxes on would be the difference between your base of $30,000 and the net sales price of $45,000, or $15,000. If you subsequently bought a house for $55,000 and fulfilled the time and residence requirements, you could defer the taxes on the entire $15,000, even though you may not have put all the money into the new property!

Another method of reducing the taxes you pay comes into effect if you own a sizable portion of your house free and clear. The government normally requires that you pay taxes in the year of sale on the full amount of profit. If, however, you receive less than 30 percent in cash and the remainder is to be paid to you in at least two or more payments, you can pay taxes on your profit as you receive it.

Finally, there are capital gains. There are two methods of figuring capital gains. Briefly, the first is to take the total gain, divide it in half, and tack this amount onto your regular income tax. If you are in the 25 percent or less tax bracket, this is usually the advisable method, as you end up paying only 25 cents or less on each dollar of profit. Alternatively, you can pay a flat tax rate of 25 percent on the first $50,000 and about 35 percent on the balance.

Some wise sellers, if they have a very large profit from the sale of their homes, use the income-averaging method to spread the gain out over five years and then combine it with the capital gains method.

If you are going to have a profit on your home sale, you should see your attorney, accountant, and/or investment adviser *before* the sale. You might save yourself a considerable amount of money.

TWO

Protect Yourself When You Sell by Owner

13

Don't Waste Precious Time

Some sellers are wasting their money hiring the services of a broker. Some houses actually sell themselves. These are well-located, highly desired pieces of property, and they usually sell very quickly. There is always a chance that your house could be one. It is important, however, that every seller be realistic and consider the possibility that his or her house isn't one of these chosen few. (While no complete statistics are available, many lending institutions figure they make eleven purchase money mortgages on homes sold through agents for every one they make on homes sold direct.)

A Chinese philosopher once said, "The only item of real value that we possess in our life is time." At one point or another, we've all undoubtedly realized the truth of this statement. The important thing, then, is not to waste time, and one of the most wasteful uses of it is trying to sell by owner a house that could be marketed only by an agent. I have seen sellers trying to sell by themselves hold open houses for endless weekends, work countless hours keeping their house in tip-top shape, constantly yell at their children to get their toys out of sight, not go out for fear they might miss a buyer's phone call, and then, in the end, after months of futile effort, give up and list with a broker. It is a fact of the real estate business that agents know their best source of listings is sellers who are trying to sell their own houses.

Should, you, then, try to sell your house yourself?

This is a hard decision to make. Most sellers decide to sell by themselves primarily to avoid paying a commission. Since, for example, on a $45,000 home the commission at 6 percent is $2700, this is a fair amount of money to be saved. However, the amount to be saved should always be weighed against the real chances of your saving it; that is, can you really make a sale?

I would never suggest that sellers totally give up on selling a house on their own. A trial selling period, as long as a reasonable time limit is given, is the final test of whether the home can be sold by owner. (Besides, for someone who has never done it before, this can be an exciting and educational experience.) I would suggest, however, that before making the decision to sell by yourself, you carefully consider the true marketability of your home and thus avoid wasting your most precious possession—time. Here are the hard facts regarding selling by owner.

LOCATION

The single most critical factor when you are selling a home by owner is location. Even if you were to put a full-page ad in the local paper describing the merits of your property, prospective buyers who do not like the general area or the immediate neighborhood would be lost to you because they *would not stop.* All these potential buyers might be turned into actual buyers if only you could tell them that the neighborhood isn't really that bad; that the neighbor across the street who left her garbage on the lawn is moving out in three weeks or that the fellow down the street who is pulling the transmission out of his '57 Chevy has never worked on his car before and will be done working on it soon. But because these potential buyers don't stop, you never get a chance to explain.

If you have a bad neighborhood, an agent is essential. An agent talks to buyers *before* they see your house. If you have a bad neighborhood, the agent is able to explain the situation (if it, in fact, is explainable). The agent can point out the merits of your house that may outweigh the poor location, such as good condition or excellent price, and can try to minimize the bad neighborhood. You could do all these things too, if you ever had a chance to talk to the potential buyers.

How, then, do you determine whether you have a good neighborhood, a mediocre one, or a bad one? This is more difficult than it may sound. Many sellers automatically think the neighborhood in which they live is terrific.

The best way to judge your location is to compare it with the location of the "perfect home." The perfect home is situated in a neighborhood of other homes which are comparably designed, whose landscaping is tastefully done and well maintained, and which present a picture of residential bliss. There are no detracting features, such as a nearby house which has broken windows, paint chipped off, or the lawn overgrown with weeds. A few children of varying ages in the neighborhood are desirable as chances are the buyers will have children of their own and will be looking for playmates for them. But too many children will make the neighborhood seem noisy and crowded.

In addition, there can't be a turnpike or freeway off-ramp in back of the home or a steel plant at the end of the block. Even a shopping center or school too close, say five or six houses away, detracts from the location (although further than that, it becomes an asset).

Finally, even if a home is perfectly situated within a neighborhood, the neighborhood itself must be one in which buyers want to purchase. Generally these are in areas of growth, rather than decay, that are far enough away from the city center to avoid much of the smog and congestion, yet close enough to allow reasonable commuting, given the high cost of gasoline and the time involved going back and forth. The schools must be well regarded in the community (although with busing becoming more common, this is less of a consideration). And, finally, the area should be an "in" community. How does a community get such a reputation? Somehow, people just seem to know where the "good" places and the "bad" places are to live. The greatest number of buyers are always attracted to the good areas.

If the location of your house doesn't quite measure up, you should consider carefully your chances of selling it by owner. The poorer your location is, the more you need an agent. If you really have a bad neighborhood, in the terms we've just outlined, you have almost no choice. To sell you will need help.

CONDITION, PRICE, AND TERMS

Assuming you have a good location, the next important items to consider are the condition of your home and how competitive your price and terms are. If your house is run down, many buyers who stop by won't be interested. (Although some will be looking for a house they can fix up themselves and will show interest if you dramatically reduce the price and offer better terms.)

The advantage an agent has here is that the agent, presumably being objective, is able to tell the buyer just how your house ranks in competition with all the other houses available on the market. If your house is in bad shape, but the price is low and the terms favorable, the agent can point this out to the buyer and the buyer will probably *listen*. If your house is a bit high in price and requires a larger down payment than most, the agent can point out that it is in supersharp condition (if it is) and most buyers will *listen*.

Agents are able to draw on their experience and educate the buyer as to what's available on the market and how your house stacks up. Some agents will even take buyers on a tour of a half dozen houses before they show the one they think the buyers will purchase, just so the buyers will recognize true value when they see it.

Selling by owner, you cannot do this. If you begin talking about how your house compares with others on the market, the buyer will probably turn a deaf ear. After all, you have only one product, one house to offer. Your judgment of other houses is naturally suspect. The agent's judgment, however, is far less likely to be suspect than yours, on the matter of comparative value. The agent has dozens of houses to sell. Whether or not the agent, in fact, is objective, the buyer is much less likely to question his or her motives here.

There are two answers to this problem. The first is to hope that your potential buyer has already seen a lot of houses and knows the market. This buyer will then have enough background to know how your house stacks up against others.

The second is to see to it that your house is, in fact, in good condition and competitive when compared with others on the market. One way to do this is to compare it with the perfect house in terms of condition, price, and terms.

The perfect house has reasonably good landscaping at the front, back, and sides. All the lawns are mowed, the shrubs trimmed and, ideally, the flowers in bloom when the buyer comes by. In addition, the house is freshly painted inside and out. The bathroom and kitchen fixtures are modern (preferably without chipped porcelain), the floors polished or vacuumed (with the carpet in good shape), and the ceiling without spots. Also, the perfect house is large enough for the typical family (at least 1300 square feet) and has at least three bedrooms and two baths and an enclosed garage (although this is optional in some areas). The back yard is gardenlike, with ornamental plants, fruit trees, or growing vegetables, yet these items seem to practically take care of themselves (sprinklers, not too much lawn, yard not too big) so that the property can credibly receive the designation "low maintenance."

The perfect house also has a few things left undone— a bare patch at the side that needs planting or a wall in the guest room that needs shelves. This is so prospective buyers can see where they can "improve" or add their own touch to the home.

To be competitive, your house must be priced at or near the price of other homes in its neighborhood. For example, if other nearby homes are selling for $40,000, your home should also be close to that price, assuming it's similar in most other ways. If you're not sure how to compare your home with others, see Chapter 2 on appraising.

And finally, you should be able to offer at least as good terms as other houses on the market. In general, the more money that you are willing to finance by yourself, the more attractive are your terms. If, for example, you own your house free and clear and are willing to give a buyer a 90 percent mortgage (10 percent down), you've got the most attractive terms possible. On the other hand, the more difficult you make it for a buyer to get financing, the less attractive are your terms. For example, if you refuse to go FHA or VA or if you insist on all cash down to you (you won't take a second), you've got the toughest financing available. These are important considerations, and Chapters 6 and 8 will aid you in making a decision.

An agent presumably already knows the prices and terms most frequently found on other nearby home sales and will be able to advise you accordingly. If you sell by owner, you will have to scramble for this information yourself. Much of it will be volunteered free by agents trying to list your property. If you use the methods outlined in Chapter 2 be sure to apply them to terms as well as price.

If your property is close to the perfect house in condition and if you can offer truly competitive price and terms, you meet the second major criterion for selling by owner. The further away you are from the ideal, however, the less chance you have of successfully selling by yourself.

SALESMANSHIP

A good agent has certain selling qualities which are assumed by the buyer and others which the agent actively demonstrates.

Most buyers will assume the agent knows at least a minimum amount of real estate law and practice and that the agent knows how to protect the buyer's rights (in the next section we will see that in many instances this is not so). On the other hand, most buyers will assume, unless you are able to demonstrate differently, that you, the owner/seller, know none of these things. This will very likely make the buyer hesitate to deal with you.

There are several ways you can overcome this liability as a direct seller. One is to educate yourself in real estate law and practice. This is time-consuming and hardly worthwhile unless you plan to enter the field. A second and very effective method which I have seen work on many occasions, is to get a professional to assist you in the formal part of the deal. This can be a broker, perhaps a friend, who agrees to handle all the paperwork for a set fee. Alternatively, you could get an attorney to do this work. This should satisfy most buyers both as to your good intentions and as to your competence in handling a deal.

One quality that a successful agent has that you may or may not be able to exhibit is salesmanship. Salesmanship is hard to define. It's the

sort of thing you can instantly recognize when you see it, but is very difficult to put your finger on in the abstract. It has been described as the
ability to sell ice cubes to Eskimos.

It has been my experience that salesmanship is a quality that cannot be
learned. It is a talent which can be improved through training, but which,
if you don't possess it, cannot be attained no matter how hard you work.

A few years ago a limited study done in Southern California revealed
that the most successful real estate salespeople were either those who had
previously been shoe store managers or those who had sold ads for the
yellow pages. While that may at first seem humorous, it is perfectly logical. Both those occupations require that a person deal constantly with the
public in a selling capacity. In such a situation, one who could not sell
would not last long. The main difference between selling ads or shoes
and selling real estate is the size of the product. The requirement to sell,
that is, to convince someone to buy, is still there.

I have seen people trying to sell real estate who simply couldn't. They
might have the right buyer in the perfect house and yet somehow manage to turn the buyer away from the deal. It might be as simple as forgetting to ask the buyer directly, "Do you want to buy this house?" Or it
might be overtalking about virtues of the dishwasher or the flooring to
the point that the buyer became bored and left.

A good salesperson knows when a buyer wants to purchase even without asking and knows how to get the buyer to act. For example, once Ben
instinctively knew that the buyer liked a home, he would whip out a sales
agreement and say something like, "Hypothetically, let's see how the deal
would look if you bought this house." Then he would carefully complete
the agreement, going over it with the potential buyer as he wrote. Just as
he finished the last line, Ben would "accidently" drop his pen and pretend he couldn't find it. The buyer, of course, would pick it up, but before he could return it, Ben would mention some point in the agreement. The buyer would be left standing there, holding that pen, considering the contract. Now, Ben would suggest he sign. The psychological
need to use a ready pen should never be underestimated. Invariably, if
the buyer really was interested and the house was right, the pen technique would work.

How can you know whether you can convince someone to buy your
house?

You may already know. By the time individuals get around to selling a
piece of real estate they have probably had some experience in selling
other things. If you were successful in your previous efforts as a salesperson and you liked it, you need not worry. When the right buyer shows
up, you'll instinctively know how to sell. On the other hand, if you've had
bad experiences selling, this may be your clue to leave the sale of your

home up to a professional. If you're not sure, there's only one way to find out whether you can sell real estate. Try.

My suggestion is that every seller who is remotely interested in selling by owner give it a reasonable attempt. Once you're ready to proceed on a direct sale, set a time limit. It could be one week or four, but more than a month really is unreasonable unless you've got a lot of time to blow and are a bit of a masochist.

Say to yourself you're going to give it your best shot. Read the following chapters on protections. And work hard. After all, the most you can lose is time.

14

Success in Showing

ADVERTISING

Showing a house to a prospective buyer usually follows placing an ad in a local paper. One of the most important aspects of this process is getting an ad that sells. If you're not in advertising, don't waste time trying to come up with a good ad all by yourself. Real estate companies spend millions of dollars annually with advertising companies trying to come up with ads that produce. The creative departments of these ad agencies are intimately familiar with buyer psychology, and they possess skill in writing and designing. Use the advertising ideas that the experts have found successful. There are many books on the market that tell the direct seller how to write ads. The purchase of one of these is a wise investment.

Certain precautions should be exercised when creating or borrowing an ad, however. Regulation Z of the Truth-in-Lending Act of July 1, 1969, applies to creditors advertising loans and covers the field of real estate. Most real estate agents are covered by Regulation Z. *Most direct sellers are not.* However, the distinction between when a direct seller is and isn't covered usually hinges on whether the seller *regularly* extends credit, and this may be open to some interpretation. Rather than take unnecessary chances, the direct seller probably should follow the provisions of Regulation Z, which are provided here as a convenience.

Regulation Z comes into effect when you advertise the financing of a home rather than mentioning merely the price. Although such general description as "liberal terms available" does not come under the rule, the advertising of any specific piece of financing information automatically triggers the need to advertise other pieces of information. The only item that can be advertised by itself is the annual percentage rate of interest.

The advertising of any of the "trigger terms" in column A automatically requires that *all* the disclosures in column B also be advertised:

A

The amount of the down payment or use of the words *no down payment*

The amount of any one installment

The number of installments

The period of repayment

The amount of finance charge expressed in dollars or, the statement that there is no finance charge

B

The actual cash price

The total number of payments

The amount of each payment

The regularity of the payment—monthly, annually, etc.

The annual percentage rate of interest

The amount of the down payment or the fact that there is no down payment

An advertisement which includes *any* item in column A without *all* the disclosures in column B is in violation.

The penalties for violating Regulation Z are severe. For willfully giving false or inaccurate information or for failing to provide required information, the individual who places the ad is subject to criminal liability, punishable by a fine not to exceed $5000 and/or one year in jail. There are also other penalties that could be recovered by a buyer.

Although it is not clear when a direct seller falls under Regulation Z, the motto "better safe than sorry" would probably be appropriate here.

One final note when you advertise property for sale. The Civil Rights Act of 1866 and the Federal Fair Housing Act of 1968 prohibit discrimination in the sale or rental of housing on the basis of race, color, religion, sex, or national origin. The acts cover houses, apartment, and vacant land to be used for residential purposes. Any advertising not in accordance with these acts might be considered a violation of them and could result in stiff penalties.

PREPARING TO SHOW

Showing a house is an art in itself. In addition to the painting and cleaning that go on before the home is ready, certain precautions should be taken. All personal property that does not go with the sale or that the buyer might reasonably conclude did go with the sale should either be noted or removed. See Chapter 5 for details on this.

MISREPRESENTING YOUR HOUSE

Sellers have a perfectly normal tendency, when showing their home, to point with pride at their property. Most buyers accept this for what it is, "puffing up" the house. *Puffing* is actually a recognized term in the selling of real estate. It covers such claims as, "This is the most charming house in the world," or "There's never a day that the sun doesn't shine on this house." Such claims will not be taken seriously by a buyer. If someone should take such a claim seriously and then try to get out of the deal claiming fraud or misrepresentation, he or she would undoubtedly get nowhere.

On the other hand, if you make claims about your house when you know they are false, then you might be guilty of fraud. If you make claims and you don't know in fact whether they are true or not, you might be guilty of negligence. The purchaser will assume, it being your home, that you know your own property. For example, suppose you converted part of your garage into a rumpus room without telling the city or county building and safety departments and without securing the proper permits and inspections. If you *informed* buyers that the building had been done in violation of local codes and that the buyers would purchase the property at their own risk knowing that at any time the city or county might require the improvements to be knocked down and might impose fines, you probably would be on very safe ground.

On the other hand, if you told buyers that the rumpus room had been built in accordance with all local building requirements, or if you said that you didn't know whether it had been built in accordance with all local building ordinances, or if you said it was there when you moved in and you didn't know anything about it, you could be in serious trouble if the buyers subsequently ran afoul of the city or county and wanted to recover their losses from you, the seller.

There is one area, mentioned earlier in Chapter 13, which is worth repeating, and that has to do with any item that could affect the safety of the buyers or their property. This usually has to do with electrical, plumbing, gas, or structural defects, most particularly with gas or electrical defects.

Take the case of Marc, who was selling by owner a very old home in northern California. Marc's home had been built in the days when electrical wiring consisted of two wires strung about 3 inches apart through the walls, ceiling, or floor and separated by porcelain insulators. This type of wiring had been illegal for more than a dozen years when Marc sold. However, so as not to produce an undue hardship on homeowners, the city required rewiring only upon sale of the property. Marc was aware of this, but he didn't want to spend the money on such an expensive job.

Rather than rewire, Marc obtained some lengths of Romex cable (two or three strands of wire wrapped separately and then together in heavy insulation) which was at the time approved by the city. He carefully rewired only those portions of his electrical system that were visible: in the garage, by the washer and dryer, and around a few light switches. Then he proceeded to sell his house.

Marc never told the buyer the wiring was good, but then, again, he never told the buyer it was bad. The buyer, seeing the good Romex, assumed that the home was properly wired. A city inspection, required on sales, also did not turn up the subterfuge.

The sale was made, and the buyer moved in. The next winter during a heavy rainstorm, the wiring shorted out and a good portion of the house burned down. The buyer was not injured, though many of his personal possessions were damaged. Marc eventually had to compensate the buyer for the loss. And he had to answer some very tough questions the city asked.

The moral here is never to try to get around a problem that involves health or safety. Either fix the defect or get a statement in writing from the buyers that they are fully aware of the problem and accept the house as is. Note: Some locales will not permit a sale unless defects in the property that could affect health and/or safety are first corrected.

PROBLEM AGENTS

Finally, one problem when you are showing the house comes from agents themselves. The moment you put a "For Sale by Owner" sign in your front yard, you become fair game for every agent in your vicinity. If you find that dozens and dozens of people are flocking through your house the first few days, be sure and ask each one whether he or she is truly a prospect or an agent. Frequently agents will go through homes for sale by owner, particularly on open house weekends, hoping to eventually get the seller to list. Others may just want to familiarize themselves with your property so that in the event they show a listed home nearby and their prospect sees your sign and asks about your property, they will be able to speak about it with authority.

These agents may or may not announce themselves. Many fall back on the excuse that besides being agents, they are also potential prospects. After all, they could, in theory, buy your house themselves.

One method that is particularly effective in distinguishing agents from buyers is to have all visitors sign in. Provide a pen and notebook at the entrance and insist that all persons coming through at least sign their name (many buyers will be reluctant to give their address or phone number for fear you will pester them even if they're not interested). Also directly ask each visitor whether he or she is an agent. Few brokers or salespeople will directly lie to that kind of question.

The list you gather has a secondary value. If you have prospective buyers' addresses or phone numbers, you can call them later. Also, if at some later date you decide to sell through a broker, you can do two things with the list. You can exclude the names you have from the listing you subsequently give, specifying that if any of the people who saw the house while you were selling it by owner come back and buy, you don't have to pay a commission. Or, if you're particularly anxious to sell, you can give the list to your broker so that your agent can contact the various people who came through and try to arrange a sale.

15

Foreclosure Dilemmas

Occasionally homeowners will go from good times to bad very quickly and often through no fault of their own. Illness, the loss of a job, or other circumstances may make it difficult or impossible to continue making the monthly payments. When the payments aren't made, the lender will threaten borrowers with foreclosure and put them in a position that can most aptly be described as "between a rock and a hard place." The lender will threaten to take over the house and throw the borrowers out. But very often, the very people who cannot make such payments are the ones who cannot afford to move. In such a situation the most common reactions of the borrower are fear, frustration, and inaction.

What should you do in such a situation? First, you should be aware that the subject of foreclosure is extremely complex, with virtually every state having different laws. When faced with the prospect of foreclosure, you should contact a competent attorney for advice on what can and can't be done in your particular area.

Next, you should be aware that the situation is usually far from hopeless. Home prices have been rising rapidly in all sections of the country, and individuals who have owned their property for even just a few years will likely have a considerable equity. (The equity is the difference between the current amount owed on the loan and the amount the house will bring in the open market.) If you are facing foreclosure, you do have at least three options given these conditions: One is to sell the property before the foreclosure becomes final and use the money to start again somewhere else. Secondly, you may, under certain circumstances, obtain a new loan, pay off the old loan, and perhaps even have money left over. Finally, until certain time limits expire, you can reinstate the mortgage by making good the lost payments and any penalties that may have been imposed by the lender.

Selling the property and making up back payments are straightforward procedures; however, refinancing when faced with foreclosure is a bit more complex.

Lenders who offer mortgages on real estate are looking for two things: First, the property must be worth more than the money loaned so that in the event you don't repay, the property can be sold to recover the loan. Second, you must show evidence of ability and willingness to repay. Lenders are in the business of loaning money, not foreclosing on property. They want to receive their money back with interest, not have the hassle of disposing of a home. This means that an owner who is already facing foreclosure on an existing loan should be the worst possible candidate for a new or refinanced loan.

However, because of certain quirks in lending procedures on real estate, it may be possible for you to get a new loan. If you have maintained all your other credit obligations, the threatened foreclosure will probably not show up on any credit report. And if you still have a steady and sufficiently high income, a new lender may act favorably on a request for a new loan. However, the new lender may request information on the status of the existing loan, and under no circumstances should you lie or try to conceal the fact that the foreclosure is imminent. You might, however, point out that you hadn't been making payments recently because of plans to refinance and that you simply didn't think it was necessary to waste money on monthly payments since, as soon as refinancing was complete, the old loan would be paid off anyhow.

Some individuals who have been refused refinancing have obtained it by having financially solvent relatives or friends cosign loans. In cases where lenders would not allow this, some unscrupulous owners have temporarily transferred title (faked a sale) to a financially solvent friend or relative and then had that person obtain new financing.

The key to any of the three alternatives to foreclosure—sale, refinancing, or reinstatement—however, is to act quickly before you lose your redemption rights to the property. The word *foreclosure,* in fact, is often defined as cutting off the borrower's rights to redeem the property.

Since time, therefore, is truly of the essence in a foreclosure, it is extremely helpful to know how much time you have before you lose your property. There are in reality three "clocks" running in foreclosure. The first clock can be called *default decision.*

As mentioned earlier, lenders do not like to foreclose on property. They are set up to spend a great deal of time appraising property, preparing documents and doing other paperwork, funding money, and doing everything else necessary to originating a loan. Once the loan is made, however, they usually put it on a computer and forget about it. They don't want to hear about that loan again.

When the borrower fails to make a payment, however, the computer sends a warning to the lender. The lender must now consider what action to take. Failure to make a payment in almost all mortgages is sufficient cause for starting foreclosure proceedings. (Failure to pay taxes or insurance or to maintain the property also are usually sufficient grounds for foreclosure, but are rarely used.) But if the lender starts foreclosure, there will be costs to pay, sometimes mounting into thousands of dollars, and there will be time lost during which the original money loaned will not be earning interest. Also, there is the public image of the lender to consider. Remember, a person's property is more than just a house, it is a home. A lender who forecloses too quickly and too often can get the reputation of a home wrecker, particularly if the local press makes an issue of it. (Never underestimate how sensitive lenders are to public opinion.)

Most lenders, therefore, will not start foreclosure procedures immediately. Rather, they will attempt to contact the borrower and determine the cause of nonpayment. If the borrower indicates a willingness to repay and the lender thinks there is any chance at all of being repaid, foreclosure will be stalled; the lender will not file a notice of default, the first step.

The default decision clock starts running as soon as the first payment is missed. How long it runs depends on how good the borrower is at convincing the lender that payment will eventually be made. The clock stops running when the lender finally decides that the borrower won't make good and files the notice of default or when the borrower makes up the payments.

How long does this clock usually run? The answer differs from state to state and usually depends on how difficult and expensive foreclosure procedures are. A recent study indicated that in Illinois, where foreclosure can take up to two years after the default notice has been filed, lenders tended to wait on the average as much as six months before filing. In Texas, on the other hand, where foreclosure can be concluded in as little time as five months, lenders only waited three or four months before filing. This does not mean, however, that a lender has to wait. It may turn out that your lender is the exception and files immediately.

While the default decision clock is running, the borrower can resort to any of the three alternatives: sale, refinance, or reinstatement.

Once the default decision clock runs out, the *foreclosure sale* clock begins. This clock runs from the time a notice of default is filed until your property is actually sold. It is a precise clock, with the time specified by state law. Each state, however, has different time limits. Once you reach this stage of foreclosure, if not sooner, you should see a competent attorney to find out what the time periods are in your state. Real estate brokers can also sometimes provide this information, as can state law books commonly found in most libraries.

How long the foreclosure sale clock runs depends to a great extent on whether you are in a state that uses the older *mortgage* system of real estate borrowing or the relatively newer *deed of trust* system. Deeds of trust are used in about a third of the states, mostly in the West.

If you have a mortgage, where there are just two parties to the loan, the borrower is known as the mortgagor and the lender is known as the mortgagee. After filing the notice of default the mortgagee normally has two recourses. One is to petition an equity court to sell the property to recoup the money loaned. The other is to sue the mortgagor in a court of law and obtain a judgment (which could be used to force sale on the property). The course taken usually depends on which is speedier in a given state. In either case the procedure takes lots of time, often up to six months or longer.

If you have a deed of trust, the foreclosure procedure is usually much quicker. There are three parties to the loan: the borrower or mortgagor, the lender or beneficiary, and a third party called the trustee. When the mortgagor buys the property, the trustee receives title and the right to sell in the event of default (nonpayment). The trustee can then sell the property "on the steps of the county courthouse to the highest bidder" and issue a trustee's deed.

In California, for example, which uses a deed of trust, the foreclosure sale clock runs thusly: From the time the notice of default is filed, the beneficiary must wait ninety days before proceeding. During this ninety-day period the mortgagor may redeem the loan simply by making up all back payments and any penalties the beneficiary may have assessed (these can sometimes run into the hundreds of dollars). After the ninety-day period the trustee must advertise the property for three weeks. During this twenty-one-day period the mortgagor can redeem the property only by paying off the entire mortgage plus penalties and costs. At the end of 111 days the house is sold to the highest bidder, which is usually the beneficiary. The foreclosure sale clock stops. (The beneficiary also usually has the option of forgoing the trustee sale and foreclosing through court action—a lengthy and costly procedure and, thus, seldom used.)

While the foreclosure sale clock is running, the borrower can normally sell or refinance the house and, subject to certain limitations, can often reinstate the loan.

Now the last or *redemption* clock begins to run in states where redemption is allowed. In the instance of the California deed of trust just discussed, the sale is final and afterward the borrower cannot redeem the property. But in many other states redemption is allowed. In the case of a mortgage, the borrower has the right to redeem the property for a set period of time, established by state law, by paying off the mortgage and costs. The redemption clock time limit varies.

It should be noted that the reason a redemption period is allowed is that a *deficiency judgment* is also allowed. A deficiency judgment is given when the property sold at a foreclosure sale does not bring enough money to cover the mortgage. The lender can then apply the judgment to other property of the borrower and force sale to recover the loss. At least three states—California, North Carolina, and Montana—have *purchase money* laws which do not allow deficiency judgments on mortgages which were part of the original *purchase price* of the property. Even in those states which have deficiency judgments the effect of the procedure is greatly minimized by the fact that the judgment often can be applied only to the borrower's other real estate, not to personal property, checking or bank accounts, cash, etc. Shrewd borrowers who have had deficiency judgments against them often record their other property in relatives' names and never pay the judgment (although, of course, there is a moral and legal obligation to do so).

The redemption clock runs for as long as the state redemption period allows. As with the foreclosure sale clock, you should check with an attorney to find the exact length of time for your area, although a guide to redemptions is given in the appendix.

Redemption is usually taken to mean reclaiming real property from someone else who has taken legal title to it, such as the lender. Thus during the equity or redemption period, it is not normally possible for the borrower to reinstate the original loan. During this period the borrower has the right to redeem the property, not the mortgage. In some cases it is also not possible to refinance during this period.

One additional problem that can arise comes from the use of a *receiver*. Many mortgages provide that during the foreclosure sale period the lender may appoint a receiver, whose duties are to see that the property is not damaged. Normally the receiver will be happy to have the original borrower remain in the property as long as it is apparent that the borrower does not intend to damage it in any way. Often an arrangement for payment of a nominal rent can be made. If, however, the receiver determines that the borrower intends to destroy part or all of the property out of vengeance or wrath, the receiver may move to have the borrower evicted. This could seriously affect that borrower's ability to use any of the three positive alternatives to foreclosure. If you should find yourself in this situation, work with the receiver. Creating a hostile atmosphere may be to your disadvantage.

Finally, there is one last option that a borrower has when faced with foreclosure—*consent*. In some cases where the borrower has very little equity, the lender will agree to forgo a deficiency judgment if the borrower will simply "deed over" the house. In common parlance this is called "walking away from it." In New England a similar method is referred to as *entry foreclosure*. Here, if the lender can gain possession of the property by peaceful entry, that is, by consent of the borrower, foreclosure can be obtained. The lender, however, must record a notice of entry, and the borrower usually has from one to three years to redeem the property. A deficiency judgment may also hold in this case. Contact the lender directly if you want to consent to foreclosure. Note, however, that some lenders will not agree to it.

In the case of rental property, borrowers faced with inevitable foreclosure have been known to "milk" the property during the time allowed by the various clocks. In residential rentals this simply means they will pocket the rent, but not pay any expenses such as taxes, insurance, mortgage, utilities, or maintenance. Most modern loans have provisions that allow the lender to step in and take over rent collection in such circumstances.

The best way to avoid foreclosure, of course, is to make your monthly payments. But, if you can't avoid it, don't give up all hope. Common sense, appropriate legal advice from a competent attorney, and a little bit of luck can help you get out of your house with almost all your equity, often in the form of cash.

16

How to Avoid Closing Difficulties

Once you've found someone to buy your home, your concern should be hanging onto that buyer. Agents are well aware of the uncertainties most buyers experience, and to avoid problems, they get purchasers to hand over a deposit and sign a sales agreement as soon as they express an intention to purchase. Agents understand that buying a house is not like making a grocery store purchase. Even buyers who seem to have made up their minds may, after a short time, begin reconsidering. It's the thought of spending all that money and tying themselves to a huge thirty-year mortgage that does most buyers in. Unless they are formally committed on paper, they are likely to get cold feet at any time.

Your problem selling by owner is twofold—you need to get a deposit from the buyer and you need to get a signed sales agreement. If you are experienced enough to fill out the sales agreement yourself, and if your buyers are experienced enough to know what's going on and to look out for their interests, your problems are solved. Unfortunately, the vast majority of direct sellers handle real estate transactions infrequently and don't know how to fill out sales agreements.

If you are in this situation, your best bet is to go with your buyer to someone who can fill out the agreement for you. An agent friend may be willing to do the paperwork either for free or for a small fee. Or you could make arrangements with an attorney to fill out the proper agreement. The important thing here is time. You want to get your buyer to sign immediately. Waiting overnight is too long.

A problem, however, is inherent in bringing in another person to fill out the forms. This third person may introduce new questions that could result in the loss of the deal. If the person who fills out the forms asks about items that you and the buyer have not discussed, or even if this person is too formal, too casual, or unsure of exactly what to do, the buyer may become uncomfortable and begin to back out of the deal. The best way around this problem is to be sure you thoroughly discuss all the items you and the buyer want in the sales agreement before you get to formally filling out the contract. It is a mistake to wait for this third party to clear up all but the most minor points. If you expect the third party to close the deal for you, you could be in for a rude awakening. It might turn out that when all the terms are out in the open, you don't have a deal at all. The buyer might be expecting you to take back a second at 7 percent interest while you assumed it would be 10 percent. You might have assumed the buyer was going to pay at least half the closing costs, while the buyer may be expecting you to pay more than half since you're saving a commission. Reread Chapter 6 on sales agreements to be sure all the hazards outlined there are taken care of before you get to the broker or attorney's office. A really experienced buyer may bring you a sales agreement and deposit signed and ready to go. If so, be sure you check it over with your broker or lawyer before you sign.

Having the buyer make out a signed deposit check for at least $500 before the formal signing is a good idea. Only don't take the check from the buyer. Let the buyer hold onto it until you've finished making out the sales agreement. The sales agreement is really a receipt for the deposit, and you need to give this to the buyer who hands you a check.

Also, if you ask that the check be drawn to an escrow officer you've already established (see Chapter 12), the buyer is likely to feel comfortable about this and go along with it.

In addition, be sure that your buyer has the capacity to sign a contract. In most states individuals who are mentally incompetent either because of insanity or old age cannot be held to contracts they sign. The same goes for individuals who are habitual drunkards. Be sure your buyer is not a minor (the age of maturity varies from state to state, but is usually between eighteen and twenty-one years). If a woman signs the contract, it is a good idea to have her husband sign also. In most states the contractual power of women, married or single, is now equivalent with that of men, but in certain areas a married woman may need her husband's consent to dispose of community property. If a corporation is buying your property, be sure that it is within the powers of its charter to make such a purchase and that the person signing is authorized by the corporation to do so. This is a job for your attorney.

Now go back and reread Chapters 1, 2, and 5 through 13. The questions they raise and the protections they suggest are in most cases just as applicable to the person selling by owner as to the individual selling with a broker.

17

Don't Count Your Money Until It's in Your Pocket!

There is one thing an agent learns very quickly in the real estate business which would benefit every direct seller to learn: Don't think a deal is closed until you've got the final check in your hand.

Real estate agents normally do the legwork in closing a deal. When you sell direct, you must do this work. It involves getting inspections, clearing liens from title, getting mortgage statements, and a dozen other chores, as discussed in Chapter 12.

It may turn out that you can't clear title because of some lien on your property you weren't even aware of. This is unlikely, but every so often it does happen. Or your buyer may not be able to get adequate financing to complete the deal. This happens fairly often. Or you may have a bad buyer who will try to win concessions from you right up until the time the title to the property is transferred. This rarely happens when an agent handles the deal because the agent acts as insulation between buyer and seller. In direct deals, however, it can be a definite problem.

An example of this type of bad buyer is Efrem. Efrem agreed to buy Mr. and Mrs. Bertleson's home for $25,000 in a direct sale. The Bertlesons carefully outlined all the terms of the agreement, including a 20 percent down payment and an 80 percent loan including interest rate and terms. Efrem agreed, and they even shook hands on the matter.

They proceeded together to an attorney that the Bertlesons had hired to fill out the sales agreement. Efrem was jovial all the way, and the sellers glanced at one another convinced they had finally sold their property and thinking about the antique store they would buy with their money.

At the attorney's office, Efrem had a lapse of memory. He seemed to remember that the Bertlesons had agreed to take back a 10 percent second. When the sellers protested that that was not at all what they had agreed upon, Efrem seemed confused. He said he was sorry if he had misunderstood, but he had only enough money to put down a maximum of 15 percent. Unless the Bertlesons would take back at least a 5 percent second, there could be no sale. This was $1250. The sellers wanted all cash, but they had their spirits up high believing that their house was sold and they despaired of starting over. In the end they agreed to the 5 percent second. Efrem handed over a $500 deposit. The sales agreement was drawn up and signed by all parties. Again they shook hands.

During the closing, Efrem proved to be a terrible pest. He jumped from one lending institution to another trying to get a ¼ percent lower interest on his new mortgage, delaying the deal. Then he insisted the sellers leave their lawn mower and garden tools as part of the sale. To get the deal over with, the Bertelsons agreed. Then he insisted that the sellers repaint several rooms inside the home. The Bertlesons absolutely refused. Efrem threatened not to go through with the deal. As a compromise, the sellers threw in several gallons of paint.

Finally, the appointed day arrived. Escrow had been completed. All that remained for the sellers was to sign their payoff papers on their old loan and the deed.

They signed and were told to expect a check in a few days. All that remained now was for the buyer to sign his final papers (giving the exact breakdown of costs, prorations, and loan amounts) and deposit the remainder of the down payment, and the deal would close.

The Bertlesons went home happy. Two days later they called the escrow officer. Efrem hadn't signed.

They called the next day. He still hadn't signed.

When they contacted him, Efrem seemed disenchanted with the deal. He said that he had meant to put down only 10 percent. He didn't think it was fair for him to have to put all his money in the property by putting up 15 percent in cash. When the sellers pointed out that he had signed an agreement, he said that didn't matter; he wasn't going to sign the final papers and deposit the final monies as the deal stood. He wanted the Bertlesons to take back a 10 percent second.

The sellers were outraged. They said they would call off the deal and Efrem would lose his $500 deposit. Efrem countered that if the sellers didn't give him back his deposit he would take them into court. He would say he had made a mistake and thought he was only putting 10 percent down. He would claim that the sellers and their attorney had coerced him into signing a false document.

The Bertlesons considered. Efrem seemed crazy enough to pursue the matter to court and even if he lost, their money would be tied up for some time, and then there would be additional attorney's fees to pay.

Should they then just forget the deal? But they had opened an escrow, and they already had attorney's fees to pay. Most important, they were planning ahead. They had spent their money from the sale.

In the end it seemed more practical to give Efrem what he wanted than to fight. After all, the Bertlesons argued, they were still getting the same amount only in the form of a loan rather than cash. They conceded and took back a 10 percent second.

Efrem was not crazy. He was a shrewd buyer who judged his sellers very well. He knew he would buy the property only if he could get it with 10 percent down, and he also knew that the sellers wanted only cash. So he persistently gave them little tests. He didn't insist on the entire 10 percent second at once, just half at first. When the sellers agreed, he knew he would get it all and more—the garden tools, lawn mower, and paint. He knew the Bertlesons had committed the great selling error—they were counting their money. Every time Efrem threatened to back out of the deal, they felt as though they would be losing that which they already possessed—a sale.

The Bertlesons should have dumped Efrem at the first sign of deceit. The instant he claimed not to have understood what was perfectly clear only moments before, they should have insisted he perform exactly on the terms of their first agreement, the one they had first shaken hands on. If he had refused, they should have found another buyer. As it was, they needed cash to begin a business and they were forced to quickly sell their second, now $2500, getting only 60 cents on the dollar, or $1500. They had lost $1000 in cash by continuing with the deal.

Bad buyers will seek out direct sellers. Often these buyers know a great deal more about real estate than they ever let on. And they are always testing to see just how far they can go with an inexperienced seller. The best defense against them is to understand that your house is never sold until you transfer title and get your check.

THREE

Protect Yourself When You Buy

18

House Hunting and Financing Hints

One curse of our modern times is that when we go to buy anything it almost always costs more than we expected. That's particularly true with houses. Over the past five years homes have appreciated at an average annual rate of between 10 and 15 percent, depending on the area of the country. What that means is that you as a buyer are going to have to pay $40,000 to $50,000 or more for a home that just five years ago was selling for half that price. Today less than 15 percent of the homes available sell for under $35,000. Taxes also have skyrocketed, and as of this writing, interest rates remain high. The problem for most house hunters, then, is not just how to buy a dream house, but how to buy any house.

There are answers to that problem, but they tend to be painful. You can put a larger down payment into the house to reduce your monthly payments; if your spouse is not working, you can increase the family's income by having your spouse go to work and use the increase to make house payments; or you can go to extraordinary means to get financing and then stretch to the breaking point making payments and hope that somewhere down the road your family income will increase to ease the burden.

Any of these measures may be necessary for the average family to get a home in today's market. Building groups estimate that over 70 percent of the population cannot afford today's average house by any other means.

A house is important—it's shelter, it's security, and it's an investment, and as such it's worth stretching for. The critical thing, however, is not to stretch past the breaking point. It is important that you protect yourself so that you aren't forced into foreclosure in a year or so and lose not only the money you invested, but your good credit as well.

It has traditionally been accepted by most lending institutions that a buyer can afford a home that is 2½ times his or her annual income. If, for example, you make $15,000 a year, you can afford a home that costs $37,500. However, upon looking closely, you may discover that you cannot buy what you expect in a home for under $50,000.

Should you be satisfied with a smaller home or should you try for the one closer to your dream house? It has been my experience that the most important thing is to find a home that you are happy with. If you get a house at a very good price, but it is too small for you or your family, or its design is not to your liking, or its location is not what you want, you will live day in and day out regretting the purchase, long after your pleasure in the price is forgotten. If you're going to live in the house, pick the very best you can get.

In today's market that can be a big chore. Assuming that you can come up with the 20 percent down that is typically required to purchase, you must be able to live with the monthly payments on the remaining 80 percent loan. At 8 percent interest, an 80 percent loan on a $37,500 home comes to monthly payments of principal and interest of $220. An 80 percent loan on a $50,000 home for the same period comes to $294. The difference is $74 a month.

Remember also that the more expensive house has higher taxes. If the cheaper home has taxes of about $1100 a year (typical for that size residence), a house that costs a third more will also probably have taxes of about a third more, or about $1466 a year. That works out to $92 a month for the cheaper home and $122 a month for the more expensive home—a difference of $30 a month. Finally your fire and hazard insurance will also be higher. A typical price is $140 a year for a homeowners policy on a $37,500 home and $170 a year on a $50,000 dwelling —a difference of $30 a year. The breakeven works out like this:

$37,500 home after $7500 cash down	80 percent loan at 8 percent	$50,000 home after $10,000 cash down
$220	Loan payment (principal and interest)	$294
92	Taxes	122
12	Insurance	14
324	Monthly payment	430

The more expensive house would cost $106 a month more. For a family on a limited budget, that's a sizable amount of money. Assuming an income of $15,000 a year, the $430 payment amounts to more than a third of the monthly income *before* deductions for income taxes, social security, and the like.

Do you want to get involved in something like that? If you're financially conservative, chances are you'll bow out and take the cheaper home. Most people today, however, are paying the price for a home closer to what they want. They have come up with a variety of ways of accomplishing this.

In going for the more expensive house, many families with sizable savings have put more money into the house. By putting 50 percent or $25,000 down on a $50,000 home, the monthly payments can be reduced to $321 a month on our 8 percent, thirty-year mortgage. That's $110.50 less than on an 80 percent loan.

It's an effective way of reducing the payments, but expensive. That money might be better invested in areas where it will make a high return. It might actually cost more than $110.50 in lost profit to keep the money in the house. This method should only be used by someone with very limited income and as a last alternative.

Most buyers, however, don't have to worry about the best place to invest their money. They don't have that much cash lying around to invest. Consequently they are stuck with taking out a loan of 80 percent or higher.

Most lending institutions, however, will not even give a mortgage on a home unless the buyer's gross monthly income is four times that of the total house payments, assuming the buyer has no outstanding debts which run for more than six months (such as car payments). That means that, in theory, just to qualify for a loan on a $50,000 home, a buyer should be making $1720 a month, or roughly $20,640 a year. To qualify for a $37,500 house, a buyer should be making about $15,750 a year.

The answer, of course, is to increase the monthly income by one means or another in order to qualify for the loan.

One method is to have a spouse get a part-time or full-time job, assuming that both spouses are not already employed. If a spouse providing a second income has been on the job for six months or longer, most lenders will usually accept that income in figuring the qualifications for a loan. Note: Discrimination against women in qualifying for loans still exists to a limited extent in some lending institutions, but is disappearing.

A method not recommended is to falsify the loan application. Most lenders have only two means of knowing a buyer's income—one is what the buyer puts down on the loan application and the other is a letter of verification from the buyer's employer. If the employer is willing to lie or hedge a bit about the wages of the employee/buyer, the lender can easily be fooled. Only if the lender is suspicious will it normally ask to see a buyer's income tax records to verify salary. This chicanery is mentioned here only to point out that it should be avoided. In most cases, lying willfully on a loan application violates state and/or federal law and may subject the applicant to stiff fines and/or imprisonment. In actual practice, buyers who are discovered to have falsified are often just turned down on their loan application.

Finally, you can try to increase your own income either by looking for better-paying work or by taking an extra job. This second alternative, however, is not too desirable, for most lenders will not allow the total salary from a second job to be included in calculating a loan qualification.

If you've increased your income to the point where you can qualify for the loan, you should still reconsider taking it out. Will your spouse, for example, continue to work for five years or more in order to continue helping with the house payments? Will you be able to physically maintain a second job over a period of years? If your second income stops, will you be able to keep up the payments from a reserve of savings until the extra income can get started again? Are you prepared to handle the increases in taxes and insurance that will surely occur on your house? These can easily boost monthly payments $10 to $50 a month *each year*.

Most of us can't really know the answers to these questions. We simply hope for the best and dive in. If that is your intent, take heart from the following information. An individual making $15,000 a year and getting annual wage increases of 10 percent a year can expect to be making almost exactly $22,000 in five years. If the wage increases are only 7 percent each year, this buyer will still be making $19,660 in five years.

My feeling is that it is reasonable to take a risk on the future in qualifying for a high loan—if the period of time is not greater than five years. If an individual's job is steady or if transferring from one employer to another is easy, and if the buyer understands that there's always the chance of losing everything, why not gamble?

Tables are provided to help you make your decision on how far to stretch your budget and to protect you from stretching too far. Table 1 shows you how much you can expect to pay in monthly payments for principal and interest on a thirty-year loan at varying interest rates and loan amounts. Table 2 shows how increasing a down payment affects the monthly payments on a loan.

To use Table 1, find the nearest loan amount and go across to the interest rate being charged. That is the mortgage payment. But remember, it is for *principal and interest only*. Taxes and insurance have to be *added* to this amount.

TABLE 1
THIRTY-YEAR LOAN

Loan amount	Interest rate			
	7%	8%	9%	10%
$25,000	$166.50	$183.50	$210.25	$219.50
30,000	199.80	220.20	241.50	263.40
35,000	233.10	256.90	281.75	307.30
40,000	266.40	293.60	322.00	351.20
45,000	299.70	330.30	362.25	395.10
50,000	333.00	367.00	402.50	439.00
55,000	366.30	403.70	442.75	482.90
60,000	399.60	440.40	483.00	526.80
65,000	432.90	477.10	523.25	570.70
70,000	466.20	513.80	563.50	614.60
75,000	499.50	550.50	603.75	658.50
80,000	532.80	587.20	644.00	702.40
85,000	566.10	623.90	684.25	746.30
90,000	599.40	660.60	724.50	790.20
95,000	632.70	697.30	764.75	834.10
100,000	666.00	734.00	805.00	878.00

To find the monthly payments of a loan amount not shown on the table estimate between the two closest figures, or for exact amounts use this calculation:

	Interest rate			
	7%	8%	9%	10%
For each $1000 of loan multiply by amount	6.66	7.34	8.05	8.78

TABLE 2
EFFECT OF DOWN PAYMENT ON THE MONTHLY PAYMENTS OF A $50,000 HOME AT 9 PERCENT INTEREST FOR THIRTY YEARS

Down payment	Monthly payment (principal and interest)
$ 5,000	$362.50
10,000	322.50
15,000	282.50
20,000	242.50
25,000	202.50

Some buyers have enough income to qualify for loans, but lack the money required for a down payment. The alternatives here are much brighter. If you can qualify for a VA loan, you can purchase a home costing up to $70,000 usually with no down payment at all (although there may be several thousand dollars in closing costs).

If a VA loan is not a possibility for you, there is FHA and conventional financing. On conventional financing most banks will lend up to 80 percent. Most savings and loan institutions will lend up to 90 percent. Some banks, savings and loans, and mortgage bankers will go as high as 95 percent on a PMI loan if you have superior credit. (Note: As we discussed in Chapter 6, a PMI is simply a conventional mortgage insured privately. Ask your bank or savings and loan association about this type of loan. Don't take "such things don't exist" for an answer. PMIs do exist, although you may have to shop around to find a lender who's willing to handle the 95 percent ones.)

Or, you can look for a home where the seller is willing to carry back a second mortgage. The thing to remember here is that the lender of the first will not normally allow more than 10 percent of the price to be in the form of a second, assuming an 80 percent first. This means that you must come up with 10 percent cash.

Finally, there is the matter of ballooning or kiting. As noted in Chapter 9, this occurs when a buyer purchases a home at one price, then falsifies a sales agreement at a higher price in order to get a higher loan from a lender. Needless to say, this is illegal and should be avoided. The trouble one can get into doing this is not worth the potential gain.

Assuming that you can comfortably make the monthly payments, there are few dangers and many benefits in putting up a small down payment. The greatest benefit is that you end up buying with someone else's money. You use leverage, and this can result in the greatest profit when it comes time to sell. Suppose you buy a $40,000 house and put down only 10 percent, or $4000. The house appreciates at a rate of 10 percent a year for three years and then you sell. Forgetting closing costs for a moment, what's your profit?

At the end of three years you sell for $53,240, or a profit of roughly $13,000. But you only invested $4000. Over three years that's better than a 300 percent return on your money!

That's the reason, as long as you don't get in over your head on monthly payments, that it's hard to go wrong buying a house in today's market.

One last point that should be taken up has to do with the *variable-rate mortgages* that have come into vogue since 1974. A variable-rate mortgage is simply one in which the interest rate the borrower pays varies either up or down. The fluctuations are usually tied to the amount it costs lending institutions to borrow money. The more it costs them, the more it costs the home mortgage borrower.

Many buyers are afraid of variable-rate mortgages. They see the danger as dramatically increased monthly payments should the interest rate suddenly skyrocket. This fear is partly real and partly imagined.

First, most variable-rate mortgages are written so that (1) fluctuations in interest charged can only occur at six-month intervals, (2) the maximum fluctuation per interval is only ¼ percent, and (3) the total maximum fluctuation either up or down over the life of the loan is only 2½ percent. This means that if you obtain a loan at 9 percent, in most cases the interest rate could increase to no more than 11½ percent. And, in the event inflation goes down, the interest rate could potentially drop to as low as 6½ percent.

Secondly, legislation is currently in the works to allow the lending institution to add on additional years to a mortgage as an alternative to increasing monthly payments. This means that rather than raise the payment as the interest goes up, the loan would be extended for as many years as needed, up to a maximum of forty.

Finally, it is still possible to avoid the variable-rate mortgage and get the old fashioned fixed-rate mortgage. As of this writing, no federal savings and loan associations are allowed to make variable-rate mortgages. Only state-chartered savings and loan associations may do so. If you want a fixed-rate mortgage, see your federal chartered lender.

Variable-rate mortgages are the lending institution's answer to a market where unexpected inflation can suddenly threaten to put them out of business. A few lenders have tied these loans to the current rate for mortgages (offering the loans at ¼ to ½ percent below the regular mortgage rates as an inducement). Others have tied them to the prime rate, which is the short-term rate charged to a bank's best customers, usually institutions. As the cost of money increases during an inflation, both these rates tend to rise and, correspondingly, so does the rate for the variable-rate mortgage. Many lending institutions today, however (particularly those on the West Coast), tie their variable-rate mortgages to the index for the cost of money at the Federal Home Loan Bank Board (FHLBB) in their area.

Since these indices did not rise and fall in *direct* relation to the great inflation of 1974–1975, some observers have argued that variable-rate mortgages are not really issued by the lenders as inflation protectors, and some have even suggested that the lenders' real motives are boosted profits.

While additional profits are certainly a motive, this argument stems basically from a misunderstanding of the functioning of the FHLBB during the last inflation. During that period, lenders, particularly savings and loan associations, were faced with few new deposits and severe withdrawals as investors took their money out to place in higher-yield investments. (Lenders are limited by law in the amount of interest they can pay on deposits; they were offering 4 to 7½ percent while inflation was approaching 12 percent.) This situation of greater withdrawals than deposits is called *disintermediation* and if continued long enough can put a savings and loan association out of business. To make matters worse, because withdrawals exceeded deposits, these lenders had no money of their own to lend and therefore had no way to create earnings to pay their expenses. Also, since the savings and loan associations supply a great portion of the nation's home loan money, there were few mortgages available for consumers.

The salvation of the lenders was the FHLBB. It lent the associations money at its own interest rate and they, in turn, were able to lend this money to mortgagors. (In some areas this was the *only* mortgage money available to buyers!) The lenders now could earn money, and thus stayed in business.

However, the FHLBB index (its price for money) is variable, fluctuating according to money market conditions. The money the lenders were loaning out was locked into thirty-year home mortgages at fixed rates. Should the FHLBB index rise, the savings and loan associations could conceivably lose enormous sums of money.

The solution was to tie the home mortgage rate to the FHLBB index, and thus one of the most common forms of the current variable-rate mortgage was created. It benefits the lender and it benefits the consumer by providing mortgages that would otherwise not be available.

Don't be afraid of variable-rate loans. But don't rush into one either. Check them out and compare them against fixed rates. Remember, while the interest rate can go up, there's always the chance that it also might go down.

In order to be sure you don't overlook any loan possibilities, check the following summaries.

FHA LOANS

TO QUALIFY

Any borrower may qualify provided he or she makes in gross income (before taxes) at least 4 times the monthly payment (including principal and interest on the loan, taxes, and insurance). In addition, the borrower must have good credit and must have no long-term debts (loans, car payments, etc.) which will bring the ratio of the gross income to the monthly payment below 4 to 1.

MAXIMUM LOAN

$45,000   1 unit
 48,750   2–3 units
 56,000   4 units

DOWN PAYMENT

Based on sales price plus closing costs, or FHA value including closing costs, whichever is less. FHA loans are made in increments of $50, rounded down.
3% of first $25,000
10% of next $10,000
20% of balance

NONOCCUPANT MORTGAGES

85% of maximum loan as computed above.

IF THE BUYER IS A VETERAN (FHA-VA)

(served on active duty not less than 90 days, discharged other than dishonorably)
0% of first $25,000
10% of next $10,000
15% of the balance

VETERAN TERMS ARE AVAILABLE ON SINGLE UNITS ONLY.

VETERAN TERMS ARE AVAILABLE EVEN IF BUYER HAS PREVIOUSLY OBTAINED A VA LOAN.

TERM OF LOAN

30 years or three-fourths of remaining economic life of property, whichever is less.

VA LOANS

TO QUALIFY

The buyer must meet one of the following three requirements:
1. Have been on active duty during World War II or the Korean conflict and (a) discharged or released other than dishonorably having served 90 days or more, any part of which was during the period from September 16, 1940, to July 25, 1947, or from June 27, 1950, to January 31, 1955, or (b) discharged by reason of service-connected disability from periods of active duty, any part of which occurred during either of the above two wartime periods.

2. Have been on active duty after January 31, 1955, discharged or released other than dishonorably, and have been on continuous duty for 181 days or more, any part of which occurred after January 13, 1955, or have been discharged from active duty by reason of a service-connected disability.
3. Be presently on active duty (other than for training purposes) and have served at least 181 days in that status.

(Note: Veterans with World War I service only are not eligible. The Congress is continually setting expiration dates for VA benefits and continually extending them. It is a good idea to call a lender to be sure the program you qualify for has not by chance expired, before you make a deposit on a house.)

MAXIMUM LOAN

No maximum, though loans rarely exceed $70,000.

DOWN PAYMENT

Usually none

OCCUPANCY

The buyer must intend to occupy the property.

CONVENTIONAL LOANS

TO QUALIFY

Qualifications vary, but for a typical 80% loan the buyer must make in gross income (before taxes) at least 4 times the monthly payments (including principal and interest on the loan, taxes, and insurance). Good credit and no long-term debts which reduce income below 4 times the monthly payment are also requirements.

MAXIMUM LOAN

95%. Most conventional lenders such as banks and savings and loan associations will loan 80% of their appraised values of the property. Using PMI many may raise this amount an additional 15%, but the buyer must have exceptionally good credit and a higher income, and the house must be in perfect condition, have at least three bedrooms and two baths, and must be in a desirable location. Banks will often loan 50 to 66⅔% to buyers who qualify at less than 4 to 1 provided they put down the balance in cash.

OCCUPANCY

On 80% loans there is not usually an occupancy requirement. On loans of higher amounts, there usually is.

LENDERS

There are four sources of conventional loan money—savings and loan associations, banks, mortgage bankers, and private lenders.

Savings and loan associations are primarily in the business of making real estate loans. They are among the most liberal of lenders and often have interest rates ¼% lower than banks. They also often charge fewer points.

Banks are the most flexible of the lenders. They will occasionally bend the rules for a good customer. They can make personal as well as real estate loans.

Mortgage bankers are usually middlemen for out-of-state lending institutions. When money is available (a big lender wants to get into your area), they frequently have the best rates and terms. But they are sporadic. Check with them by phone first to see if they have money or are going through a dry spell. (You'll find them in the yellow pages.)

Private lenders are usually a last resort. They will often make loans on property that institutions won't touch, but they'll charge higher rates. They often advertise in local papers. Escrow officers also often know private lenders.

19

How to Handle a Selling Broker

Buying a home differs from almost every other type of purchase in one significant way—it's extremely difficult to see what you are buying.

When you go into a grocery store to buy a can of tomatoes, all the cans are conveniently arranged on the shelf for you to pick and choose by size, price, and brand. When you go to buy a car, each dealer has dozens or even hundreds of models on a lot for you to examine. But when you go to buy a house, especially a resale or used home, often considerable distances separate each product. You have to travel from one to the next. This traveling and the time it takes makes comparison shopping very difficult. In order to really see what's available, what the prices are, what the market is at the moment of your purchase, you have to spend days or weeks of solid effort.

ADVERTISING TRICKS

Many buyers begin their house hunting efforts by consulting the local paper. The residential real estate section of a paper is often a good percentage of the classified advertising, in some papers more than half. Usually the advertising is organized by area, not by price, and this can make house hunting extremely difficult, for within any given area the prices may fluctuate enormously. In addition while in one area $40,000 may buy a three-bedroom, two-bath home, in another it may get nothing more than a one-bedroom shack.

Some *exaggeration* is the rule rather than the exception in advertising. A "Cape Cod dream cottage" may in reality be more of a nightmare once you see it. Or a "ranch-style rustic home" may be a converted barn. Anyone who has ever gone house hunting usually has a favorite tale of humorously exaggerated claims.

Much more serious a tactic is extreme exaggeration or the *bait and switch* game used by a few unscrupulous agents. Basically it goes like this:

Jim and Rita are looking at the ads and they see what appears to be a miracle house—it's got four bedrooms and two baths, is in a great location, and costs only $27,000 with a low down payment. Enthused, Rita and Jim call the agent and are told that yes, such a place does exist, but the agent isn't sure if it's been sold. If they rush down to the office, they might just get it before someone else beats them to it.

Upon arriving at the agent's office, out of breath, Rita and Jim learn that the house has been sold. "Sorry," the agent says, "I told you it would go fast. But we have another." Now our buyers are escorted by the agent on a tour of homes none of which even comes close to the advertised property. In the end, if the agent is a "good salesman," Rita and Jim may end up buying one of the other homes.

In fact, the dream home was just bait to get buyers in the doors of the agent's office, where they could be switched to another home. Did the advertised house really exist? Perhaps. One agent ran an ad for such a home for six months after it had actually sold. When a buyer finally complained to the local district attorney's office, the agent said he had forgotten to remove the ad from the paper. In other cases advertisements have almost lied about a home's assets. Closets and porches have been called bedrooms; sinks in the garage, bathrooms. And "mistakes" have occurred regarding price and terms.

Anytime you see a "miracle" advertised in the real estate section of your paper, you may have found an unscrupulous agent. So, beware. If it were truly a steal, the agent, or someone in the agent's office or even a friend would have already bought it. If the "miracle" is for sale by owner, the seller is probably simply exaggerating. However, since most direct sellers have only one house to sell at a time, there's not much chance of a bait and switch, so it's at least worth a look.

Most advertising that agents do serves two purposes. The first is to get listings. Agents know that sellers often check the local paper to see who advertises heavily and then list with these. Secondly, the ad is designed to bring in buyers. Since it is virtually impossible to know whether or not you will like a house until you're physically inside it, agents know that no matter what they say in their ads, more than nine out of ten buyers will be disappointed when they finally see the property. So they make the ads as alluring as possible, hoping to get buyers to call and then to find the right house for them.

An important rule to remember is that when you call an agent because you've seen an ad, that agent is not answering the phone to give out information. The agent is answering the phone to get your name, address, and phone number and most important, to make an appointment with you.

The basic reason for this is competition. Agents cooperate on the majority of listings, and in many cases any agent can sell you a particular house. Agents believe, with some good reason, that buyers are totally disloyal. They will buy from whomever they are with when they find (or are talked into) the right place.

If an agent simply gives you the information you need on a piece of property, such as price, terms, location, and size, and it is not exactly what you want, it is so easy for you to say, "Sorry, I'm not interested," and hang up. After all, why should you continue on with an agent who doesn't have the property you want?

Agents often believe that they must prove to you that you need them. And the easiest way of proving this is by not giving you all the information you need so you'll stay on the line, keep asking questions, and eventually meet with them. They may not refuse outright, but after a few pleasantries and the identification of the house you called about, you will often find the agent turning every question you ask into a demand for an appointment. If you ask how large the home is, the agent may quote you a size and then mention that he or she has several other homes in the same area at different sizes and ask what size you were looking for. When you respond, the agent may suggest that he or she has such a home, but the only way to tell if it's for you is for you to make an appointment to see it.

Some offices have a policy of never revealing the address of advertised property to callers. If you ask directly for the address, agents will often respond that the owner has requested that the property be shown only by appointment (which may or may not be true). If you ask again for the address so you can just drive by and see the outside, agents may respond that you can't really do justice to the home by seeing it from the outside. The implication here is that the agents are first protecting the homeowner from intrusion and secondly protecting you from yourself. In fact, agents are usually protecting themselves. They are afraid that if you drive by and don't like the house, you will never call back. If you drive by and like the property, the agent worries that you may call another broker (particularly if another broker has a sign on the property) or a relative or friend in the real estate business.

All this goes to say that when you call about an ad, don't expect to be given the information you seek without spending some time getting it. Be prepared to spend at least a few hours and probably an afternoon with the agent. If you've got a lot of time, it can be fun. If, however, you're short on time, forget altogether about checking the agents' ads.

DEALING WITH THE BROKER

After the hassle of checking out ads, many buyers resort to searching for a home on their own. This is exhausting and probably fruitless. Traveling up and down streets looking for homes for sale may be all right if you've pinpointed the area you want, but don't expect to cover an entire city that way. Besides, some sellers who have listed their homes don't have signs on them, although this is a rarity. Your best bet is to simply contact an agent and then let the agent show you properties. This has many advantages, and many disadvantages which you should be aware of.

1. *Should you have one agent or many?* Many agents belong to multiple listing services. These are cooperative organizations through which brokers share their listings. By means of the multiple listing service, a broker may be able to show you 50 to 80 percent or more of the homes available in your area. On the other hand, many offices do not share their listings, particularly the good ones (which usually means the lower-priced ones). Thus, it is important not to limit yourself to one agent. Go out with as many agents as you can manage in the time you have available.

A word should be said here about the payment an agent receives for showing you homes. An agent may spend hours, even days, with you, driving you many miles to see one, two, or a dozen homes. You should understand that in almost all cases, the agent receives no compensation for this service *unless* you ultimately purchase a home on which the agent can collect a commission.

Many agents are very adept at making you feel you are in their debt for their efforts. They may occasionally remind you of the number of houses they've shown to you. Or they may casually grumble about the expenses of being a real estate agent—an impressive car in which to drive you around, gas, their office expense, their time. After a while, you may begin to feel that you owe an agent for his or her services—that after all the agent has done, the least you can do is buy a house.

Put such guilt feelings aside.

The agent in almost all cases works for the seller, both legally and morally. The agent is paid by the seller, via a commission, to procure a buyer. If an agent fails to show you a home that you of your own volition want to buy, you owe that agent nothing. The agent hasn't earned a commission and doesn't deserve to be paid. And every agent knows this, for it's specified in virtually every listing agreement—the agent will be paid a commission only upon procuring a buyer *ready, willing,* and *able* to purchase on the seller's specified terms. If you've gone out with an agent for several days sincerely looking for a home and that agent hasn't found it for you, you don't owe the agent. The agent owes you for wasting *your* time. In real estate, the agent is the hunter and you are the game. And the game never owes the hunter for being a lousy shot.

When an agent begins to turn the screws, mentioning all that he or she has done for you, it's time to get another agent. For what is really being said is that this agent can't find the house you sincerely are looking for, so won't you buy something less than you want in return for that agent's efforts? In school, a student may get an A for effort, but in real estate, a salesperson deserves nothing for it unless it's accompanied by a sale.

2. *Many buyers are concerned about getting the right agent.* The right agent is simply one who will find you the house you are looking for and not pressure you into buying something you don't want. Is this agent more likely to be a broker than a salesperson?

As we saw in Chapter 1, a broker has usually passed a rigorous exam, has served an apprenticeship, and is licensed by the state to sell real estate, whereas a salesperson has usually passed a less rigorous exam and is still serving an apprenticeship under a broker. Is it better to deal with a salesperson or a broker?

It depends. Usually brokers will be more commanding when it comes time to present your offer. Drawing on years of experience, the broker can often convince a seller to take less. On the other hand, a broker running an office with several salespeople usually won't have the time to spend taking you around the countryside looking at homes. Ideally, you should get the salesperson to show you the homes and the broker to present your offer.

Some buyers, in trying to find a "good" agent, will ask friends for recommendations, particularly friends who have recently bought or sold homes. This could be risky, as a good many agents will offer any buyer or seller whom they've dealt with a finder's fee of $25 to $100 or more for sending new prospects their way. Unless you know and trust your friends very well, their recommendation might be biased by this fee.

3. *What should you tell the agent?* Agents and buyers often play a cat-and-mouse game about how much money the buyers really have, what their income actually is, what kind of house they truly desire. Much of the deception that goes on is unnecessary. However, a certain amount is necessary in order to protect the buyers' privacy.

In terms of the house itself, you should probably tell the agent the maximum amount that can be spent. You should know how big a loan you are likely to qualify for and how much you will need to put down. You might check your agent's competency by telling him or her your income and cash available and seeing if the agent comes up with the same answers. If the answers are different, find out why, and be sure some hanky-panky like balooning the mortgage isn't involved.

While it may be necessary to tell the agent your gross income and any long-term debts you have, it is not necessary to reveal much more, although if you have a credit problem you might want to mention that. It's not necessary to tell the agent if you've been divorced one or more times. It's not necessary to tell the agent if you own any other real estate. It's not necessary to mention any other assets, such as cash, stocks, bonds, gold, unless you plan to use them in the current transaction. You might need to reveal all this information once you find a home and apply for a loan, but no one need know while you are just looking.

4. *Get the best information.* Once you've told the agent what you can spend, you should insist that the agent tell you the best areas of town. Often at this stage, the agent will indicate that there are certain areas where you can't possibly buy because you can't afford the homes. And at the same time the agent will often indicate areas where you are most likely to find a home in your price range.

Remember, location is the most important item in buying a home. And the agent is not necessarily thinking about getting you into the best possible area, but rather in making a sale. If one area has a dozen houses for which you might easily qualify, while another has only one that you could just barely get into, which area do you think the agent will suggest?

Insist on seeing homes in the area that is just above your reach. If you can afford only a $35,000 house, it obviously would be ridiculous to spend a lot of time looking in an area where all the houses were selling for $100,000 or more. But it might be worth your time searching out an area where the homes sell for around $40,000. You might find one priced lower, or you might try a few offers at less than the asking price. This can be frustrating, for everything you look at may seem to be just out of reach. But time spent in this kind of searching can result in getting a far better home.

5. *Watch out for the broker who offers to get you a VA loan on a home when you know you don't qualify or the broker who offers to put you into an FHA home even though you're not planning to live in the house.*

VA loans are very desirable from a buyer's point of view because normally they involve no down payment. However, in order to qualify, you must have been on active duty in the armed services for a minimum of 180 days during certain specified dates (see loan summaries in Chapter 18). Most buyers simply do not qualify for VA loans. Occasionally, however, brokers will offer to get around the qualifying problems by using a substitute buyer.

An unscrupulous agent may ask you whether you have a friend or relative who qualifies. If you have, the agent will probably turn all smiles and begin showing you homes that you could only buy VA (probably because you couldn't come up with the necessary financing). Once you've found a home you like, the agent will say that in order to buy it, your friend or relative will have to apply for the loan and sign the sales agreement. You put up the money, and your friend or relative, who might be called your "partner," buys the property. Since these loans are available only to buyers who intend to live in the property, your partner will need to lie a bit on the loan application. Actually, the lying is more than a bit, because on a VA loan buyers must normally affirm that they are coming up with all the cash to buy the property from personal funds. When the sale goes through, your partner issues you a deed to the property. But, so things don't look fishy, you don't record that deed for a month or two. At the end of that time you record the deed and apply to have your partner's loan transferred to your name at a cost usually under $50.

If it sounds like a sweet deal, that's because it is. It's also illegal. VA loans are provided by the government as a kind of reward for service personnel who have served their country in time of military conflict. It is one thing for a veteran to buy a home using VA benefits and then, after a few months, decide he or she doesn't like it and sell. The Veterans Administration normally has no complaints about this. However, it is quite another thing to buy never intending to move in and knowing all along that the purchase is a phony one. The difference is intent.

Both cases appear the same on the surface—a purchase and then a quick sale. However, should there be an investigation and should the facts come out that the veteran never moved into the house, that a deed was issued at the same time as the sale, and that you supplied the cash for the transaction, you could lose more than just your money and your house.

Further, even if the VA never finds out about this kind of collusion, there is another risk. The partner could sell or encumber (use the property as collateral for loans) the house before the deed was transferred to the real buyer.

The substitute-buyer ploy is used successfully more often than many people suspect, but every so often someone gets caught. And that risk far outweighs any benefits. Don't get involved with it.

Another ploy is sometimes used with FHA loans, which are intended to help buyers purchase homes at minimum down payments. In order to qualify, the purchaser must intend to live in the property. The reason is that a buyer who lives in the house is more likely to keep up the property and make the payments than a buyer who rents to tenants who don't pay.

Occasionally a buyer looking for rental property will be told by the agent to apply for an FHA loan. The agent will suggest something like, "Just say you intend to live in the property. If you don't end up living there, who'll be the wiser?" It's surprising how often this ploy results in a sale. In many cases, the buyer may get away with it. Occasionally, however, especially when the buyer has purchased many homes with FHA loans, the government may get wise and descend in wrath. Again, the risk far outweighs the benefits.

6. *Think twice about a repossessed home.* Many brokers will suggest that you consider purchasing a repossessed home if you indicate that you are looking for a bargain or that you don't have a lot of money with which to work. Be careful of these, for there are bad deals as well as good.

Most repos for sale today are offered by either the VA or the FHA direct from the Department of Housing and Urban Development (HUD). These homes may come completely refurbished or as is.

The refurbished homes usually look brand new. They've been repainted and recarpeted if necessary and usually come with guarantees on the appliances. However, they are almost always priced at or slightly above current market value. And in order to purchase one, you must meet all the qualifications for a regular VA or FHA loan (except that for the VA loan you don't have to be a veteran). The drawback to these homes is usually their location. Homes in excellent areas simply never complete the full foreclosure process. When an owner in a desirable area goes into foreclosure, almost always someone in the lender's office, a neighbor, or even a broker will "pick up" the house and resell it. The area makes this worthwhile. However, in undesirable areas, repos are often available by the dozens. Since the single most important factor is location and since the terms for a refurbished repo are virtually the same as for any other house, you are probably better off leaving these alone. Both while you are living in the house and when it comes time to sell, you are far better off buying in a good location.

The as-is homes, however, are a different story. The vast majority of these are sold by HUD. They are also usually in undesirable areas, but since they are often auctioned off to the highest bidder, you may be able to purchase one at 25 percent or more below market value. For someone who likes to fix up property and then sell, hoping to make a profit, these can make excellent investments. To purchase, however, you must usually come up with cash. HUD often allows a period of time, usually three weeks, in which you can secure financing from a lender. For more information on these types of homes, contact your nearest HUD office. (Addresses are given in the appendix.)

7. *Watch out for the high-pressure agent.* You'll recognize a high-pressure agent the moment you meet one. There's intimidation in the eyes. Often as you get into the car to inspect a house, this salesperson will say something like, "We're going to sell you a home today." There's a certain determination in the voice that may make you think that you're going to have to buy even if you don't find what you want. With this type of agent, you could be closer to the truth than you think.

There are various ways of pressuring a buyer into purchasing a home. One method is the "kidnap."

This technique was used to perfection by Ken, who had a two-way radio in his car. The secretary in his office would have all the listing books at her elbow, and when Ken wanted a house in a particular price range and location, she would quickly look it up and radio him the information.

When buyers came to Ken's office, usually from an ad in the paper, he would invite them to leave their car in his parking lot and take his car to look at some homes. As they drove around, Ken would question the buyers about their finances and quickly learn how much they could afford. Then his secretary would radio Ken the information on the various homes that were available. Often there were a dozen or more homes. Ken would drive the buyers to the various homes. Usually the buyers were impressed with his service. Sometimes the buyers would like one of the homes and a sale might be made. But, as is often the case in selling real estate, none of the homes satisfied most of the buyers. Perhaps the floor plans were wrong, or the location bad, or the financing poor, or maybe they just weren't ready to buy.

After four or five homes the buyers might get tired of looking and ask Ken to take them back; they would try again another day. Ken would smile and begin the "kidnap." He would say there was just one more house they absolutely must see, and off they'd go again. If the buyers didn't like this house, there'd be "just one more" and so on. Ken would continue, through all the houses available, if necessary, wearing down the buyers' resistance with exhaustion. When the buyers would complain and demand to be taken back to the office, Ken would smile and go right on talking about the next home as if nothing had been said. Sometimes, if only a few houses were available in the buyers' price range and they had seen them all, Ken would begin a second tour. Sooner or later, the buyers would wake up to the fact that Ken was not taking them back to his office until they agreed to purchase a home.

During the time that he was a broker, Ken made a very good business out of the kidnap technique. However, on more than one occasion, obstinate buyers refused to get back into his car and either walked or took a cab to their own. On one occasion Ken's nose was flattened by a large, irate buyer. In that instance Ken did return the buyers to their car. But in more cases than not, Ken actually made the sale through this technique.

Ken is now out of real estate, and I know of no other agents who would go to the extremes he did. Nonetheless, his example does illustrate an important psychological weapon of the high-pressure agent—mental kidnapping. When you go out in an agent's car, you automatically, unless you're a very strong personality, become subject to a certain control by the agent. This is partly actual—the agent does determine where you are going—and partly imagined—only the agent knows your destination and only the agent knows how long you'll stay and when you'll return. In a sense, you must rely on the agent to take care of you while you're out in the car, and this reliance is the first wedge an unscrupulous agent will use in bullying a weak buyer into signing a sales agreement.

If you notice this not-so-subtle pressure when you go out with a broker, the obvious solution is to take your own car. You'd be surprised at the flap some agents will raise when buyers insist on driving their own car. A few will even refuse to show the property. They know the psychological one-up-manship that sitting in the driver's seat gives.

Another trick of high-pressure agents is the "buy it quick" technique often used with new buyers. As a buyer, you can recognize this when an agent begins by saying the particular house you are going to see is a steal, there already are several interested prospects getting ready to sign, and it won't be on the market overnight. Usually the setup for this occurs in the following manner. The agent takes you to three or four houses, all roughly in the area or price range you want, but not at all what you are looking for. Then the agent says, "Well that's all there is," and scans the listing book. Suddenly the agent shows surprise. There's a red mark or notation on one of the listings. The agent may say something like, "I thought that house was sold. If it's still available, you must see it." And off you go while the agent continues with the spiel about it surely will be sold overnight.

When you arrive, it's close to what you want. The agent maintains the pressure. "If it's what you like, sign now. Don't take a chance on losing it." If you're the typical new buyer you might consider: You've just seen three or four other houses that aren't even close. This house at least approximates your needs and desires; you'd better act fast.

Chances are you'd sign.

If you did, you probably were taken. The first three houses were shills, homes purposely selected to be the opposite of what you wanted, to give you a warped sense of what was on the market, and to make the final house seem close to what you wanted by comparison.

Of course, there's always a chance that the final house really was the "perfect" one. But even if it was, you probably could have slept on your decision to purchase and still gotten it the next day. Usually, deals in residential real estate will wait overnight. The moral here is to give yourself enough time to reconsider, to "cool down" and think it through. It's positively amazing how one night's sleep can change your perspective. You might wonder how you ever considered that house yesterday that seems so awful today. Although you could be running the risk that someone might buy the house out from under you while you wait, you might not be missing a good house, you might be missing a bad one.

Some high-pressure agents are not above trying to convince a buyer that a house is terribly underpriced and that not to buy immediately would be close to insanity. Unless you've seen enough homes to know prices very well, don't take the broker's word for it. Always ask yourself why, if the home is so underpriced, doesn't the broker buy it? (Don't let agents tell you it's illegal for them to purchase a home they have listed. It's not, as long as they make full disclosure to the seller.) Remember, a low price by itself may be caused by factors not easily recognized: an undesirable location, awkward floor plan or lot location, or terrible neighbors. It's better to lose one or two "buys of a lifetime" than get stuck with a white elephant.

Buyers who are being transferred into an area and have only a very limited amount of time to look, or buyers who have sold their homes and must get out are particularly susceptible to this type of pressure. If you're in this situation, you should make every effort to take a few extra days to house hunt and get the right home.

8. *Every salesperson you go out with will want to "close" you.* This means getting you to put up a deposit and sign a sales agreement. There is nothing wrong with being closed on the right house. Too often, however, you really haven't found the property you want and the salesperson is trying to close you on the "next best" piece of property. Usually this means the best piece that the agent happens to have to show you that day. Always remember, tomorrow will bring an entirely new set of houses onto the market.

Closing can be very simple when you've found the right house. The agent may say, "Shall we make an offer?" And you'll respond in the affirmative. On the other hand, if the property isn't quite right, closing can be a long, strained process wherein the agent seeks to persuade you to sign and you try politely to get away. If the agent is persistent and clever, you may end up with a "next best" house.

Closing actually starts the moment you meet the agent, who begins by building your confidence in his or her knowledge of real estate and the housing market. It usually reaches its climax when you're standing in the house in question or have returned to the agent's office or with the agent to your own home.

The climax begins with the agent trying to determine your reaction to the property. "What don't you like about it?" is often the first step. The agent knows that more often than not, selling begins when the buyer says, "No." When you are required to verbalize your objections to a house, the agent can begin to deal with them. For example, you might say that the price is too high. The agent could ask how much too high and you might respond, "$2500." Now the agent may point out that the home is comparably priced to others in the area, or, if it is not, that the additional amount you are asked to pay (the $2500) is compensated for by additional qualities such as upgraded carpets, insulation, or fresh paint. If this does not move you, the agent may then seek to make you appear to be a penny pincher or even a fool who does not know what is to his or her advantage.

One method of doing this is to ask you how long you plan to live in the house. If you, for example, say ten years, the agent may break down the $2500 price difference over that period of time, saying, "Over ten years, that's only $250 a year or about 75 cents a day. Isn't it worth that much to you to get the house you want?" Or the agent may use the inflation technique. If the house is selling for $50,000, the agent may say you can expect inflation to be at least 5 percent a year for the next year, or $2500. "Isn't it silly to worry about that $2500 now when you'll be getting it back in a year anyhow?"

Both of these types of arguments are very convincing. Unfortunately, they are also deceptive. In both cases they try to rationalize paying more than market value for a home. True, if it were your dream home, you'd probably pay anything to get it. But in that case the agent wouldn't have to resort to such arguments. We're talking about "next best." When you purchase a home, it is worth exactly what you pay for it the day you buy it. It doesn't make any difference that it'll be worth more a year from now; almost any home you buy will be worth more then. It doesn't make any difference that you can rationalize the overpayment over a ten-year period; it's still money out of your pocket.

Or, you might object that the home is poorly located or not well kept (the two other most common objections). To your objection that the home is run down, your agent may point out its other benefits to you, for example, that it is in a perfect location, has the right price, and has the large master bedroom you insisted upon. The agent may further state that with a little elbow grease, detergent, and paint you can turn the disaster you are being shown into a doll house.

All this may be true, but by maximizing the benefits to you and minimizing the effort needed to clean up the place, the agent has not given you a fair balance. There may be other houses that meet your needs that are already in good shape. And it may take a lot more elbow grease and money to put a run-down house into shape than it appears to someone who hasn't tackled the job. Remember, just putting 1000 square feet of medium-grade carpeting into a home (most homes have much larger areas than this) can easily run $1500 or more. To have someone paint a house inside and out can easily cost $1000. To do it yourself can cost $300 or more just in paint and materials.

To the objection that the house is too far away from where you work, the agent may reply that it really isn't that far because everything is relative. If you're now traveling thirty-five minutes on the freeway and the new home will require you to travel fifty minutes, the agent may point out that you are objecting only to fifteen minutes each way. Isn't it worth a half a hour a day to live in a finer community, better home, etc?

Maybe it is. But be sure you travel that fifty-minute route before you decide. It may take longer; it may wear you out so you don't handle yourself as well at work; it may make living in that home a nightmare. Even though it is a little less than a 50 percent increase in time on the freeway, studies have shown that merely increasing your road time by half can almost double your fatigue, particularly if you have to fight rush-hour traffic.

Many agents' technique in closing is to get you to raise objections and then to deal with them. Since agents already know the most common objections and have on hand a ready supply of answers to them, they are way ahead of you. They have the answer even before you can get the objection out of your mouth. This makes you look a little bit foolish. After you run out of objections, all the agent has to say is, "If you don't have any other objections, I'll begin writing the sales agreement."

You will be hard-pressed to find an answer . . . and you may very well sign. If you do, you've been closed.

At this point, many people, realizing what's happening, try to get out of the closing by saying something like, "I want to think it over. I'll decide by tomorrow."

A quick agent will not let you go so easily, since what you are really saying is "No." By tomorrow you may see another home with another agent, and the commission to this broker will be lost.

To get you back on course, the agent may first put you off your guard. This is done by apparently agreeing to let you have more time. Once you've heard this, you relax. The agent may then casually ask if you really were sincere about purchasing the home. Of course, you'll answer you were. (Otherwise you'd be wasting the agent's time.) Now the agent will begin to raise all the objections you've previously raised one by one in a role reversal and ask if any of them still bother you.

Since the agent already has answered them, you probably will be forced to say they don't. But, if one still does, the agent may then proceed to answer it again. Finally the agent will say something like, "Since you don't have any real objections to the home, if you're really sincere (not wasting my time), you're going to buy, aren't you?"

You've been closed again.

The important thing to remember is: *Just because you can't verbalize your objections doesn't mean you don't have any.* Often just sleeping on the purchase overnight will clarify your real reason for not buying. How do you get out of being closed if this happens? Be honest. Tell the agent you don't know why you don't like the place, but you just don't and you're not going to buy it until you've slept on it overnight. You have no objections other than one—you don't want it now.

Should the agent persist in asking to know why (a sophomoric game played very well by many brokers), in order to begin closing you again, simply leave. Walk, run, or drive away. Be glad you got out of there with your wallet.

9. *Don't wait until a broker's listing runs out and try to buy the house for less, directly from the seller.* If you do, the chances are that you'll simply be wasting your time, and you might lose the house you really want. Most agents' listings provide that they must be paid a commission if an individual to whom they showed the house purchases it even after the listing expires (usually for up to six months—See Chapter 3). Furthermore, any really good well-priced home won't sit around while you wait for a listing to expire. If it's a good deal, someone will buy it. And finally, the sellers may not agree to give a buyer who waits the full commission or any portion of it. The sellers may figure they deserve the commission for handling the sale themselves.

20

Checkpoints for the House

When you buy a residence, the purchase is usually made out of personal preference—you like or feel comfortable in one particular home, whereas none of the others you see seem to please you. Personal preference is, of course, important, for if you're going to live in it, you'd better like it. But before you dash out and fall in love with a house, there are certain things you ought to consider for your own protection. This chapter provides a checklist of some of the points you should consider about every house you see, even the "perfect" one.

1. *Size.* Although it may seem strange, the best time to consider the future sale of your new home is when you are buying it. Two, three, or ten years from now it will be too late to reconsider and get a home with another bedroom or bathroom. The time to buy so that you can sell in the future is now.

Most lending institutions consider a prime house to be one that has at least three bedrooms and two full bathrooms. (A full bathroom includes a sink, a toilet, and either a shower or a tub.) Such houses fulfill the requirements of the majority of buyers and are the easiest to sell. A two-bedroom home is more difficult to dispose of than one with three. Having only one bathroom also makes a house difficult to sell. Before you sign a sales agreement to purchase that absolutely smashing one-bedroom home with the huge living room, consider what your problems may be when you are the owner and decide to sell.

2. *Floor plan.* Certain arrangements in houses are considered standard by lenders, while others are looked upon as awkward. Some obviously awkward arrangements are bathrooms that connect directly with kitchens (this is even illegal in certain areas) or front entrances going right into bedrooms. Other awkward arrangements, however, are less obvious, for example, the home entrance to the garage going through a bedroom, bedrooms entering directly into living or dining rooms without first entering a hall, halls excessively long, kitchens which have no direct entries to dining rooms, entrance to the back yard only through the garage, the front entrance opening directly into the living or dining room without even a small distinct entry area, the dining room an extension of the living room (a common arrangement, but still awkward).

In general, the more standard the floor plan, the easier it will be for you to live in the home and eventually to sell it. Some apparently awkward floor plans are handled in such a manner by the architect that they are attractive and quaint. This is the exception, however, rather than the rule.

3. *Lot.* The lot a home is built on can also be awkward. A standard lot is either rectangular or square. A lot that is long and narrow, that is wedge-shaped, or that has weird angles is likely to give you trouble when it comes time to sell. In general, the larger the lot, the better, although a large lot has inherent in it the problem of maintenance.

Certain lots in tracts are referred to as "key" lots and are considered less desirable. A key lot has the *back* of another lot butting up to one side as well as the rear. Normally the back of one lot butts up only to the back of another lot.

4. *Additions.* With the price of homes skyrocketing in today's market, many owners have decided to add on a room or porch or other improvements. In many cases these additions are done without benefit of city or county inspection or approval. When the local governing body discovers what's been done, as often happens at the time of a sale, all kinds of problems can arise. Often, because the work was completed without regular inspections, the local building and safety department will require that all the new work be torn down, even though it may meet local code requirements. In some cases, a fine may be imposed on the builder.

When looking for a home, you should pay particular attention to anything that looks as if it has been added on. A two-car garage door on the outside with rumpus room on the inside is a giveaway. A bedroom that juts out of the house at a peculiar angle is another.

In a tract area, if possible, try to see at least one other similar home. You may discover that all the houses were built with three bedrooms and that the fourth bedroom in the house you are considering was added by its present owner.

If you suspect that an addition has been made, question the seller. Usually the seller will confess and request that you not make a fuss about it to the city. If this is the case, you can take the house as is, require the seller to bring the building up to code (in which case you may lose the deal), or just forget the property.

If the seller says everything is up to code, but you're still suspicious, take a few hours to check out your suspicions. Most city building departments keep on hand the building plans of every recently constructed home in the city. A quick check there should reveal if any addition was made with building department approval.

As a final precaution, you might write into a sales agreement a clause specifying that the house is being purchased subject to its meeting all local building codes.

5. *Boundary lines.* When you look at a piece of property, don't assume that a fence or hedge at the sides and back mark the boundaries. The hedge may belong to a neighbor, or the fence may be 10 feet inside another neighbor's yard. To be safe, ask the seller where the exact boundary lines are and then ask for an up-to-date plot map to verify this. If none is available, you might condition the sale on the lot being so many feet wide and deep and along the boundaries the seller mentioned. Also, if possible, ascertain whether there are any boundary disputes with neighbors. You don't want to inherit someone else's headache, so require that these be cleared up as part of the purchase.

6. *Defects.* Don't take an agent's or a seller's word that there are none. Check out all the floors, walls, and ceilings in the house yourself. If there is a history of cracked slabs in the area, insist on a structural engineer's report. (Cracked slabs often cannot be repaired. If a new slab must be poured, this can cost $5000 or more.)

If you have any questions about the wiring, as you may have in older homes, insist on an electrical report. If the water runs out of the toilets very slowly when they are flushed, if water is present under the house or in the basement, or if anything else looks strange about the pipes, insist on a plumbing engineer's report. You may have to pay for all these reports yourself, but they usually cost less than $100 apiece. You probably won't need more than one or two, however, and the trouble you avoid will undoubtedly be well worth the expense.

7. *Sewer.* Ascertain from the seller and/or the agent whether the house is connected to a main sewer line or has a septic tank or cesspool. If it's not connected to a regular sewer line, *always* insist on an engineer's inspection of the septic tank or cesspool. These can clog or fill up over the years and can be very expensive to repair. If the owner volunteers that the house has recently been hooked up to a city or county sewer system, ask whether the assessment for that hookup has been paid, and if it has not, insist on its being paid as part of the sale's terms.

PREPURCHASE CHECKLIST

1. Is the house big enough for you to live in comfortably? Is it large enough to resell easily?

2. Is the floor plan awkward?

3. Is the lot conventionally shaped (rectangular or square) and large enough to allow an easy resale, but not so large as to make maintenance a problem?

4. Has the seller put on any illegal additions?

5. Do you know the exact boundary lines? Are there any boundary disputes with neighbors? Will the seller clear these up before the deal closes?

6. Is the house free from defects? Have you had a competent engineer check out any area you suspect is at fault?

7. Is the house hooked up to a sewer? Is the sewer assessment paid? If the house has a septic tank or cesspool, have you had an engineer verify that it is working properly?

8. Is the heating system adequate? Is the house insulated?

9. Have you checked the roof for leaks?

10. Is the water heater leaking? Is it old or new? Can you get the seller to replace it?

11. Have you insisted upon a termite inspection?

12. Have you checked all windows and appliances to see that they are not broken?

13. Have you asked the neighbors whether there are any problems with the house or the neighborhood?

8. *Heating and insulation.* Make sure the house has an adequate heating system. I shall never forget an old friend of mine who bought a new nine-unit apartment building in Minnesota in the middle of summer. He never thought to check the heating system, but promptly rented out all the units. At the first cold spell, he had nine angry tenants complaining about the lack of heat. The contractor had neglected to install heaters. Needless to say, the expense of installing heaters in a completed building was astronomical.

While it is unlikely that your home would not have a heating system, the heater it has may be inadequate. In the past decade many builders saved costs by cutting down on the size of the heaters they installed. Units that are too small may work constantly, be inefficient, and end up not fully heating the home. While heating engineers recommend so many BTUs per square foot of home, I have found this method of judging heating systems to be inadequate. Much depends on the layout of the house, the height of the ceilings, whether the vents are on the floor or in the wall near the ceiling, whether the heating ducts are insulated in fiberglass, etc. A good way to find out about the heater in a house you are considering is to casually mention to the owners that you are thinking of having a new heater installed in any house you buy and are wondering whether they would recommend it in this house. The sellers may exaggerate, but if they think you're already going to get a new heater, the truth about the current system may come out.

If the owner admits the current heating system is inadequate, you might want to reconsider purchasing. A new heating system can cost $1000 or more. And it's not usually feasible to insist on a new heating system as a condition of sale.

Besides the adequacy of the heating system, be sure and check to see that it works. Ask the seller to turn it on, even if it's the middle of summer. And in colder climates, make the workability of the system a condition of the sale.

Insulation is becoming more and more of a necessity in these days of increased fuel costs. If the house you are purchasing is not insulated, you might consider the fact that if you buy you will probably have to insulate it yourself within a few years.

9. *Roof.* The roofs of older houses have a nasty habit: they tend to leak. And if they leak on your new oriental rug or expensive furniture, it can be disturbing and costly.

If you buy your home in the middle of a hurricane and it's dry as a bone inside, you probably don't have to worry about roof leaks. But if you buy in the middle of a dry summer, watch out for a wet winter.

At the very least you should walk around the outside of the house looking at the roof. On a shingle roof, check to see whether any shingles are missing. On a composition or tar and gravel roof, look for any holes (they often show up looking like abrasions). On a tile roof, look for missing or cracked tile. On a metal roof, check the condition of the metal. If you are in the least bit concerned, insist that the home be inspected by a roofer. If there is damage, make the fixing or even the replacement of the roof a condition of the sale. If the roof leaks and you don't make the seller pay to have it fixed, you'll end up paying for it yourself.

10. *Water heater.* Water heaters last anywhere from ten minutes to ten years or more. A water heater that doesn't leak today may turn into Niagara Falls tomorrow. About the best you can do is ask the owner how old the heater is. You can figure that the *average* heater will serve only about five to seven years. If it's already eight years old and not one of the super-deluxe models guaranteed to last a dozen years, you can figure it's due to go out any day.

You can try to make the seller replace it, although most sellers will balk at this. "Why replace a heater that's working fine?" they may argue, and you'll be hard-pressed to find an adequate answer. If the heater is leaking, however, or if it begins to leak within three months after you purchase the house, complain like heck to the agent and/or seller. You may get a new heater out of it.

11. *Termite damage.* Always insist on a termite and pest report, even if you have to pay for it. (The fee is usually around $25.) Most lenders will want this inspection anyway, and if there is damage it could save you many thousands of dollars. In most areas, the seller is responsible for correcting any termite damage while the buyer normally pays for any preventive work.

12. *Windows and appliances.* Check all the windows for damage; check all the appliances to see that they work. Don't assume an oven will work just because the stove works. Check them both. It has become common practice in recent years for the buyer to insist on the workability of all appliances as a condition of sale.

13. *Neighbors.* Never be embarrassed to talk to the neighbors; in fact, make a point of doing it. Ask them how they like the neighborhood, its strong points and its weaknesses. Ask whether there's ever been a fire or problem with the house you're considering. By talking a few minutes with one or two neighbors, you may learn more than you could from spending days with the seller and/or broker.

21

When Buying Direct from a Builder or Seller

BUYING FROM A BUILDER

Probably the biggest problems in buying a new home from a builder arise out of the model home concept. Builders of large tracts and even of small ones have to tie up large amounts of capital and pay substantial interest payments on new homes while they are under construction and, once finished, until they are sold. Building homes is, to a large extent, a race against time. If builders cannot sell their new houses within a given maximum time—usually anywhere from six to eighteen months—they may lose all that they have invested and find themselves in foreclosure. To facilitate the sales of new homes, builders almost invariably put up model homes, often before they have even done the preliminary grading of the tract. The purpose of the model homes is to show prospective buyers what the new houses will be like and to get advance sales. A successful builder will be able to sell as much as half a tract of homes even before construction begins. On the other hand, builders have put up model homes only to discover that for one reason or another no one would buy them. And they have gone on to scrap the tract, leaving the models standing like lonely scarecrows in an empty field.

The danger with a model home is that it may not truly represent the production homes of the builder.

Many builders rigidly adhere to a moral code of honesty and make their model homes no better and no worse than production models. Some others, however, change both the quality and quantity of construction in the model homes. It is this latter group that the buyer must watch out for. In a typical case of an exaggerated model home, the size of the rooms will be larger; the floor coverings, paint, and fixtures of higher quality; the appliances, landscaping, and wall coverings (including expensive wallpaper) not included in the production models; and even additional window spaces and sliding glass doors added to the model not found in the production home. Buying from such a model home is somewhat comparable to walking into a new car dealer's showroom and seeing the top-of-the-line car completely outfitted with all the optionals only to find, after a purchase, that you've bought a stripped-down model.

When inspecting model homes of a builder it is a good idea to ask the salesperson *exactly* what differences there will be between the model home and the production model you will buy. Don't accept vague generalities such as, "The homes are almost identical," or "You'll get essentially what you see in the model." Pin the representative down to exactly what differences there are. Will you get the same brand and quality sink and dishwasher? Is the garbage disposal shown in the model extra? Does your production home come with the two-oven stove shown in the model? Will your home have any landscaping or fencing? Will you have to pay an extra fee to get a lot as large as the one on which the model home is standing? Will you have to pay extra to upgrade the carpets in order to get the same quality as in the model home? Will the production home be the same number of square feet? These are just a few of the questions you might want to ask. Don't hesitate to ask as many more as come to mind.

If you decide that you truly like the home and want to buy it, be sure you have the builder add an amendment to the purchase agreement stipulating all the differences between the model home and your production model and be sure you understand and agree to these differences. It is a good idea to include a statement that the production model is to be identical in all ways to the model home except in those ways you and the builder note and agree upon.

Before you buy, you should check out other items besides the house itself. For example, you should demand that the builder supply you with the most current edition of the local city's master plan, zoning map, and map showing where schools and parks are currently located and are planned. You should also be given information on all elementary, junior high, and high schools and if possible what the teacher-to-student ratio is in these schools and whether bus service is available. If the builder won't or can't supply all this information, you should make it a point to go to the city hall and the school district office to get the information yourself.

Furthermore, you should obtain from the builder a map showing all improvements, particularly streets and lighting, planned as part of the construction phase in which you are buying and those planned for later phases. Often builders construct houses in units. In the sales office you may see a plan outlining a huge development, but the builder may be currently working on only a very small portion of this. The full development may hinge on how well sales on the current construction phase go. If they go poorly, it may be years before streets, lights, or parks are finished. If they go very poorly, these improvements may never come in, and you could end up sitting in the middle of a half-completed tract.

Finally, you should demand information on any greenbelts or common areas of the tract. Many builders, either because it is good business or because local zoning and planning departments demand it, dedicate certain portions of tract area as open to all. It is often an advantage to obtain a home near one of these spaces.

DEALING WITH THE BUILDER

When you purchase a home direct from a builder, the tendency is to let the builder take care of everything. Often the builder is also an agent and gives the impression of knowing so much about the real estate business that a buyer may feel awkward asking questions.

Question as much as you can.

When builders or agents offer their own houses for sale, they become primarily sellers and are subject to all the weaknesses of any other seller. I would be quite suspicious of a builder who got upset with me for questioning anything at all about the house I was buying or the tract it was in. Here are a few items about which you should be particularly careful:

1. *Make sure you don't have to come up with the full down payment until the house is completed and signed off, that is, until it has passed final inspection by the local building department.* In most cases a deposit of $500 or less should be sufficient to hold the property until that time. If a builder insists that you must complete the deal even though the house is still under construction, be very suspicious. A shaky builder may be planning to use your deposit money to help finance the construction of the building. While this may work out all right if the house is eventually built and you successfully buy it, too many cases have been reported (particularly in Florida) where after spending the buyer's deposit the builder still could not finish construction. The buyer lost both the deposit and the house. To protect yourself you should insist that the deposit be placed in a neutral escrow where the builder does not have access to it. Further, you should insist that the deposit be returned to you in the event the building is not completed within a reasonable period of time and specify a particular date.

Some builders may require that as evidence of your good faith you deposit into escrow the full down payment and get approval from a lender before the home is completed. If you have fallen in love with the builders' house and can't persuade them to accept a small deposit until completion, then be sure that you will get your full down payment back if the home is not completed to your specifications for any reason. A clause stipulating this in the sales agreement is one way of handling it.

2. *Be sure you get a copy of any state or local subdivision reports.* Many states and local areas require builders to file extensive reports on their project if they intend to subdivide a large parcel of land into more than a specified number of lots (usually from four to six units). If such reports are required in your area (you can call the local building department to find out in case the builder doesn't offer the information), insist on seeing them. They are public and in most cases must be presented for your viewing before a sale can be completed. In some states buyers must sign a statement that they have been given a copy and have had time to read the public report. *Don't sign such a statement until you have read the report.* Otherwise, you may lose your right to protections included in it.

Usually such reports state an opinion as to the quality of the subdivision and additional information indicating whether or not the builder has complied with state and local codes regarding streets, lighting, sewers, etc. In most areas builders cannot complete projects without such compliance.

3. *Check the deed for any covenants, conditions, and restrictions.* All three terms simply refer to agreements inserted in a deed to control the use and acts of future owners. Builders almost always insert such items either for the protection of future owners or by demand of local building departments. If the builder you are buying from says none are included, be very suspicious. Check with the city or county recorder where such items are normally filed. If it turns out that no conditions, covenants, or restrictions have been recorded, ask the builder why not. Normally included are restrictions on the height of walls that may be built between houses, the color of homes (often no pinks or purples are allowed), the height of additions that may be added on, etc. Such agreements that buyers make when they purchase are normally for the benefit of everyone in the tract and should be included. When you sell your house, these agreements will pass on to the next buyer.

When you check the conditions, covenants, and restrictions, make sure that they are all reasonable. If there are some that are unreasonable, for example, that you are prevented from ever adding on to your house or from leasing it out in the future (such a condition might be unenforceable), you might reconsider buying that home. Restrictions on your right to sell the property are probably unenforceable, as are restrictions on selling to minority groups (these may even be illegal).

4. *Be sure that all special assessments for sewers, utilities, streets, schools, parks, etc. have been paid or will be paid by the close of escrow on your new home.* Local communities often assess builders' fees for these services (in addition to the amount you will be paying for them in your regular taxes). It is a good idea to make their full payment a condition of sale; otherwise you may end up paying for them yourself.

5. *If the home is built on a hill or if there is any indication of flooding, such as large puddles in the street after a rain, get a soil engineer's report.* Don't trust the builder's judgment on this. Too many housing tracts in the past have been built on land that subsequently did not drain properly. The cost of fixing poorly drained land after houses have been built on it can be enormous.

6. *Get an accurate plot plan.* Most builders will supply these gladly. The plan, really a map, should show your lot in relation to all the others in the tract. It also should show the exact dimensions and shape of the lot. Once you have this plot plan, make it a part of the sales agreement. That's a good way to ensure that you don't end up with something other than what you thought you were getting.

7. *Ask the builder if you're tied into any property owner's group (this will often show up as a condition on the deed).* If you are, make sure you want to belong. Such groups can have stiff mandatory dues. They can be very beneficial, however, in providing a safe and secure community with recreational facilities. Remember, though, that you may need to devote some time to the organization to see that it's running properly.

8. *Unless you are skilled at reading sales agreements, have a broker and your attorney read it before you sign.* Most builders have their own sales agreement forms. On these the printed material often goes out of the way to protect the builder, but tends to leave the buyer wide open. Don't let the builder simply fill in the blank spaces on a prepared form. A sales agreement may look harmless, but it is a legal and in many cases binding document. Remember, the builder is primarily the seller and looking out for the seller's interests.

9. *Use a reputable escrow officer or company and a reputable title company.* Often title and escrow companies will bid on the opportunity to handle all the sales in a builder's tract. Since many houses are involved, but there is only one seller and one title search, they can give the builder a much lower rate. However, the title insurance is to protect you, the buyer, not the seller. And the escrow company will handle *your* money. It is to your advantage to use a reputable company, even if you must pay extra.

How can you know a reputable company when you see it? Most large escrow and title companies must maintain a spotless reputation in order to stay in business, particularly to stay in business a long time. So age and size are one way to judge. Another is to check with the lender. If a lending institution which is going to loan you 80 percent or more of the money to buy the house is satisfied with the escrow and title insurance company, it's a good sign (but not a guarantee) that you're in good hands. Some lenders make deals with builders in order to get the loans on the entire tract. These lenders often offer interest rates lower than you, the buyer, could get by yourself. But they are also tied to the builder, and to protect the money they have already invested (remember, a small tract of thirty $35,000 houses represents a total investment of over $1 million), they might overlook a shady escrow.

10. *Be sure the house is guaranteed for at least one full year by the builder.* When you buy a new car or a new refrigerator, you expect the manufacturer to stand by the product. The same is true for new homes. Be sure the sales agreement stipulates that the builder will fix or replace any defective appliances, windows, water heaters, or other parts of the house that become defective.

If you have a large, well-known builder with an impeccable reputation, you might rely on this alone to protect your warranty. Otherwise, you might insist that the builder post a bond for a reasonable amount of money, say 5 percent of the sales price, to cover any possible defects in the house. A builder who is not willing to warrant the entire house may know something about it that you don't!

Some builders will offer an optional warranty package that buyers may purchase for an additional fee to cover any defects in the property. It may be through the builder or a separate insurance company. These warranties are only as good as the company making them. (Insurance companies are normally required to maintain minimum reserves to pay off reasonable claims.) The reason a builder offers a separate warranty package is probably to get the price of the home as low as possible. It's sort of like buying a stripped-down car with the warranty package as one of the optional extras.

Should you purchase such a warranty?

If you make the workability of all the appliances and the good construction of the home a condition of the sales agreement, you might be able to get the builder to fix any problem even without the warranty package. But if you do buy a warranty, assuming it's not too expensive, you're probably doubly protected.

BUYING DIRECT FROM A SELLER

When a buyer purchases a home direct from a seller, the motive often is the saving of a commission. In these days of 6 percent or higher commissions and homes averaging $50,000, this could be a considerable savings. Unfortunately, the direct seller usually is also counting on saving the broker's commission. In most cases the best a buyer can hope for is the saving of half the commission—still a considerable sum. However, this amount may be offset by other problems.

Haggling. When you buy direct from a seller you will quickly discover that it is very difficult to express your feelings about what's wrong with the property. Most sellers, particularly if they live in the home being sold, feel a certain pride of ownership, and to knock the purple paint on the bedroom ceiling or the fake waterfall may cause resentment on their part and may even destroy the deal. When you make a deal direct with the seller, it is best to keep all uncomplimentary comments about the property to yourself. Put the seller at ease by mentioning favorably those things which you like. A seller who knows you have good taste is not as likely to be balky when it comes to haggling over the price.

Deceit. You will receive most of the information about the property direct from the sellers. A good policy is to trust nothing the sellers say and to try to verify everything. This is not to say that sellers lie. Rather, they leave things out, exaggerate, or even bend the truth a wee bit in their efforts to snag a buyer. Whereas in an agency transaction you might trust the broker who tells you what the boundary lines are, you might want to get a new survey with a direct seller. And be doubly careful to get professional inspections of any part of the home you are not quite sure of, particularly plumbing, electrical wiring, and heating.

Bargaining. Bargaining with a direct seller takes a certain amount of courage. With an agent, you can easily say the seller is crazy to ask whatever the price is and insist that you won't pay a penny more than your low offer. Saying that to a seller's face takes guts. You must keep in mind that you don't want to offend the seller to the point where he or she won't sell to you out of principle. On the other hand, certain things will have to be said if you want to get a price lower than what's being asked. If you have a gift for gab, you shouldn't have any problems here. If not, I would think again about using an agent. (There is no reason a buyer can't hire an agent for a commission, although it's almost never done.) If you know a broker or salesperson who's active in the business, you could ask that person to present an offer for you, indicating that the agent might be able to talk the seller into a commission on the deal. Most agents will jump at this chance. But beware. The arrangement the agent makes with the direct seller may involve raising the price to you in order to cover the commission. In general, however, if you follow the rules for bargaining outlined in the next chapter, you shouldn't go far wrong.

In dealing with direct sellers there are at least two items you should handle with special care:

1. *The deposit.* Never make the deposit check out to the direct sellers, if you want to be on the safe side. If the sellers cash your check and then the deal doesn't go through, you might have to go to court to get your money back. Insist on making the check out to whatever escrow company will handle the transaction and protect the funds as outlined in Chapter 11.

2. *The sales agreement.* Unless you are very familiar with real estate, don't rely on the sellers to fill out the sales agreement. Have it done by an agent or attorney whom you trust. If the sellers insist on drawing up the agreement, don't sign it until you've had an attorney and/or agent you know and trust look it over. This point can't be overemphasized. The sales agreement is the key to the deal. All things follow from it, and if it is prepared wrong, if there is something in it which is to your disadvantage, it may cost you the deal or worse.

22

Strategies for Buying

If you fell in love with a home that you absolutely must have and you know you will kill yourself if you don't get it, offer the full price—in fact, offer *more* than the asking price. I have, on occasion, offered $100 more than the asking price on property just to be sure my offer was accepted in case more than one offer was presented at the same time. When the heart rules, don't take any chances. Pay the price.

On the other hand, if you're a bit cooler and calmer about a house, if you would like to get it, but know that you won't die if it gets away, that you'll always find another house, you should do some heavy bargaining.

In this latter case, I would never offer the asking price. The question then becomes: For how much lower than the asking price can you reasonably expect to get this house? Nothing makes buyers feel worse than to hear a seller say just as they have finished signing, "I would've dropped the price another thousand just to get out of this place."

Since every deal or sale is different, it is only possible to give some general rules.

1. *Know the market.* In order to know how your prospective home ranks in the housing market, you have to have seen enough houses to make a fair comparison. This means you must have seen houses that cost more and other houses that cost less both in the same area and in other areas. How many houses do you need to see to get a true idea of the market? If they are representative, three or four will do. If, however, the houses you see have been carefully selected by someone else to give you a distorted picture, you may need to see many dozens.

There is no formula for comparing houses when buying. A few guidelines however, can be helpful. *Within* any given area, a house with three bedrooms will sell for more than one with two, one with four will sell for more than one with three, and so on. The same applies for bathrooms. *Within* any given area, the bigger the house, the more it will sell for.

Regardless of area, any detracting features will lower the value of the home. These include such things as proximity to freeways, thruways, or industrial areas; any awkward arrangement in the floor plan; a small lot; bad neighbors; poorly maintained yard in the subject home or in nearby homes; a noisy, crowded, or narrow street; poor paint inside or out; cracks in walls, ceiling, or floors; small closets; out-of-date bathroom or kitchen fixtures; any other item in the house which you can reasonably say detracts from its appearance. (For a more thorough discussion of home appraisal, see Chapter 2.)

By the time you find a home and are getting ready to make an offer, you should have some idea of what similar homes in the area sell for and how much better or worse than similar homes this one is. Knowing this should give you a good idea of the price you can expect to pay.

Some homes will already have FHA or VA appraisals. These appraisals are the opinions of people who are experienced in appraising the value of houses. Even though they are just opinions, most sellers will abide by them religiously. Thus, you will find it difficult to get a seller to accept an offer below an FHA or VA appraisal.

2. *Know the maximum amount that you can pay.* If you can afford to pay the full asking price, then you've got considerable room to dicker. On the other hand, if the most you can pay is 5 or 10 percent below the asking price, you should make the best offer you can and emphasize to your agent that because of your finances it is your best and last offer. If you can convince the agent that you mean it, the agent has a better chance of convincing the sellers. If the sellers are anxious to sell and haven't had any other offers, they may accept your offer. If not, there are always other houses.

3. *Meet the sellers personally.* Get to know them; spend some time talking; ask them why they are selling. Are they moving out of the area? Have they already bought another house? How long has the house been on the market? Have they had other offers? Are they in foreclosure?

The object is to find out what kind of pressure the sellers are under. If it's the first day on the market for the house and they have all the time in the world to sell, they're not likely to cut their price very much. On the other hand, if they've been at it for seven months and have already purchased a new home and are making double payments, they may be willing to make a pretty good deal on the current home.

Some buyers feel that as a rule they should let houses "age" before they make an offer; that is, they should wait until the house has been on the market for a while. The trouble with this is that really good houses get sold right away, while the not-so-good deals tend to be the ones that linger on.

4. *Judge the agents.* Once you have a feel for the sellers' needs to get out, make a good evaluation of your agent and the sellers' agent. If the agents seem tough and domineering, there's a good chance they might bully the sellers into signing a low offer. On the other hand, if the agents seem unsure or new to the business, you may not be in the best position to get your low offer accepted. Remember, though, an agent who will be tough on the seller is just as likely to be tough on you, trying to get you to make a higher offer.

5. *Become a bit of an actor.* The agent who shows you the home and who will take your offer is the servant of the sellers regardless of whose listing it is. And remember, a servant cannot serve two masters. The agent is out to get a buyer for the sellers at the *sellers' price.* That's how the agent gets paid. If the agent can't get the sellers' price, then he or she will try to get as close to it as possible, for that's the next best way to get the commission. (The closer to the asking price the offer is, the more likely a sale.) Consequently, *don't expect the agent to help you get the house for less.*

Often an agent will suggest a lower offer in order to entice you into making any offer at all. But once you've expressed a desire to purchase, the agent will be doing his or her level best to get you to offer the asking price or close to it. Once the agent sees that you are interested, such phrases as, "You don't want to take a chance on losing this, do you?" or "Better safe than sorry," may emerge. Some agents may even go to the extreme of refusing to accept anything less than the asking price, knowing full well that if they do this, you will pay it.

How do they know?

An agent has to know a good deal about human behavior, and it's learned quickly from the first exposure to "buyer's fever." You can see this malady on car lots, in boat showrooms, and in home sales. It seems to occur whenever a big purchase is to be made. The buyer, who while looking at various homes has appeared matter-of-fact and calm, suddenly becomes anxious and determined. Somewhere in the buyer's mind a switch has closed, and the decision to buy, to spend an enormous amount of money and to make an incredible commitment to a thirty-year mortgage has been made. I think it's the weight of that decision that temporarily makes buyers paranoid. Once they've decided to buy, they can't stand the thought of someone else getting the house they want. The house suddenly becomes the buyers', at least in their minds, and they begin to fear losing the deal.

This is how most buyers I have seen react to a major purchase. The symptoms might not be obvious to someone who doesn't know what to look for. But agents having seen them before, can pick them out in an instant. And in that instant, agents know that they have you.

The best way to avoid being coerced into paying more than you should by an agent who knows you want to buy is to become an actor, temporarily. Once you've decided to buy, tell your husband or your wife or your children, but don't tell the agent. You might say something like, "Let's make up an offer on this house and, if it looks good, I'll consider it, but I don't really like the place. It's not quite right."

This will be enough to perk up an agent's ears, and a sales agreement will be placed in your lap before you know what happened. Look it over all the while saying as sincerely as you can, "I don't really like this house," or "It's not quite right," or "There are always other homes that I can buy." This will help convince both the agent and yourself that you're not 100 percent sold on the property. And don't sign the sales agreement.

In order to get you to sign, the agent may begin suggesting an offer of a lower price or of terms more favorable to you. Now you have to fall back on your judgment of the agent and your appraisal of the home. For how much less than the house is really worth on the open market can the agent persuade the sellers to sell? Under what pressures are the sellers?

Your own best judgment must prevail here. On some homes you might offer as much as 15 percent below the asking price and get it. On others, a 2 percent reduction is a lot. The important thing to remember is to make your offer a *sincere* one. A sincere offer is one which the seller will recognize by price, terms, or deposit as an earnest attempt to purchase.

6. *Become a juggler.* Buying a home is a balancing act. You balance price against terms against deposit. I have bought houses on which I have agreed to pay the full asking price, but on which I have insisted the full closing costs be paid by the seller. Since the closing costs are normally all cash, and since 80 percent or more of the selling price is normally in the form of a loan, this strategy saved me cash. The way to do this is quite simple. Have a clause written into the sales agreement which specifies that the sale is subject to the seller paying *all* closing costs. Many loans require the establishment of an impound account to handle the buyer's future tax and insurance payments, and most sellers who might agree to pay most closing costs will balk at this fee. However, I have, on occasion, insisted that the seller pay even this amount, and to make the deal, it has been done. Remember, almost anything can be made a condition of sale.

If you are long on cash, but want to get the price down, you might agree to pay your normal closing costs, but insist on a substantially lower price.

One way that some buyers try to impress a seller is to offer a flat amount for the property in cash. Such buyers have no intention of paying all cash out of their pocket. They simply intend to secure their own financing and include a fairly long escrow, often sixty days, in order to accomplish this. Be careful of making such an offer without an escape clause. You risk losing the deposit if for some reason you can't secure the proper financing. Most deals are written in such a way that the buyer has a certain period to apply for and obtain a loan and if the described loan is not available, the deposit is returned. In a cash offer, there is usually no such provision, and herein lies the advantage to the sellers. The sellers in such a deal know that whatever happens they will keep the deposit. If you want to get a particularly low price and are very sure you can get financing, you might sweeten the offer by including a substantial deposit —$1000 or more. A seller, impressed by the amount of money you put up and assured of an almost guaranteed sale, might lower the selling price.

However, simply increasing the amount of the deposit, for example, to the entire down payment, does not always impress sellers. Such a maneuver looks too much like what it really is—just a ploy.

7. *Give a big deposit.* As just mentioned, the deposit is mainly to impress the seller with how earnest the buyer is. A deposit of $500 or more is usually sufficient to do this, although today, many agents and sellers are insisting on at least $1000.

Your commitment when you make an offer. A sales agreement is a legal and perhaps binding contract. Don't make an offer to purchase or sign a sales agreement (or deposit receipt as it is often called) unless you intend to buy. And don't sign until your agent and attorney have had a chance to look the document over.

When you do sign a sales agreement, it is not binding until the seller also signs the exact same agreement for the exact same terms and price you offered. This is why it is critical that you get and keep a copy of the sales agreement. It is your copy which ultimately can be used to determine whether the seller has added or altered any of the conditions of the sales agreement. No matter what the agent or anyone else may say, don't sign a sales agreement without getting an exact copy. It's your protection against a bad deal.

Since the sales agreement becomes a purchase contract only once the seller signs, it is just an offer until that time. Strategy here is very important.

If you're an easygoing individual, you might think it reasonable to give the seller three or four days, perhaps a week, to sign. This will give the seller ample time to fully consider the offer. Don't do it. Normally, don't give the seller more than one day to sign, or two days if the seller is out of town.

The reason, quite simply, is that by giving the seller a lot of time you risk losing the deal. The seller can hold your offer and wait for a better one to come in. If you give the seller four days and a better offer comes in during this period, your offer will be returned and you'll have lost the deal. But if you give the seller only one day, it won't make any difference what offer comes in two days later—the house will be yours.

There's also a psychological reason to limit the time for acceptance. The time the agent presents the offer is the time that presents the best chance of getting a signature. The terms are fresh in the seller's mind, and the thoughts of a sale are tempting. If the seller knows that a decision has to be made then and there, that seller is under the most pressure to sign. On the other hand, if the agreement allows several days for a decision, the seller may put off deciding. The next day, having thought over the deal and not having the agent's pressure right at hand, the seller may decide not to sign at all.

Your agent has a commitment to you when you sign a sales agreement. You normally have the right to rescind an offer any time up until communication of the seller's signing is conveyed to you. This has some unusual possibilities, since in theory it is possible for you to rescind the offer after the seller has signed, but before you know about it. For example, you give one agent a sales agreement on another agent's property. Your agent allows the sellers' broker to present the offer. The offer is presented and signed by the sellers. While the second agent is driving back to his office, you call the first agent and tell him you don't want the house—the offer is off. The two agents get together. The first tells the second that the buyer has revoked the offer. The second tells the first that the seller has signed. Who's right? It would probably take a court of law to decide. To avoid just such problems, many agents insist on going together with any other agents who are party to the deal to the seller's home for the presentation of an offer. And many agents, once you've given them an offer, won't accept any calls from you, the buyer, until they've received word that the seller has either signed or rejected the offer.

The counteroffer. When the sellers make a counteroffer, even if it's on the same piece of paper as your offer, it's a rejection of your offer, and your commitment usually has ended. A counteroffer by the sellers is in reality a new offer to you—a compromise, usually, between your offer and the asking price. You are under no obligation to accept it. If you do accept a counteroffer signed by the sellers, it becomes a complete contract and both parties are obligated by it. The sellers, in a very real sense, are bound by the same obligation when they counter as you were when you made the original offer.

Should you accept a counteroffer? A lot depends on how good a horse trader you are. If you're pretty sure you know the sellers and you think they might come down even more, you might counter-counteroffer. There is no limit to the number of such offers that can be made. On the other hand, if your first offer was the highest and best you could go (or if you're a really shrewd bargainer) you might counter with the exact same offer you first made. This tells the seller to take it or leave it—you won't budge an inch. Or, finally, you can simply sign the counteroffer, pay the money asked, and avoid all the hassle.

You should keep in mind that by countering at all, the seller has indicated a certain amount of flexibility. How far this flexibility extends, of course, you won't know unless you refuse the counter and make another offer. You could get the house for much less, or you could lose the deal. But remember, even if you recounter at a much lower price and the seller refuses altogether, you can then recounter at the price that the seller originally countered to you, if you're willing to swallow your pride. The seller, of course, is under no obligation to accept this and may even refuse, thinking that if you've come back after all this, you must want the house so badly you'll pay the full asking price. Or the seller may simply sign to avoid the hassle. It's one of the risks of bargaining.

When you bargain over a house, you should be firm yet keep your ears wide open all the time. When the seller appears wishy-washy, don't budge. You'll probably get your way. But when the seller appears rock-like, become conciliatory. It's all a game of "chicken," and courage pays off very well here.

7. *Be sure you understand all the escape clauses.* In most areas the words *subject to* introduce escape clauses. They normally mean that the entire contract is conditioned upon whatever terms follow them. For example, should the sales agreement read, "Purchase subject to buyer obtaining a new fully amortized loan for 80 percent of the sales price including 9 percent annual interest per year payable $200 monthly for 30 years," it would probably be interpreted to mean that if the buyer was unable to obtain the specified loan then there was no sale. However, in some cases, getting a loan for very close to the terms has been judged sufficient. (Fully amortized means the loan will be paid in equal installments.)

You as a buyer should be careful about inserting a subject-to clause whenever you are in doubt about your ability to perform. This will often permit you to escape gracefully from an otherwise binding contract. (Check with your attorney about having them inserted.)

Your uncertainty about your ability to perform could be over any number of items: loans, down payment, credit report, or even a spouse's approval. Subject-to clauses can also be used when you think the house may not be able to perform. For example, the sale could be subject to a termite clearance, an electrical clearance, there being no cracks in the ceiling, or the doorbell working.

Further, most sellers will insist on a clause indicating that the sale is subject to the sellers' being able to give clear title. If such a clause were not inserted, you the buyer might conceivably sue the sellers if they had some hidden lien on the property which prevented a sale.

It is a good idea to check subject-to clauses for their time and performance factors. For example, the sellers may insist on a clause making the sale subject to the approval of a grandparent living in a distant city. This in itself may be harmless; however, unless there is a reasonable limit set for the performance, say approval within one week, the sellers could conceivably drag the deal on for months waiting for a grandparent to sign.

Similarly, if there is a clause making the sale subject to all the appliances working, there should also be a provision for an inspection by the buyer or the buyer's representative *before* the sale to determine whether the appliances do in fact work. It won't do any good to include a subject-to-workability clause if you wait until after the sale to check out the equipment. If you then find out a stove doesn't work, it's too late to stop the sale; it's already been consummated. Your alternative here might be to try to rescind the sale via a court order. This would probably cost ten times as much as a new stove.

Lest buyers think that they have found the ultimate answer to protection in a real estate deal, namely, to make every provision of the agreement subject to a condition, take heed of this advice. Your object is to get the seller to sign, but no intelligent seller will sign a sales agreement filled with escape clauses for the buyer. Such sales agreements aren't worth the paper they are written on. Such offers amount to asking the seller to take the house off the market while the buyer considers the purchase.

Your escape clauses must be reasonable. If, for example, the house you are going to purchase is on a hill where there have been slides in the past, making the sale subject to a soil engineer's report is reasonable. If the buyer's husband is out of town, making the sale subject to his approval within forty-eight hours is reasonable. Similarly, making the sale subject to obtaining proper financing should also be accepted by a reasonable seller.

One final word of caution. Escape clauses can cost you the deal when two parties are trying to get the same house. If prices are about the same, any smart seller will accept the offer with the least number of escape hatches open to the buyer.

8. *Be sure you know the difference between real property and personal property.* (See Chapter 5 for a detailed discussion.) In general, real property is defined as the land and anything appurtenant to it, such as a house. Personal property is everything else—those items such as a car and cash that you can take with you personally. When buying a home, however, buyer and seller can dispute what is real and what is personal. For example, is a light fixture real property? Are drapes personal property?

One way to avoid disputes is to identify in the sales agreement all those items over which there might be confusion. A list of items that usually cause trouble is given in Chapter 5. One item in particular, however, has given many buyers real headaches—wall coverings.

Often buyers will fall in love with the drapes in a house and insist they be included in the sales agreement. That the drapes are to be included in the sale is dutifully inserted in the contract. But, when the buyers take possession, the drapes are gone. Frantic phone calls reveal that the sellers never thought of those things in the living room as drapes—they considered them curtains. And it's curtains for the buyers unless they want to press an uncertain lawsuit.

One method that many buyers use to overcome this problem is to specify that all *wall coverings,* including but not limited to drapes, curtains, shades, etc., are to be included in the sale. Sometimes it is wise to list in which rooms the wall coverings are, particularly if not all the wall coverings in the house are to go with the house.

If a lot of personal property is included in the sale, a lender may balk at giving a full loan, feeling that the sales price reflects personal as well as real property. In such a case, a separate bill of sale for the personal property will probably solve the problem. But, be sure that you, the buyer,

CHECKLIST OF TYPICAL SALES AGREEMENT PERILS

1. Can you understand the language of the contract? If not, why not have it rewritten so you can?

2. Is a legal description for the property given?

3. Have you previously discussed with an attorney how you want to take title? Do you understand the ramifications of all the different methods?

4. Is the sale price accurate?

5. Are the terms completely specified? Are they exactly as you want them to be?

6. Are you making the deposit out to a broker, an attorney, or an escrow officer?

7. Are your escape clauses reasonable?

8. Have you itemized all the personal property that will be included in the sale?

9. Is the phrase *time is the essence* included in the agreement?

10. Will you be allowed to open escrow?

11. Is there a date set for the close of escrow? Does it allow enough time for you to obtain financing?

12. Is an equitable date set for prorations?

13. Is the date for you to take possession in accordance with your wishes? Do you have a guarantee that the sellers will be out or that they will pay rent if they are not out?

give the seller some consideration for the personal property, even if it's only $1—otherwise such a sale might be invalid.

9. *Be sure to see if the sales agreement has a clause indicating time is the essence of the agreement.* This is normally taken to mean that any periods of time given for performance of any items are strict and not to be interpreted as just approximations.

10. *Be sure that you will open escrow.* It is important for many reasons (discussed in Chapter 11) that you, the buyer, open escrow, even though you may have to pay the costs if the deal falls through. One of the better ways to accomplish this is to make it a condition of the sales agreement. However, a wise seller may also want to open escrow, and fighting for dominance here may be one of the bars to making a sale. You may have to give up this option in order to get your price—or pay more and get to open escrow.

11. *Be sure there is a date for closing escrow and that this date is far enough in the future.* The date for closing escrow should allow you time to obtain financing and to fulfill any other obligations you may have to the sale. Thirty- to sixty-day escrows are common.

12. *Be sure that all items to be prorated are prorated as of close of escrow or whatever other date you and the seller may agree upon.* (Prorating is discussed in detail in Chapter 24.) Close of escrow is normally used for this and indicates that you, the buyer, will pay the taxes, insurance, etc. only for that period of time when you actually own the property. If, however, you occupy the property before or after the close of escrow, you might want to adjust the date or prorations.

13. *Be sure a date is given for you to take possession of the premises.* When I am a buyer, I insist on the right to inspect the property one day before the close of escrow to determine that the sellers will actually be gone. If possession is given, for example, fifteen days after close of escrow, the sellers will be allowed to occupy the property for over two weeks even though you own it. If the sellers insist on such terms, you should insist that they pay you reasonable rent during that period and that the rent money be taken out of their escrow funds before the sale closes. In any event, you should have a clause in the contract specifying that if the sellers fail to get out on the agreed-upon date, they will be charged a certain rent. If possession is given after escrow closes and the former owners refuse to move out, you might have to evict them as common tenants.

24

Don't Be Cheated by Closing Costs

To protect yourself to a great extent from unreasonably high closing costs, try using the "suspicious buyer" method. This method is used by most buyers whenever they are afraid they may be cheated. Quite simply, it is to question the price and then shop around *before* making your final decision. *Before* you hire an attorney, or an escrow company, *before* you pay for termite clearances, title reports, and insurance and any of the other myriad things involved in closing, ask the cost. To help you determine if the costs are reasonable or excessive, the following guidelines have been prepared. If the costs are excessive, exercise your right in a free marketplace—*go somewhere else!* There is almost no service required to close a real estate transaction that is not offered by at least a dozen or more individuals or companies. In this highly competitive business, rates vary and in many cases can be bargained for. Be a smart shopper and you will save yourself hundreds of dollars, perhaps much more.

The distribution of closing costs between buyer and seller is largely up to local custom. In some areas buyers pay escrow charges and sellers pay title insurance. In other areas the seller pays for the escrow and the buyer pays for title insurance. In yet other locales the fees are split. Your agent and escrow officer are the best guides to what is accepted practice in your area.

A good agent will explain the costs to you at the time escrow is opened (for a complete discussion of the escrow process see Chapter 11) and offer you alternatives to get the cheapest possible closing costs. Unfortunately, this does not always happen.

In 1974 Congress made an attempt to deal with the problem of high closing costs. It passed the Real Estate Settlement Procedures Act or RESPA. RESPA was originally intended to limit closing costs; however, the final bill as passed fell far short of this. Rather than limit costs, it required that most lenders offer to the buyer a complete list of all closing costs at least twelve days before close of escrow. The idea here was that the twelve days would allow the buyer time to shop around for other services if the costs of ones offered were too high.

In actual practice the twelve-day provision proved unworkable. Many costs, such as some prorations, could not be figured to the last penny until the actual date of closing. In other cases the new law caused unnecessary delays in closing a deal. And finally, it actually added to the closing costs by requiring lenders to do additional work. Confronted with such problems, Congress passed a new law in early 1975 repealing the twelve-day provision of RESPA, although retaining the requirement that a complete list of closing costs be presented to the buyer before the deal was closed. Since in most cases such a list is presented before closing anyway, the law has almost no effect on the closing costs of real estate. It is mentioned here only to indicate the lack of federal protection in this area. (One other provision of RESPA prohibits sellers from conditioning the sale upon the buyer going to a particular title company. The penalty may be three times the cost.)

A final word of caution: Shortly after escrow is opened, you will be required to sign escrow instructions. These are a more formal document than the sales agreement empowering the escrow officer to carry out the conditions of the sale. It is critical that the escrow instructions agree completely with the sales agreement. Normally, once signed, these instructions are not revocable, and any errors can be extremely difficult to correct. If you have any doubt at all that the escrow instructions correspond completely with the sales agreement, have your broker and attorney examine them *before* you sign.

1. *Escrow charges.* Either the escrow company or the attorney handling the escrow will charge a fee for this service. Surprisingly, the fee will often depend on the selling price of the property, being at a rate of so many dollars per $1000 of price. On the surface this may seem inappropriate since the amount of escrow work in an $80,000 house is roughly the same as for a $40,000 house yet the fee is likely to be 50 percent higher. One explanation offered by many escrow companies is that they must guarantee their work. If they make a mistake in the disbursement of funds, they must make up the loss. And that loss is potentially much higher in an $80,000 piece of property than in a $40,000 one.

The rates charged by escrow companies or officers may vary enormously within a given area of the country. In some areas, one escrow officer or company may charge 50 percent or more above competitive rates. This is more likely to be the case when you are a "captive" buyer, that is, when your agent escorts you to his or her favorite escrow company (sometimes an affiliate of the real estate agency). If you walk in the front door of an independent escrow company by yourself, you may get a lower rate. Your best bet is to shop around. Call or stop by a few escrow companies to get a comparison and don't overlook the escrow services offered by many banks. They can be found in your local phone book.

2. *Title insurance.* This ensures buyers that they are getting a good title to the property. You should always want title insurance. It is your best protection against a bad transaction. Two types of coverage are available. The first is called "standard." Unfortunately, from the point of view of comparison, there are no standards for "standard" coverage. Whatever a title insurance company registers with the state insurance commissioner as standard in that company's policy is what will be included in it. And almost every company's standard policy differs slightly from the standard policy of other companies.

There is, however, another type of title insurance that is standardized. It is the American Land Title Association (ALTA) coverage (also sometimes called extended coverage). It is very thorough and is insisted on by many lenders. However, it is not usually possible to simply call various title companies and get a comparison of their ALTA rates, for the coverage under the ALTA policies may vary greatly from company to company depending on their standard coverage.

This is not nearly as complicated, however, as it may first seem. The easiest way to understand it is to think of title insurance in terms of a full cup of coffee. The ALTA policy represents a full cup. Now, if title company A has a standard policy that fills the cup up 60 percent of the way, the ALTA policy it offers will fill the remaining 40 percent. If title company B offers a standard policy that fills the cup up 90 percent, its ALTA policy will add only another 10 percent. And so on.

In order to compare title companies' rates, you must usually combine the standard rate with the extended or ALTA rate. Some title companies might argue, however, that even this comparison is inaccurate for they may offer items in their standard policy which are over and above what's required in the ALTA policy. To me this means they are filling the cup of coffee 110 percent full. If you or your house has a particular problem, you may need special coverage and will have to pay extra for it. But as for myself, the ALTA policy is the most I ever require—anything additional is coffee that just spills over the cup.

3. *Points.* Almost every time you get a new mortgage there are points to pay. A point is a discount on a mortgage equal to 1 percent of the loan amount. One point on a $10,000 loan is $100. Who pays the points in a real estate transaction is a matter of agreement (except in the case of

FHA loans where the buyer may not pay more than 1 point, technically called an origination fee). If you, the buyer, were shrewd and the sellers were not, you would have the sellers pay the points on your new loan.

The number of points charged usually varies 1 or 2 points from one area of the country to another. There are two basic reasons points are charged: One is that lenders often charge points to cover their expenses in establishing the loan. Second, the lender uses the points to offset any loss when the mortgage is sold in the secondary money market. (VA and FHA mortgages given by savings and loan associations, banks, and mortgage bankers are often resold to much larger government-controlled lending organizations.) When money is readily available, few points are charged, perhaps 1 or less. When money is tight, however, the points can skyrocket. I have seen them as high as 15 points for a loan.

To be sure you don't pay more than the minimum number of points, you should check two things. First, you should be sure that your agent is not getting a finder's fee for bringing you to a particular lender. These fees are usually 1 percent of the loan, paid by you in the form of 1 point. Secondly, you should be sure that the lender you have is not charging higher rates than other lenders.

It takes only a few minutes to check up on these things. Here's how: Take out the yellow pages of your phone book and look up savings and loan institutions. Start at the top of the list, call up the lender, and ask to speak to a loan officer. Tell the officer you need a loan and give the amount. The loan officer will tell you the best interest rate available and the points charged. Often the answer will be expressed something like "1½ points plus 50." The "plus" 50 here refers to a set fee for making up documents—it means $50. The fee varies from nothing to $150 or more. Just go down the list of lenders. You'll find out very quickly if the rates quoted you are competitive. If they're not, switch lenders. There's almost never a fee for applying for a loan and then not obtaining it. Just take your business to the lowest bidder. Remember, money is money regardless of who makes the loan.

4. *Prorations.* To prorate simply means to divide costs between buyer and seller so that each pays only that portion that is due while he or she owns the property. Taxes, for example, are normally prorated as of the day escrow closes. Since property taxes must normally be paid to the government in either annual or semiannual installments, and since the close of escrow rarely falls exactly on the date that taxes are due, and paid, they must be prorated.

Let us say, for example, that taxes are paid annually and are due November 1 for the tax year running from March 1 to the end of February. Let us further suppose that the tax bill is $1200 and that escrow closes on the first day of May. The seller is responsible for taxes for the first two months of the tax year, March and April, and the buyer is responsible for the balance. However, at the close of escrow, the seller has not yet paid the taxes on the property since they aren't due until November. The seller must pay to the buyer two months' worth of taxes, or $200. On the other hand, if the property were sold on January 1 and the seller had paid the taxes in November, the buyer would have to refund to the seller two months' worth of taxes for that period of time that the buyer would own the property during the tax year. The following items are normally prorated as of close of escrow:

Taxes (including tax reserves)

Insurance (including insurance reserves)

Interest on mortgages

Rents (if any)

Water, gas, and electric bills

Oil or coal on hand

Garbage removal

It is possible for you, the buyer, to greatly reduce (or increase) the cost of your prorations by varying the date on which the items are prorated. If the taxes are due but have not yet been paid, extending the date for prorations will require the seller to add money to the escrow, thus reducing your charges. If the prorations are made on the day monthly interest is due on an existing loan you are taking over, you won't have to pay any interest prorations. However, if the prorations are made before the next interest date, you may have to put that amount of money into escrow to make the payment. The same holds true with existing fire insurance and utility bills.

Moving the date of prorations can be a bit tricky since most sales agreements specify that they are to be made as of close of escrow. It usually is not too difficult, however, to delay or advance the date of the close of escrow.

Keep in mind also that many states allow exemptions on taxes for certain groups such as resident homeowners, veterans, and senior citizens. Be sure you get these exemptions if you are entitled to them, as they can greatly reduce closing costs.

5. *Attorney's fees.* It is possible that before escrow closes a buyer may become involved with as many as three attorneys and owe separate fees to each of them.

If a buyer (or seller) has an attorney look over the documents to a real estate transaction, a fee normally will have to be paid. The amount can be anywhere from $50 to $500 or more. There is no set schedule and the buyer should seriously consider discussing and even bargaining with the attorney for the fee *before* any legal work is done.

If the escrow officer is an attorney, he or she will have to be paid (although there probably won't be a separate escrow fee). Fees here, again, are subject to bargaining although to a much lesser degree. Attorneys who regularly handle escrow work often have a set fee schedule they will not depart from. Of course, if the attorney who checks over your documents also handles the escrow, you conceivably could save one entire fee.

On the East Coast, a third attorney often enters the picture—the lender's lawyer. The institution making the loan will often have a lawyer make up the documents, such as the deed of trust or mortgage and the note. A fee for this work will usually be charged to the buyer. It is often in the range of $200 to $300.

I personally have never seen the justification for this particular fee. Lenders' documents are usually prewritten legal forms that only require filling in the names of the parties, the amount and terms, and the description of the property. On the West Coast a single document fee covers this, and it is usually under $75.

It is possible to dicker over the amount of the lender's attorney's fees. However, it is probably best to have your own attorney do the arguing. Since the lender won't make the loan without the documents and you need the loan to make the transaction, you have very little leverage to work with.

6. *Credit report.* The fee for this is normally much less than $50, and it usually is paid by the buyer, although it can be paid by the seller if both parties agree. There is little opportunity to bargain here as the lender will usually specify which credit reporting company must be used.

7. *Loan origination and/or placement fee.* As mentioned, this is a set fee often quoted along with points. Just be sure it's competitive and that it doesn't include a finder's fee to the agent.

8. *Appraisal fee.* If you've hired an independent appraiser, you'll have to pay a fee, which you should have discussed at the time of the hiring. If you did not hire an appraiser, there should be no appraisal fee. Lenders do not normally charge appraisal fees on mortgages they are making.

9. *Mortgage service charge.* The buyer usually pays this one-time fee. It usually goes to an independent company that reports to the lender the amount of taxes due on the property so that the lender can pay them out of your impounds. It is usually under $50 and there is little room for bargaining as the lender will specify which service it wants to use.

10. *Impounds.* If your monthly payment on your mortgage will include taxes and insurance, you will have to come up with enough money at the close of escrow to cover the first installment on your taxes and at least the first year's payment on your fire insurance. The lender will set these amounts.

The only way you can effectively reduce them is by changing the date escrow closes. If you can manage to close escrow just after a tax payment was made by the previous owner, you will have ample time to establish your tax fund in monthly payments before the next tax installment is due; hence your impounds should be very low.

Many lenders require an extra month's worth of taxes and insurance as a buffer in case you don't make a payment or in case taxes rise. If the lender requires more than this amount, you should check to see if you can get a better deal from another lender. In the past, interest has not been paid by lenders on impounded money; however, new federal laws may soon require that at least a nominal interest rate (around 2 percent) be paid. Impounds are normally required on any loan that is higher than 80 percent of the selling price of the property.

11. *Notary fee.* Notarizing or witnessing documents is usually performed by the escrow officer and in many cases is done as part of the normal escrow charges. Where an extra charge is made, it shouldn't be more than a few dollars for each document notarized.

12. *Recording fee for deed and mortgages.* In most areas this fee is under $5 for each document. If you question the amount being charged, call your county or city recorder's office and ask what the regular recording fee is.

13. *Transfer tax.* Until 1967 the federal government charged a revenue stamp tax on the conveyance (transfer of title) of real estate. When this law was repealed, the states instituted their own transfer tax. To find out how much your state charges for a transfer tax, see the appendix.

14. *Other items.* Land survey, soil engineer's report, structural engineer's report, termite report or clearance, etc. are special items which the buyer, the seller, or the lender may insist upon. The cost should be arranged beforehand, and the person who will pay should be mutually agreed upon.

15. *Commission.* This is almost always paid by the seller (but it could be paid by the buyer). The amount is a percentage of the selling price arrived by mutual agreement between agent and seller. There is no set or official rate. It can be any amount, although at this writing 6 percent seems to be the most common rate. (See Chapter 3 and 6 for further discussions.)

16. *Disclosure documents.* If you are obtaining a new mortgage, there are two documents which you will receive before escrow closes. The first is a full-disclosure statement required under the Truth-in-Lending Act of 1969. It will tell you the annual interest rate, the total number of monthly payments, whether there is a balloon payment (not usually allowed), the total interest charged, and other facts pertaining to your mortgage.

The other document is the RESPA statement which will disclose the true closing costs you are paying.

If either document does not coincide with what you have been told to expect by anyone in the deal and you are concerned that you have been cheated, contact that person and demand a full explanation. If you are still not satisfied, see your attorney at once and, above all, *before you sign any more documents.* Further, if it appears that your agent has deceived you, contact the nearest office of your state's real estate commissioner for further advice. (Addresses for all state commissioner's offices are given in the appendix.)

25

What to Do about a Bad Credit Report

Almost anytime you purchase a home and obtain new financing, the lender will require a credit report. If the report does not reveal a bad credit rating, you'll forget about it, and it will just be one more item in the transaction. However, if the report reveals adverse credit information, the lender may refuse to make the loan and you could lose the deal. In this case the credit report will become the biggest obstacle to overcome, and you will remember it vividly whenever recalling the deal.

If, in fact, you do have poor credit, you may not be able to counter a bad credit report. Nonetheless, you should read what follows as it may help you improve the report just enough to get you your house. (With truly bad credit you should think about taking over an existing government-insured loan, where your credit rating shouldn't be a problem.)

If you think the credit reporting agency has made an error or has failed to state all the facts in a particular case, the Fair Credit Reporting Act of 1971 offers you certain remedies. After an adverse report has been made at the request of a lender and you have been denied credit, almost all consumers (excluding certain commercial consumers) normally have the right to:

1. Demand and be told the name and address of the credit reporting company.

2. Demand and be told the *nature, substance,* and *sources* of the adverse information unless the information was of a medical nature. (However, if the information resulted from an investigative-type source, you probably can't get the names.)

3. Get the information free if you request the information

within thirty days. (Otherwise, the credit reporting company can charge a fee.)

4. Challenge information you feel is inaccurate. This is probably the biggest advantage the law affords the person trying to get credit.

Once you've found out the nature, substance, and sources of the bad credit report, you can make your plans to challenge it. You have the right, in most cases, to have inaccurate or incorrect information reinvestigated. However, if the agency made a mistake the first time round, it may make the same mistake the second time. My suggestion is that you go directly to the source of the bad credit information. For example, if a department store has reported slow payments or a repossession when none occurred, take the matter up with the store. Be sure that the problem is cleared up with the source before you have the matter reinvestigated. Sometimes paying the source the amount due in the case of a true credit problem may result in that source not reporting the bad credit at all the second time!

Once you've cleared up the matter at the source, and the credit company has reinvestigated and made a correction, you usually have a right to:

5. Have the agency notify the lender that previously received the inaccurate report of the changes.

In the event that you can't correct the problem at the source and the reinvestigation doesn't improve the report, you have the right to:

6. Request that the credit reporting agency send your version of the dispute to the lender. If the request is made within thirty days of the original report, no charge is usually allowed.

The rights that the Fair Credit Reporting Act extends to you also apply to certain types of investigative reports, in which the credit agency sends out an investigator rather than simply reports on what information stores, credit card companies, banks, etc. have sent in. An investigative report is most often done when a consumer applies for life or auto insurance. On occasion, however, it is also done for real estate lenders. An investigator might ask your employer, neighbors, and yourself questions about your financial condition and character. Since this type of investigation, on occasion, may end up using hearsay as the basis for the report, it is often the most difficult to correct.

Under the Fair Credit Reporting Act you have the right to discover the nature and substance of the adverse report, but not the source. The nature and substance, however, may reveal to you the source. Certain remarks might only have come from your employer, others only from that cranky neighbor up the street. In such circumstances you might talk to your employer or neighbor and explain the situation. Unless you're an extremely bad character, most people will go along and agree to speak better of you in the future. Then have the agency reinvestigate. Unless challenged information can be verified, it may be dropped from your report.

The Fair Credit Reporting Act also may give you the right to:

7. Be notified if a company is seeking an investigative report and the right to request that the inquiring company inform you of the nature and scope of the investigation.

8. Have most of the adverse information in your file dropped after seven years. Bankruptcy is an exception; it stays on record for fourteen years.

9. Take any other person you choose with you when you visit the consumer reporting agency (this is often helpful in terms of moral support) to gain information about your adverse report. You do not, however, have the right to physically handle your file nor to receive a copy of your report. It is helpful, therefore, to take someone along who can jot down the information quickly as the credit company officer tells it to you (or to use a tape recorder, when allowed).

Probably the act's biggest drawback is that it does not authorize the federal government to intervene on behalf of an individual borrower who has received an adverse report. The Federal Trade Commission, however, can sometimes offer very helpful advice on how to deal with a troublesome credit reporting agency. Here's where to contact the FTC:

City and state	Office location	Phone
*Atlanta, GA 30308	730 Peachtree St., NE, Room 800	(404) 526-5836
Charlotte, NC 28202	623 East Trade St. Room 206	(704) 372-7762
Oak Ridge, TN 37830	Room G-209 Fed. Off. Bldg. P.O. Box 568	(615) 483-4735
Miami, FL 33168	Room 105 995 NW 119th St.	(305) 350-5540

* Indicates regional office.

City and state	Office location	Phone
*Boston, MA 02203	John Fitzgerald Kennedy Federal Bldg. - Room 2200-C Government Center	(617) 223-6621
*Chicago, ILL 60603	55 East Monroe St. Suite 1437	(312) 353-4423
*Cleveland, OH 44199	Federal Office Bldg. 1240 E 9th St. Room 1339	(216) 522-4207
Detroit, MI 48207	333 Mt. Elliott Avenue	(313) 226-6890
*Dallas, TX 75201	500 South Ervay St. Room 452-R	(214) 749-3056
San Antonio, TX 78212	Federal Center, Bldg. 3 630 Main Avenue	(512) 225-4521
*New Orleans, LA 70130	1000 Masonic Temple Bldg. 333 St. Charles St.	(504) 527-2091
*Kansas City, MO 64106	2806 Federal Office Bldg. 911 Walnut St.	(816) 374-5256
Denver, CO 80202	18013 Federal Office Bldg. 1961 Stout St.	(303) 837-3480
St. Louis, MO 63101	210 N 12th St. Room 1414	(314) 622-4710
*Los Angeles, CA 90024	11000 Wilshire Blvd. Room 13209	(213) 824-7575
Phoenix, AZ 85004	Amerco Towers Bldg. 2721 North Central Ave. Room 828	(602) 261-4127
San Diego, CA 92101	Bank of America Bldg. 625 Broadway Room 1132	(714) 293-5547
*New York, NY 10007	22nd Floor Federal Bldg. 26 Federal Plaza	(212) 264-1200
Buffalo, NY 14202	111 West Huron St. Room 221	(716) 842-5933
*San Francisco, CA 94102	450 Golden Gate Avenue Box 36005	(415) 556-1270
Honolulu, HI 96813	Room 605, Melim Bldg. 333 Queen Street	(808) 521-6937
*Seattle, WA 98101	Suite 908 Republic Bldg. 1511 Third Avenue	(206) 442-4655
Portland, OR 97205	231 US Courthouse	(503) 221-3629
*Washington, D.C. 20037	Gellman Bldg., 6th Floor 2120 L Street, NW	(202) 254-7700
Philadelphia, PA 19107	1406 Bankers Security Bldg. 1315 Walnut St.	(205) 597-0438

* Indicates regional office.

26

Prejudice/Your Right to Buy and Rent

"All citizens of the United States shall have the same right, in every state and territory, as is enjoyed by white citizens thereof of to inherit, purchase, lease, sell, hold and convey real and personal property." So reads the Civil Rights Act of 1866. However, until 1968 it was largely understood that it applied only to state action and did not cover private actions. In that year the Supreme Court in the case of *Jones v. Mayer* declared that the law "bars all racial discrimination, private as well as public in the sale or rental of a property." This decision, along with the Civil Rights Act of 1968, virtually eliminated the basis for any discrimination in housing.

Under the Civil Rights Act of 1968, specific discriminatory activities were prohibited. These included:

1. Refusal to sell, rent, or even negotiate on the basis of race, color, religion, sex, or national origin

2. Discriminating by changing the terms or refusing to discuss the terms

3. Discriminating in any advertising, whether at a housing tract or in a newspaper

4. Falsely stating that a property is not for sale or rent as a means of discriminating

5. Practicing discrimination in providing financial assistance for the purchase of a house by a lender

6. Discriminating in providing facilities, such as parking, or in the furnishings of a housing unit

7. Block busting, that is urging homeowners in a neighborhood into which, for example, a person of a different race has just moved to quickly sell their homes

8. Discriminating in refusing to admit a real estate broker or real estate organization to a multiple listing service

This law was intended to apply only to housing and not to industrial or commercial property. In addition, certain exceptions were included:

1. Bona fide homeowners selling their own property and not discriminating in advertising nor using the services of a broker, providing the homeowners reside in the property and do not own more than three such houses

2. A building in which rooms or units are occupied by fewer than four families living independently of each other as long as the owner occupies one such unit

3. A religious organization, which may limit the occupancy, sale, or rental of its property to persons of the religion unless membership in the religion is restricted by race, color, or national origin

4. A private club that is not open to the public and that provides lodgings noncommercially and incidental to its primary purpose, which may limit the occupancy or rental of its lodgings

If you feel you have been discriminated against in real estate, you can seek a remedy under the Civil Rights Act of 1968 by appealing to the Department of Housing and Urban Development as long as you file your complaint not more than 180 days after you were discriminated against. You should report the discrimination to Fair Housing, Department of Housing and Urban Development, Washington, D.C. 20410, or to the nearest HUD office.

More than thirty-five states and/or cities have passed similar housing laws and if you have been discriminated against you may seek help from your state or city. These include:

Alaska	Hawaii
California	Indiana
Colorado	Iowa
Connecticut	Kansas
Delaware	Kentucky

Maryland	Washington
Massachusetts	West Virginia
Michigan	Wisconsin
Minnesota	District of Columbia
Nebraska	Dade County, Florida
Nevada	Aurora, Peoria, Springfield, and Urbana,
New Hampshire	Illinois
New Jersey	Ann Arbor Michigan
New Mexico	Kansas City, Missouri
New York	Omaha, Nebraska
Ohio	New York, New York
Pennsylvania	Philadelphia, Pennsylvania
Rhode Island	Mercer Island, Washington
Vermont	Charleston, West Virginia

If you have been discriminated against in a way that is not covered by the Civil Rights Act of 1968, you can seek a remedy through the Civil Rights Act of 1866, in which almost all discrimination is prohibited. You will, however, probably have to pursue this action in the form of a suit in federal court.

The Civil Rights Act of 1968 has criminal provisions for anyone who uses threats, intimidation, or coercion. If you have been so discriminated against, you should report the matter to the police and/or the FBI.

Largely because of the Supreme Court decision and the Civil Rights Act of 1968, discrimination in housing has in most states of the country ceased to be a problem. Nonetheless, if you should stumble into an area where you are discriminated against because of your race, color, religion, sex, or national origin, you should exercise your rights as a free member of our society. The law is on your side.

27

How to Get out of a Bad Deal

It's been said before, but it bears repeating: The best way out of a bad deal is to avoid getting into it in the first place. Having said that, let's consider what your options are if you do find yourself in a bad situation.

As the buyer, you stand to lose your deposit if you back out of a deal; however, your liability does not end here. The sellers may sue you for specific performance, which means they may go to court to force you to complete the transaction. In addition, the sellers may sue you for damages if the property is resold and brings less than it would have in the deal you backed out of.

In actual practice this rarely happens. Most sellers are satisfied to have kept the buyer's deposit money, particularly if it was a substantial sum. If you were a smart buyer, however, you might not even lose the deposit money. Now is the time you will be thankful you put all those escape clauses in the contract. When you suddenly find out that the wonderful house you're going to buy backs up to a sewage treatment plant, you bring to the seller's attention the clause giving you three days to get the approval of your aunt in Schenectady. Your aunt simply doesn't approve. Or use any of the other escape hatches you've installed in the contract.

If you've deposited your money in escrow, you recall the provision you had inserted that it will be paid back to you if escrow doesn't close within a certain number of days and if the provisions of the sales agreement have not been fulfilled.

But perhaps you don't have any escape clauses. Or perhaps the seller intends taking you to court to get you to buy.

Your first step should be to consult with an attorney, if you haven't already done so. You should keep in mind that most real estate contracts rely on the good intentions of the parties for them to be carried out. If one party doesn't want to go along, it could be that the contract, particularly if it was filled out by someone other than a good lawyer, will be so illusory (the meaning will not be clear) that it will not hold up in court.

Occasionally, buyers will want out because they innocently signed a contract that is extremely one-sided in favor of the seller. If you have such a contract, the one-sided terms themselves may be enough to invalidate the contract under the Uniform Commercial Code.

If you're dealing with an agent, scream loud and long that you've been cheated, if you have, and that you want out of the deal and your deposit back. You might not get back your deposit, but you stand a good chance of getting out, if the agent can persuade the seller to let you go.

Many agents may try to coerce you into completing a deal that you don't like or want. Think twice before you give in to such persuasion. You may have to spend many years in a house you don't care for if you don't fight back. If an agent tries to pressure you, tell that agent that you are going to see your lawyer, and do it. If the agent begins telling you of all the dire things that will happen if you don't complete the sale, point out that an agent isn't supposed to give legal advice—only bring buyer and seller together. And then go see your attorney.

In almost all the cases that I have seen where buyers wanted to back out of a deal that had escape clauses, they have done so and have received their deposit back. In those cases where there was no escape clause, the buyers were allowed out but lost the deposit. Most residential sellers that I have seen would rather concentrate on selling their house than fighting an expensive battle with a reluctant buyer in court. In several cases involving hardship, such as a sudden loss of employment or a death in the family, the seller has allowed the buyer to back out and returned all or part of the deposit. Finally, a really good agent will step in and quickly resell the house so that the seller really isn't suffering a loss.

Although you may lose your deposit and you may be forced to complete a transaction, this isn't very likely. In any event, don't give up until you've exhausted all your options. (See Chapter 12 for a further discussion.)

FOUR

Protect Yourself When You Buy a Condominium

28

Be Sure It's What You Really Want—Thirteen Problem Areas to Watch Out For

Before prospective buyers purchase a condominium, or condo, they should take a moment to consider the sacrifices and the responsibilities of "team" living. This is not to say that one shouldn't purchase a condominium, rather that a condominium demands a type of lifestyle different from that afforded by a single-unit home. The fact that nearly 2 million condo units have been built, nearly three-fourths of these in the last six years, indicates that many people have found the lifestyle of the condo acceptable.

When you purchase a condominium, you are actually buying a hybrid, a cross between a house and an apartment. While developers are quick to point out that you will have the benefits of house and apartment, the best of both worlds, so to speak, you may also end up with the drawbacks of both.

If you buy a condominium, don't expect to be master of all you survey. As a homeowner you are in charge of all your property—front yard, side yards, back yard and house—but as owner of a condominium you control only the inside of your unit. Once past the front door you are just one of many owners, a member of a team. And as is the case in team sports, in a condo there will be times when you will have to forgo your personal preference for the good of the whole project.

If you buy a condominium, your fixed expenses will probably be higher than if you purchased a home at a comparable price. In addition to taxes, interest (and principal) on a loan, and insurance, a condominium also requires that you pay dues to a homeowner's association. Since these dues must cover the cost of all operating expenses, including maintaining all the landscaping, setting aside reserves to cover future maintenance work (such as repainting the building), setting up additional reserves to pay for repair of electrical, plumbing, and heating systems (including repairs to the swimming pool, if there is one), they can be fairly high, occasionally as much as 30 percent or more of the mortgage cost of the unit. Some projects lease their recreational facilities from the developer, and this is an additional cost that must be met.

Also, don't think you can simply move into your condo and forget about everyone else. You will want to attend the meetings of the homeowner's association if for no other reason than to protect your own interests. To see that matters get taken care of correctly, you may find yourself appointed to or applying for an administrative position (nonpaying of course) in the association, which can require a good deal of time. And you may be called upon to come up with cash and time when emergencies such as a fire or structural damage occur to someone else's unit in the building.

Most condominium buyers, however, are more than willing to give the added time and money necessary for condominium living for one big and two little reasons. The big reason is convenience. When you live in a well-run condo, you never have to worry about mowing the lawn or painting the outside of the house. All external upkeep will be taken care of. This is probably the single biggest reason people buy condos.

A secondary reason is the recreational facilities. In a condo very often a recreation hall, swimming pool, putting green, and tennis courts are included in the project. As an owner you have use of these facilities, something as a homeowner you very likely could not afford to have on your own property.

Another reason is companionship. Some individuals are gregarious either naturally or because of their situation in life. A condominium provides neighbors who are not simply tenants who move in and out, but solid owners. And friendships are often easier to make here.

Given these three reasons for purchasing, it is not difficult to see that condominium purchasers fall into two main categories. According to a study conducted by the Department of Housing and Urban Development in 1975, 58 percent of condominium owners surveyed were forty-five years old or older, most without children living at home. Of the remaining group, half were under thirty-five years of age, with most of these in their twenties and, again, without children. The conclusion is that the majority of buyers of condominiums are either young marrieds or couples whose children have grown up and left home. In the trade this latter group is often referred to as "empty nesters."

Before defining exactly what a condo is and what problems to watch out for, a word should be said for condos as an investment.

When purchasing real estate, the anticipation is that values will go up. While this is true of real estate in general, it has not necessarily been true of condominiums. Those projects built near recreational facilities or close to working areas have in general done quite well. Others, however, have not done well at all, with many units going into foreclosure in 1974 and 1975. Condominiums suffered perhaps more than any other type of real estate during the recession of the midseventies. (Two recreational areas where condominiums did not do well were the Lake Tahoe–Reno area in California and Nevada and the Ft. Lauderdale area in Florida. Both these areas suffered heavily in the midseventies, primarily because of overbuilding.)

The important thing to remember about the appreciation of value in a condominium is that the *entire* project must appreciate in order for your individual unit to go up in price. While it is possible for a unit's owners to improve the inside of their condo—upgrading the carpeting, hanging decorative wallpaper, repainting, etc.—all units are maintained by the homeowner's association on the outside, including painting, mowing of lawns, landscaping, etc. Usually there is nothing individual owners can do to make the outside of their unit outstanding; in fact, most condominiums' bylaws prohibit unit owners from in any way making their units externally distinguishable from any other units. Consequently, with minor differences caused by interior upgrading, any one condominium unit will be worth no more than any similar unit in the project. For any unit to appreciate in value, they all must. In a large condominium with, for example, 200 similar units, it is easy to see that before prices can rise, the demand must be very large to compensate for the large supply. Individual condominium units suffer from the same handicap that often keeps homes in a tract where all the houses are identical from rising dramatically in price—lack of uniqueness.

When you buy a condo, you should be sure that it is, in fact, a condominium and not some other type of ownership. There are at least two other types that are often confused with the condominium—a *cooperative* and a *planned unit development* (PUD), often called cluster housing.

The word *condominium* comes from Latin and combines two elements: *dominium,* meaning "control," *con,* meaning "with" (other people). It broadly means shared control over property with other people. The concept can best be understood in terms of Figures 1 and 2.

In a traditional *single estate,* or ownership of real property where an individual owns a single home on a lot, the ownership covers more than just the surface of the land. Imagine invisible lines extending from the edges of the lot all the way down to the earth's core and in the other direction all the way out to infinity—this is the area owned in a single estate. Often, owners who have retained mineral rights deep below the surface can sell these to a mining, oil, or gas company. Similarly, owners are protected from anyone building anything directly over their property (although not necessarily from someone erecting a tall building next door that cuts out the sunshine).

To understand a *condominium estate,* imagine horizontal lines now intersecting the vertical lines of Figure 1. These horizontal lines bisect the vertical planes and prevent them from continuing upward or down-

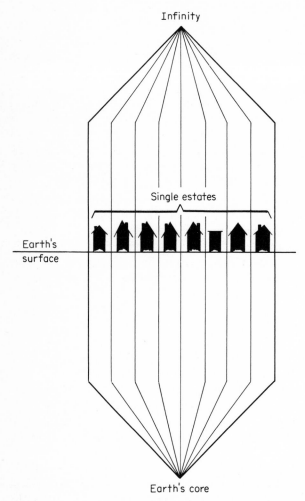

Figure 1 Traditional real estate, where ownership extends both above the property to infinity and below to the center of the earth's core. (*Based on a chart taken from "Questions About Condominiums," Department of Housing and Urban Development, U.S. Government Printing Office: 1974 0–557–488.*)

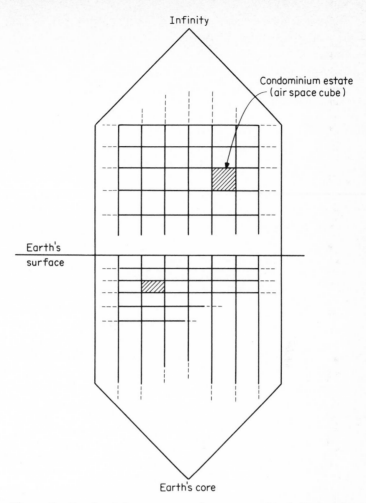

Figure 2 Condominium estates, where ownership is limited in the vertical as well as the traditional horizontal planes. (*Based on a chart taken from "Questions About Condominiums," Department of Housing and Urban Development, U.S. Government Printing Office: 1974 0–557–488.*)

ward. They form cubes of air space often called *space estates.* In real life the horizontal and vertical lines will appear as the ceiling, floor, and walls of the condominium. Individual ownership applies only within the air space cube. Ownership in common with the other dwellers of the building applies to the supporting structure, the land (down to the earth's core) and the air space above the building.

When you purchase a condominium, you in reality purchase two estates (or ownerships). You buy a single, undivided estate within your own air space cube. If, however, that were all you bought, your ownership would hang suspended in space. So you also buy an undivided or common interest in the building and other property. This undivided interest extends right up to the boundaries of the land the condominium building rests on.

A type of ownership often confused with a condominium is a *cooperative*. A coop involves ownership in a corporation which then holds title to a real property. In addition, the coop owner holds the right of *tenancy* within an air space cube within the real property. Essentially, a diagram of a coop is the same as that of the condominium (see Figure 2). The important difference, however, is that in a condo you *own* the air space cube while in a coop you, in essence, rent it.

The advantage of a condo over a coop include these:

1. In a condo your mortgage covers only your own unit. This is enormously important. If the owners of another condo unit in your building cannot pay their mortgage and foreclosure results, you are not affected. In a coop, there is a single blanket mortgage covering the entire building. If one owner cannot pay, the remaining owners must make up the difference. If a majority or even a large minority of owners cannot pay (as may happen during a severe recession or depression), the entire building may go into foreclosure and you could lose your interest, even though you were still able to pay your own way. This also applies to taxes.

2. When it comes time to sell, your position is much better in a condo. You are able to sell your own unit often without regard to other owners (some condo deeds provide a *first refusal right* to the homeowner's association). Most important, the purchaser is able to obtain financing without regard to the other owners. In a coop in order to sell, you must find someone who will buy your stock in the owning corporation— often a much more difficult task.

3. In a condo you have the option of paying off your mortgage at any time. In a coop you must continue to make payments on the blanket mortgage unless all the owners agree to pay it off—something which almost never happens.

4. In a condo you normally can't be forced out unless you fail to meet your monthly payments on your individual mortgage. In a coop you can be forced to leave for failure to meet your

lease agreements, that is, for failure to pay rent. In addition, you could be forced to leave because other owners found your conduct objectionable.

5. Finally, in a condo you are liable only for your own unit (and indirectly for the undivided area). If someone has a suit against another owner in another unit, it is not normally your problem. In a coop, a suit is usually filed against the entire corporation, including your unit interest. You are liable for all debts of the coop up to the value of the individual unit.

This is not to say that condos are all good and coops are all bad. Coops do have certain advantages over condos.

1. In a coop you have some control over your neighbors. Just as you can have an objectionable tenant evicted, so too can you have an objectionable coop owner evicted. In a condo this is far more difficult, if not downright impossible. Further, as an owner in a coop, if you don't like the building or the other owners, or if you just feel like a change, you can simply "walk away" much as a tenant can—if you don't mind forfeiting your original investment. In a condo you would be faced with foreclosure on your mortgage.

2. In later years when the building begins to decay, a coop usually has no difficulty in raising money via a new blanket loan for renovation or major repairs. Since each unit is individually owned in a condo, there is often no similar way to raise money. In order to fix the building, each individual owner must donate money to the homeowner's association. (A few states have enacted provisions allowing for a blanket mortgage in such cases.)

3. In certain cases it may be advantageous to sell the entire building, as when a developer is willing to pay a good price for it. In a coop this usually takes only a two-thirds vote of the owners. In a condo it normally takes a 100 percent vote of the individual owners; thus one owner in a 200-unit condo could block such a sale.

Before 1970, of the approximately 400,000 such units built, 85 percent were cooperatives and only 15 percent were condominiums. Since 1970, however, of the more than 1 million units built, over 90 percent have been condos and less than 10 percent coops. Many of the coops have been created by a transfer of ownership from individuals who built moderate-income housing under FHA 236 plans as tax shelters and then bailed out by selling the project to the tenants as a coop.

A separate type of condominium ownership that is often confused with a conventional condo is the planned unit development. Figure 3 shows a typical PUD.

A PUD combines some features of individual home ownership with some features of the condominium. PUDs are horizontal, with no units occupying air space cubes (although there may be community walls). Ownership of a unit includes the ground down to the earth's core and the air space above it to infinity, as in ownership of a single estate. Separate ownership, however, ends at the walls of the unit. The property around the unit, including parking areas, common greens, walks, recreational areas, etc., is owned by the homeowner's association. The owner must pay dues to the association for the upkeep of the common area.

The biggest advantage of the PUD over the condo is the decreased density. Usually there is more common area and less building, that is, fewer units per acre.

One should be careful of the term *townhouse*. This is a most misused word. It can be and frequently is used to describe an individual housing

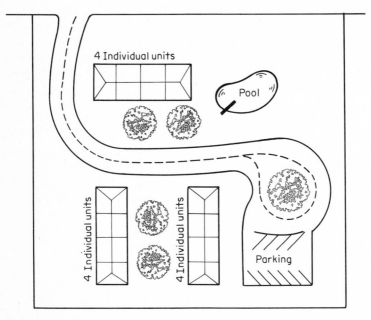

Figure 3 Typical Planned Unit Development (PUD) design.

unit, a condominium, a PUD, and on some occasions, even a coopera-tive. The word *townhouse* usually just means a home which has a common wall with another home.

When purchasing a condominium, there are certain problem areas prospective owners should consider which are different from those nor-mally involved in buying a home. These include the following:

DENSITY

This is probably the single biggest problem area when buying a condo and yet the one often least considered by prospective purchasers. Den-sity doesn't necessarily mean how physically close together units are, but rather how many units are placed on an acre of ground. The number of units per acre varies enormously from one condo project to another. If the project is several stories tall, it is possible to have many units per acre and still have a lot of open space. On the other hand, in one- or two-level condos there might be very little area left for grass and open space. Many studies have been made to determine the optimum units per acre for condominium living. Almost all have arrived at the conclusion that with certain exceptions, the fewer units per acre, the more satisfied and happy the owners. The optimum level is about *six* units per acre. An acre is 43,560 square feet. Assuming each unit is about 1500 square feet hori-zontally, six units would be 9000 square feet, leaving over 30,000 square feet for recreational facilities, parking, pathways, lawns, etc.

The big advantage of having so few units per acre is increased privacy. One unit's windows do not face the windows or doors of another unit—a big complaint among cramped condo owners. Children have play areas away from the living areas so they tend not to bother owners. Cars can be parked far enough away from the units to reduce noise and smells.

Just increasing density even slightly can lower the pleasure of living in a condominium. In a private study conducted in California, forty owners in a unit with a density of 6.3 units per acre were compared with sixty-four owners in a project with a density of 9.4 units per acre. Only 15 per-cent in the lower-density project complained about a cramped lifestyle, while more than 60 percent complained in the denser unit.

As mentioned earlier, there are exceptions to the density rule. If the neighborhood surrounding the condo is a park, there is less objection to high-density living. On the other hand, if the surrounding neighbor-hood is composed of other condos or of apartments, even low density can be objectionable. If the project is located very close to a recreational area, for example, a ski resort or shoreline, increased density is offset by the desirability of location. As many as thirty units per acre can be located unobjectionably near such facilities. Usually in such cases many owners use the condo as a second or vacation home and many units are unoccupied much of the time.

Developers are well aware of the density problem. They have two ways of handling it. One way is to build fewer units per acre, make them in small clusters rather than large buildings, and provide pleasant views and a large amount of recreational facilities. This, however, usually results in very high-priced units and restricts the number that the builder can sell. The alternative is to disguise a high-density project and try to trick buyers into thinking it really is a low-density one. Many techniques are used here. One of the most common is staggering the buildings in the project. The average person can easily judge the size of a building if it has straight walls; if, however, the walls are staggered and walkways meander and trees are placed at unusual spots, it can become very difficult to judge size. Another technique is to have a large grassy open area in the front of the project. The average person, then, is less likely to notice tiny, cramped garden areas inside. This illusion is simply a matter of one's first impression. If one's first impression is of roominess, later cramped views will make less of an impression.

In a disguised high-density condo the parking will often butt right up to the back of the building or perhaps be underneath it. However, there may not be any windows facing the parking so from the inside the impression will be that cars are not around. When a car starts, however, noise and smells often enter the units.

An open patio is also a common feature of a disguised high-density condo. Closing in a patio for each unit not only takes up a considerable amount of space, but requires a lot of additional open space to keep that closed-in patio from looking cramped. A developer will therefore often build a patio without walls. This will seem to give the individual unit some private territory, but this is an illusion. The open patio really just adds additional space to the common area, making the project appear roomier than it is.

The big advantage of the disguised high-density condo is that because the builder can put more units on an acre, they can be sold for less. An important adage to remember when buying a condo, however, is not to be penny-wise and density-foolish.

LIFESTYLE

Another problem with condominiums, and one that many buyers overlook, is the lifestyle of the unit as a whole. A young couple buying a condo might reasonably hope to have other units in the project likewise occupied by younger people. An elderly couple might buy with the expectation of there being very few children in the project. Both these expectations can be dashed, however, if proper care is not taken before purchase to see what sort of lifestyle the project as a whole will offer.

In existing condominiums, the solution to this problem is simple—just walk around and see who lives there. In a new development, however, the answer is not so simple. Perhaps less than half the units have been sold at the time you buy. How will you know who will occupy the remainder? You could try asking the developer—the seller. Many developers are honest and will reply that their project was built for young marrieds or for people with children or for elderly couples. They will honestly try to dissuade someone from buying if that person would not enjoy the lifestyle. However, with the recession in the midseventies and with the overbuilding of condos in many areas, some builders were faced with the choice of selling to anyone or going into foreclosure. It's not difficult to imagine what choice many made. On the other hand, there are some few unscrupulous developers who would lie to make a sale regardless of the economic conditions.

How can you protect yourself? I am sorry to say that you probably can't. Rules and conditions written into the deed restricting pets or children are often unenforceable.

My suggestion is that if you are interested in a condo and the lifestyle is a major concern, you should wait until it is 75 to 85 percent sold before buying your unit. If you're afraid you might miss out, you might ask to put a deposit down to hold the place for a month or more while you decide, but make sure it will be returned if you don't buy. During this time you can observe who's filling up the condo and decide whether they will coincide with your desired lifestyle.

LONG-TERM RECREATIONAL LEASES

This is an abuse that has become known as the "Florida problem" because it occurred so often in that beautiful state. The problem arises when the developer retains ownership of the recreational facilities and leases their use to the homeowner's association. The developer will often point out certain advantages to the purchasers of such an arrangement. For example, the owners will probably not know how to properly maintain such facilities while the developer, a pro in the business, can handle it easily. This is a valid argument.

The abuse of the long-term lease, however, comes from its payment schedule. In many cases such leases were written with high payments and escalator clauses tied to a national cost-of-living index. As the cost of living increased, so did the monthly payments on the lease. In the last few years the cost of living has skyrocketed, and payments on some of these leases have gone up similarly. In one condominium project in Florida, the developer reportedly made $200,000 profit on the project and another $200,000 profit on the recreational lease over the first 2½ years of its existence!

When the owners objected, they found that the homeowner's association was tied to the long-term lease. It couldn't be broken. If they refused to make their monthly dues payments to the association for the lease payment, their property could be tied up to force payment.

The easiest solution to this problem is not to buy a condominium that provides for a long-term lease to anyone for any purpose whether it be recreational facilities or building maintenance. If you fall in love with a condominium that does have a long-term lease to the developer or some other party, don't buy until you've had your lawyer look over the declaration of conditions and other documents and fully explain the ramifications of the lease.

UNDERESTIMATED COSTS FOR MAINTENANCE AND REPAIR

Operating a condominium is somewhat like running a small company. There is the need to have cash on hand to pay current operating expenses—maintenance and minor repairs. And there is the need to set aside reserves to pay for future repairs and replacements. In a new condominium there is an additional expense rarely mentioned by any developer—the cost of replacing parts of the structure or equipment that were inadequately designed in the beginning. This can include inadequate heating and cooling systems; inadequate structural support for the building; plumbing or electrical systems that were inappropriate; swimming pool pumps, filters, and heaters that were too small. Often these defects do not show up until after expiration of the one-year warranty commonly given to buildings by many developers.

When purchasing a condominium, a prospective buyer will usually ask the developer how much the dues to the homeowner's association will be. Developers tend to underestimate costs for two reasons. First, they don't really know what the eventual costs will be and therefore often base their estimates on the initial operating costs, which may be very low. Secondly, operating and maintenance costs have increased dramatically over the past few years and are likely to continue to increase.

Therefore, no one can accurately tell you what the dues will be after a year's ownership in a new condominium. A good rule of thumb to follow is that costs may be 25 to 100 percent higher than the developer estimates. Of course, when buying an already established condominium unit you should be able to get a highly accurate cost figure by examining the dues the current owner is paying.

LOW-QUALITY CONSTRUCTION

It is much more difficult to judge the construction in a condominium than in a single-family home. You usually can't crawl under the unit, check the attic, or easily examine the plumbing and wiring. Traditionally, buyers have relied on city and county building inspectors to provide them with at least minimum construction standards. However, studies have shown that these inspectors nationwide are overworked and often pass inspection on construction that does not meet minimum standards. What, then, should a buyer do?

A buyer of a condominium should insist on seeing engineering reports. Every responsible condominium developer should have these available for prospective purchasers to see. Usually they are conducted by independent companies and contain important information on the structure.

Secondly, a prospective buyer should always ask to see two adjoining units, never just one unit alone. Then, while the buyer remains in one unit, the spouse or a friend should go into the other and talk loudly next to the wall and bang on it. In a well-constructed unit there will be double walls between units (see Figure 4); voices will barely pass through, and

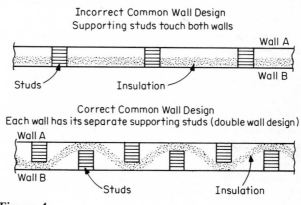

Incorrect Common Wall Design
Supporting studs touch both walls

Wall A

Wall B

Studs   Insulation

Correct Common Wall Design
Each wall has its separate supporting studs (double wall design)

Wall A

Wall B

Studs   Insulation

Figure 4.

bumps and pounding on the wall will be muted. If sounds pass through easily, it's a good indication that the builders have skimped on the construction between walls, an essential area. And if they skimped here, there's a good chance that they skimped everywhere.

Finally, responsible developers will leave a certain portion of their money, perhaps only 1 or 2 percent of the selling price, in escrow for at least a year after the units have been sold to provide a reserve fund to pay for correcting any poor construction that shows up. This protects the buyer in case the builder should go bankrupt and not be able or willing to honor any warranties.

If this escrow reserve is not included in the regular selling papers, it will do little good to insist it be included for your unit. Even if you succeeded, the amount would be negligible in comparison with a problem that might be building-wide. To be adequate, this reserve must be set aside from every unit's sale.

COMPLEX DOCUMENTS

When purchasing a condominium an individual gains undivided title to many common areas, and, as we have said, it is necessary to establish a homeowner's association to take care of these. The mechanism for creating the association is a document or series of documents outlining the responsibilities and obligations of each unit owner. These are normally incorporated into the deed and become legally binding.

One of the most serious problems in condominium ownership is the complexity of these documents. Usually, they are far beyond the understanding of the average buyer, and in some cases they are beyond the comprehension of the average lawyer. Occasionally, a trivial provision innocuously inserted in the master deed may effectively prevent the homeowner's association from functioning efficiently. Since 100 percent of the unit owners must usually agree to any change, altering this document may be extremely difficult, if not impossible.

A further problem stems from the fact that condominium estates are created by the laws of each state, and consequently no standard form is used nationwide. This, unfortunately, means that there is no established norm which prospective condo buyers can use to compare their documents.

The situation is not hopeless, however. One aid to the consumer comes from the Department of Housing and Urban Development through the Federal Housing Administration (HUD-FHA). If a condominium is built using financing insured by HUD-FHA, the government under the National Housing Act attempts to oversee the operation to the extent that the builder must conform to minimum building specifications (often set quite high). Further, when a consumer purchases a condominium and government-insured FHA financing is used (under section 234, Condominium Program), the sales agreements, homeowner's association bylaws, and other documents are standardized. In short, if you buy a *new* condo and the builder is able to offer you an FHA-insured loan, many of the items you need to watch out for have already been checked out by the federal government. To a lesser degree this is true with VA loans also.

Unfortunately, a great many condos are not built using government-insured financing. In such cases it is up to the purchaser to investigate to determine both that the construction is adequate and that the documents are appropriate. I suggest that any buyer, before making a purchase, take the documents to an attorney who specializes in or at least is familiar with condominium work for an opinion.

Enabling Declaration. One of the most important documents in a condominium sale and the one that probably causes the most problems is the *enabling declaration.* It is also sometimes referred to as the master deed, the declaration of conditions, covenants, and restrictions, or the plan of condominium ownership. These are some of the areas in the enabling declaration to watch out for:

1. *Legal descriptions.* There must be a section which describes the units and the common elements of the condominium. It is critically important that all such descriptions be accurate. However, if title insurance is purchased, normally the title company will insist on the accuracy of this area of document. The lender will also be watching out for its accuracy. Of more immediate concern to the purchaser are the provisions which specify how the common property such as streets, parking lots, and recreational facilities are held. They are usually owned by a nonprofit homeowner's association or are leased to the condominium owners by the original developer. If they are leased, the buyer should watch out for the cautions noted earlier.

2. *Percentage interest.* Another section of the declaration will specify an owner's percentage interest in the undivided portion of the project. This is usually expressed in terms of a ratio of a unit to the total number of units. This ratio is of great import for it will determine among other things the voting power an owner has in the homeowner's association, the amount the owner will have to pay for maintenance operation assessments, the amount of real estate tax to be assessed against the individual owner, and the amount of money a lender will loan.

There are at least four different ways the ratio can be determined: by market price, by builder's value, by the amount of living area, and by equal shares (each owner has equal interest regardless of the size or value of the unit).

Since the ratios are often initially determined by state law, there is little an individual buyer can usually do to change them. However, the buyer should watch out for clauses which allow the ratio to be changed once the condominium is established. This could adversely affect your responsibilities and payments.

3. *Changes.* Any changes to the declaration normally require the consent of 100 percent of the owners. This is an important clause and any deviation from the 100 percent figure should make the buyer wary. What this means is that no changes can be made unless the buyer of each unit agrees. This is tremendous protection for each unit owner. Unfortunately, it also severely limits the ability of a homeowner's association to respond to unexpected problems.

A related problem has to do with delegating the policy-making powers of the association's board of directors. Sometimes duties are delegated in the declaration to a professional management company at a high and escalating fee. Since it takes 100 percent of the owners to change the declaration, the developer or the management company could buy just one unit and prevent the board from changing its policy. To avoid this, authority should probably not be given to the board in the declaration other than to hire a manager who will be under its control. All authority for all other operations probably should be in the bylaws, which can be changed by a majority of owners.

Bylaws of the Homeowner's Association. These establish rules for any future owners, tenants, or employees. They also establish many conditions which determine how pleasant living in the condo will be. A prospective purchaser should check these out carefully. Here are some of the things to watch out for:

1. *Enactment of the bylaws.* The bylaws are a secondary agreement and they require assent by all the unit owners. To avoid problems, it is a good idea for the bylaws to provide that merely occupying or renting any unit indicates that the owner ratifies and accepts the bylaws and agrees to comply with them.

2. *Administration of the condominium.* The bylaws should provide that someone, usually the developer, will administer the condominium until the first annual meeting of the owners. They should also specify if, at that meeting, the administration will be turned over to an association board of directors elected from the owners.

3. *Voting rights.* The bylaws should specify what constitutes a quorum for doing business at a meeting, the method of voting, the use of proxies, and the manner in which board members can be removed for objectionable action. They should also specify which bylaws can be amended and how (usually only a majority vote is needed).

4. *Term, qualifications, and responsibilities of the members of the board of directors.* These should be spelled out in the bylaws.

5. *Items relating to individual owners and their rights and responsibilities as co-owners.* The bylaws should clearly specify the collection of monthly charges and special assessments, including the means to force payment from those who refuse (including the developer); the use of the common areas; the establishment of a budget and reserve funds; provision for professional management where needed; the right of entry to the project and rules governing conduct by owners, visitors, and tenants; the rules for the use of recreational facilities; provision for fire insurance on the common area; provision for liability insurance; restrictions on changes in the exterior of individual units; and restrictions governing the use of the property for residential purposes as provided by local and state zoning ordinances and other items of mutual interest.

Purchase Agreement. Finally, a buyer will have to sign a purchase agreement. This is basically the same sort of agreement that is signed when purchasing an individual home, the dangers mentioned in Chapter 23 also apply here. The buyer of a condo should also check to see if the sales agreement contains the owner's percentage interest in the condo and how it is determined; refer to and make a part of the agreement the other condo documents; fully disclose any and all pertinent facts regarding the project, including those contained in federal, state, and local reports as well as in engineering reports.

Don't sign a sales agreement until you've had time to think it over. Don't be pressured into thinking that if you don't sign immediately, you'll lose the best deal of your life. (See Chapters 19 and 21.) The best advice is to wait until you can think it over. You could be committing your life savings to something you may not really want. Be sure, *before* you sign. Remember, your signature protects the seller more than it protects you.

OPERATIONAL PROBLEMS

There are always going to be problems in setting up the homeowner's association. Often the most enthusiastic and best-qualified owners will be the first to get on the board. But even in a condo with a well-thought-out set of bylaws, there will be many problems in getting the organization off the ground, and many frustrations. Usually the board will meet once a month, but individual committees, such as finance, recreation, maintenance, may wind up meeting weekly or more often as problems arise. In condos I have seen, the "burn out" rate for the best managers is very high. Spending long hours on a thankless job, these people quickly lose interest. All buyers, therefore, should understand that at some time during the first few years of the condo's existence, they will probably have to take on an administrative responsibility just to keep the project going.

The difficulties in operation can be large in a condo with a responsible developer, but in one with an irresponsible developer they can be enormous. It is a great help, especially in the beginning, if the developer works with the infant board of directors, guiding and teaching its members how to handle the job. Some developers, however, give no such transitional aid. A wise buyer will pay careful attention to the commitments the developer makes in the documents. A well-created condo project will find the developer retaining control until at least 51 percent of the units are sold and then remaining as a counselor until the very last unit has been disposed of.

NONPAYMENT OF DUES

In order for the homeowner's association to operate, it must receive money in dues on a regular basis from the owners. If an owner does not pay, there must be a reasonably efficient way for the association to force payment. This can include anything from establishing a lien on the owner's interest in the property to filing suit to tie up the owner's other assets. It is of great importance that the developer as well as the individual owners be subject to these enforcement rules. There have been cases where, for example, only 60 percent of the units were sold and the developer, instead of paying 40 percent of the dues, paid only the difference between the actual maintenance and operating costs and the dues from 60 percent of the owners. This can be a figure considerably lower than the owed 40 percent and can severely weaken the association's financial position.

SALES MISREPRESENTATION

This can happen with any purchase of real estate. In terms of the condominium it usually is most flagrant with regard to promises made by the sales personnel concerning the tax savings offered by condominium ownership. There are no great tax advantages to condominium ownership beyond those a buyer would get from purchasing a single-family house. Normally, interest and taxes may be deducted if the property is a residence. The homeowner's association dues are not normally deductible. If the condo, however, is used as an investment and rented out on a full-time basis, all reasonable costs can usually be deducted and the property depreciated just like a rental house.

Another problem has to do with a completion date. Developers tend to be overly optimistic with regard to how long it will be before a project is completed. A verbal promise that your unit will be ready by July may find you still waiting in October. Since project completion depends on a large number of factors, many beyond the builder's control, it is not usually possible to force the builder to complete by a specified date. The buyer's best protection is to keep an eye on the work in progress. Don't sell your old house, change jobs, or commit an arrival date on furniture until the building at least looks finished. And even after it appears to be completed, several weeks or longer may be required for local and/or federal inspections.

Often taxes and dues will be understated by the condo developer. The usual reason is that the developer does not know these figures in advance. Property taxes are usually paid on bare land until the project is completed. Once it is completed, however, the property is reassessed, often jumping the figures up three- to fivefold. In buying a new condo, be sure and ask whether the tax figures given to you are based on current evaluation, that is, on the land only. If they are you can figure they will rise sharply within a year when the property is reevaluated.

There is also the problem of deposits. Developers often insist that the buyer put up a deposit to hold a condo under construction until it is ready. There is nothing wrong with this as long as the sum is small and refundable. One hundred dollars should be sufficient to hold a condo until it is completed. Be suspicious of developers who ask for more; they may be planning to use your deposit to help finance the construction. You don't want this to happen, for if something goes wrong and construction can't be completed, you might lose your money. Often developers will agree to return the deposit minus the cost of a credit report or other minor costs involved in qualifying the buyer. This should be perfectly acceptable to most buyers.

RESELLING OR RENTING PROBLEMS

Some documents in a condo give the homeowner's association the right of first refusal when an owner sells. Others go much further—they give the association the right to clear prospective purchasers before the owner is allowed to sell. Many states do not allow either condition. You should be wary of any condo that gives the association the right of first refusal, and you should stay away from one that allows it to pass judgment on prospective buyers. This is a restriction on your right to dispose of real estate and could cause enormous difficulty when you want to leave quickly. The same applies to renting out of your unit. An additional problem for condos located in recreational areas is that often there are restrictions against renting for periods of less than one month.

Another problem in reselling or even renting a condo has to do with restrictions in the bylaws against signs or advertising on the condo property. Most condos won't allow these. It may be difficult to direct prospective buyers or renters to your unit if you can't post signs anywhere (not even on your front door in many cases).

Finally, the complex documents and the difficulties involved in reviewing them has led many lenders to avoid loaning money on condominiums. When you want to resell, you may find it difficult to obtain financing other than from the original lender on the property. This, too, could hamper a resale.

CONVERSIONS

There is another form of condominium which we have not yet talked about—the *conversion*. A conversion is basically taking a building designed for apartment rentals and converting it to condominium usage.

In addition to all the things a buyer should watch out for that we have just listed, a potential buyer for a condo conversion should consider the extent of the conversion. Prospective buyers must remember that they own not only the unit being purchased, but also the plumbing pipes, electrical equipment and wiring, water heaters, air conditioners, etc., common to the building. Many developers are conscientious and when converting check out all this equipment and repair or replace that which is damaged or worn. Some, however, are in it for the fast buck and sim-

CHECKLIST OF MAJOR CONDOMINIUM PROBLEMS

1. Is the development too dense? A density of six units per acre is optimum; ten or more units per acre is crowded.

2. Is the lifestyle right for you? Older couples (empty nesters) or young marrieds? Too many children?

3. Are there any long-term leases in the enabling declaration?

4. Are the costs for maintenance and repair underestimated?

5. Is the construction of high quality? Check for sound-proofing.

6. Can you clearly understand the documents? If not, take them to a lawyer who can.

   a. The enabling declaration (also called the master deed; declaration of conditions, restrictions and covenants; or condominium ownership): Are the legal descriptions accurate? Can the document be changed only by a 100 percent vote of the owners?

   b. The *bylaws:* Do they spell out how the condo will be operated and by whom? Can a simple majority change them?

   c. The sales agreement: Do you remember all the dangers to avoid when signing any sales agreement? Does this agreement incorporate all the other documents? Have you seen engineering reports?

7. Judging from the bylaws, are there likely to be operational problems?

8. Are there provisions for enforcing payment for home-owner's association dues from the owners, *including the developer?*

9. Are you facing high-pressure selling? Will your deposit be refunded if you don't buy? Do you have to put up more than $100 on an uncompleted building? Does the project look as though it could be finished by the date the builder estimates?

10. Are there any restrictions on your reselling or renting your unit?

11. If it's a conversion, was a thorough job done? Or were just cosmetic changes made?

12. Is the building really designed for the condo lifestyle?

13. Are you prepared for condominium living and the problems of a homeowner's association? Why not wait overnight before signing?

ply do a cosmetic job. They fix just that which can be seen. This may mean that soon after the developer has sold all the units there could be large and unexpected repair bills requiring the individual owners to come up with substantial sums of money. This is particularly a danger in buildings over five years old, and the risk increases with the age of the building.

Before buying into such a structure it is important that you obtain and examine a copy of engineering reports. These should be conducted by independent companies on all aspects of the building, including condition of plumbing, mechanical and electrical components, the heating and cooling systems, the roof, and the structure. In addition, the enabling declaration or bylaws should provide for substantially higher reserves than in new condos to repair items as they wear out.

The other large problem with conversions stems from the fact that the building was designed as an apartment house and not a condo. Common walls may not be as thick as owners would like. Units may be packed together too densely. The overall design may be poor, with doors and windows of adjoining units opening onto each other. These design problems are usually not correctable.

Usually higher-priced apartment buildings make the best condo conversions. These usually have large units with spacious grounds—just the sort of thing a condo owner expects. An inexpensive building designed for a highly transient tenant usually makes the worst conversion.

FIVE

Protect Yourself When You Buy Rental Property and Become a Landlord

29

Pitfalls to Avoid When Buying Rental Property

The money to be made in residential real estate in recent years has caused many people to turn an inquisitive eye toward the rental market. If they could just buy a home or multiple-dwelling unit, rent it out, and then, in a few years, sell, they could make a substantial profit.

There is no question that thousands of individuals are doing just that today. However, as with most things in life, there is a great chasm between the idea of successfully renting out property and the doing of it. It can be a difficult task for an individual inexperienced in such matters. But with a little luck, some common sense, and a watchful eye out for things to avoid, it can be done, and quite profitably.

Most people start off buying a house, a duplex (two units), a triplex (three units), or at most a fourplex (four units) when first jumping into the rental market. For our purposes we will in most cases consider the individual who buys a house to rent out, although the same rules will apply for the larger dwellings.

The first pitfall is the idea that you will make money from the rental income. While this may be the case with very large buildings (ten or more units), it is rarely so with smaller ones. In a house you will be lucky to be able to meet the monthly payments and maintenance expenses from the rental income. You will do somewhat better in two- to four-unit dwellings, but you certainly won't get rich.

Mortgage costs and taxes are currently at close to the highest level they have been in this century. Yet rental rates, although they have risen sharply, have in most areas not kept pace. One of the biggest reasons is that a family that can afford to make the huge monthly payment on a home ($400 to $500 a month for just taxes, principal, interest, and insurance is not uncommon on a $40,000 home) will more than likely buy, rather than rent. Consequently, the rental market tends to be composed largely of those who cannot afford to buy, and this group also cannot afford to pay high rent.

Maintenance costs on a rental are also high and rising. To rent successfully, you must set aside reserves from each month's rent in order to pay for those items that need to be repaired (leaking faucets, a broken water heater, a fan that goes out on the heating system, etc.) and to pay for cleaning the rental between tenants. Some owners don't keep such reserves and often think they are making monthly profits when they see their income topping their mortgage and tax payments. They are deluding themselves. Just let a water heater go out and they will have to come up with the repair money out of their pockets, and there will go their so-called monthly profit.

Finally, there is the matter of vacancies. Even in an excellent rental area, there will be periods, usually just after a tenant moves out and while you're cleaning the rental, when you won't receive any rent. A conservative estimate is that in good areas you should figure at least one month out of the year for vacancies; in an exceptional area, two weeks or less may be closer to the truth.

How much money should you set aside for vacancies, repairs, and maintenance? Most successful rental managers I have known have felt that between 10 and 15 percent was usually sufficient on a dwelling of four or fewer units. On a rental with income of $300 a month, this means that every month the unit is occupied you should set aside in a separate bank account between $30 and $45. Thus, when no rent is coming in but you're still making payments, or when a water heater goes out and you have to replace it, you can dip into this fund.

It should be apparent that with high mortgage payments and taxes and reserves for vacancies, repairs, and maintenance, it will be very difficult to meet, let alone exceed, your monthly payments from the monthly rental income. Why bother then?

The answer comes when it's time to sell. From 1972 to 1977 residential real estate appreciated at an average annual rate of 11 percent in most urban areas. This means that if you bought a home in 1972 for $25,000, in 1977 you probably could have sold it for $42,125, a profit (excluding sales and purchase costs) of $17,125. That profit makes up for a lot of rental headaches. It even makes up for having to take $50 a month or so ($3000 over five years) out of your pocket just to meet monthly payments. Of course, these are just average figures. Some investors made much more and others much less.

In addition, for most people, owning rental property offers decided tax advantages that often offset the entire loss that may be encountered from low rents versus high costs. While the homeowner normally may deduct only interest and property taxes from regular income (income from your usual occupation), the owner of a rental may normally deduct interest, property taxes, repair and maintenance costs, cost of finding a tenant (including advertising), costs of adding to or fixing up the property (usually as long as such costs don't exceed 5 percent of the total value), and depreciation. All these costs with the exception of the last are deducted on a one-for-one basis. That is, for every dollar of cost, you deduct a dollar from your regular income. Depreciation, however, is on a "plus" basis. Since a rental can be expected to produce income for only a set number of years before it decays, the government allows owners to deduct each year from the income a certain amount of the used-up life of the building. On used homes, the maximum amount on which the deduction is based is currently 125 percent a year for a minimum of twenty years. Here's how this works: You take the total purchase price, say $40,000, and deduct one-twentieth of that amount the first year. On a $40,000 building this means in the first year you take 125 percent of the cost:

$$
\begin{array}{r}
\$40,000 \\
\times \quad 1.25 \\
\hline
\$50,000
\end{array}
$$

Now you divide the sum of $50,000 by the number of years remaining, twenty in our example:

$$\$50,000 \div 20 = \$2500$$

Thus, in the first year the deduction is $2500. In a 30 percent tax bracket this means a savings of $750 in actual cash. For later years you subtract the amount already deducted in previous years, take 125 percent of that amount, and divide by the number of years remaining.

The reader should take careful note, however, that setting up the depreciation schedule and knowing what to deduct on income tax forms is no job for an amateur. In addition, anyone taking accelerated depreciation (in which a percentage larger than 100 is used, as in our example) may run into the problem of recapture of depreciation upon sale or foreclosure. Therefore, this very brief description of tax sheltering offered by real estate should be taken only as a report of what others have done in the field. Readers should consult with their own accountants or tax lawyers before taking any action. For additional suggestions on sheltering as well as reports on how individuals are making profits on larger rental buildings, I recommend *How to Buy and Sell Real Estate for Financial Security* (New York: McGraw-Hill, 1975).

To a very great extent, how well one does depends on how successful one is in avoiding the pitfalls of buying rental property. Several of the worst are as follows:

1. *Location.* Since the profit on a relatively small rental purchase of one to four units will usually come at the time you resell, it is wise to purchase a unit in a location with an eye toward resale. A further consideration to be made when purchasing a rental unit is the *tenant market* in the area. It may very well be that for reasons totally out of the control of the prospective owner, such as the lack of local industry, there is very small demand for rentals locally. If so and if a large number of vacancies are already available, a prospective buyer would do well to look elsewhere.

How can you find a good rental area? After you've located a good area for resale, several methods are advised. Drive around and see if there are "For Rent" signs on nearby houses or buildings. In a good area you will seldom, if ever, see any such signs.

Check the newspapers servicing the area. See how large the rental section is. Check to see at what price the rentals are being offered. Note their location. Then, do some footwork. Call several owners or stop at "For Rent" signs and inquire about the property. You can say you are thinking about buying a house to rent in the area and would like some information on local rentals. Or, if you prefer, you can pretend you're a tenant and seek information using this subterfuge. Whatever method you use, don't feel bad about seeking out such information. Most owners are happy to talk about their property. And once you buy yours, you'll be returning the favor when prospective buyers come by to question you.

You should talk to as many owners as possible to get an overall picture. Questions you should ask include: "How long has the apartment or house been for rent?" (If you pose as a tenant, most owners will tell you it just came on the market. Checking back issues of local papers to see how long a unit has been on the market is a good way to verify this information, and it also tells you whether the owner has been forced to reduce the price to get a tenant.) "Is there usually a problem in getting tenants?" "How long do the tenants usually stay?" (If all the renters in an area are transient workers for a large corporation, and that company changes location, you could be stuck with a dead house.)

Once you've checked the papers and the area, you should consider: (*a*) Is the property you are thinking about purchasing able to bring in enough rent to meet or come close to meeting the monthly payments and will you be able to sustain a monthly loss over a long period of time, if necessary? (*b*) Does the number of other rentals constitute an oversupply? (*c*) Is there a good supply of tenants for now and the future? If your answers are favorable, you should now turn your attention to the house itself.

2. *Exterior of house.* When renting, you should remember that no tenant will keep up a home as well as the owner. Consequently, when buying a house to rent, you want a unit with as small and maintenance-free front, back, and side yards as possible. Remember, however, you're going to eventually want to sell, so the yards must be large enough to interest a prospective buyer. A happy compromise is often average-sized yards where the previous owner has put in a lot of cement and patio work, planted many self-sustaining shrubs and trees, and installed an extensive sprinkler system. It is best to avoid large lawns, flower and vegetable beds, and any areas that require much gardening. From a great deal of experience I can assure you that a "good" tenant is one who will occasionally water a lawn. In my many years of renting to tenants, less than a handful have ever made any attempt to maintain a garden or flower bed in a yard.

If possible, it is best to hire the services of a yard maintenance service or gardener. Often the minimum service required can be obtained for under $50 a month.

The importance of maintaining the yard in a rental cannot be over-stated. A bad yard, particularly in the front, will cause the neighborhood to deteriorate, causing you, the owner, to lose potential profits when you sell. A poorly maintained yard will also make it difficult for you to rerent the house. You may be able to slap a coat of paint on the outside of a house and make it look good for a prospective tenant, but you can't grow a lawn, shrubs, or trees overnight. Good tenants will usually pick the homes with the most pleasant yards, leaving the less attractive houses with the less desirable tenants.

3. *Interior of houses.* Purchase a home that offers low maintenance inside as well as outside. The typical tenant will not make any extra efforts to keep up the inside of your house. White or light-colored carpeting that requires great care to avoid staining is out. So are light-colored curtains and drapes. Wallpaper is another no-no, as just a little tear on one corner can require redoing an entire wall or room. Screens or other types of easily broken room dividers should also be avoided unless they can be cheaply replaced.

Ideally the walls will be painted in light, neutral colors that most people will find compatible. The paint should be rubber-based to allow for quick repainting, except in the bathroom and kitchen, where high-gloss enamel should be used to allow for easy washing. The carpeting should be closely woven—no plushes or shags—in a dark color such as green, brown, or red that will tend to hide stains. If wall coverings such as curtains and drapes are to be supplied, they should either be of a heavy kind not easily damaged or be very cheap so that they can be inexpensively replaced.

If you haven't already gotten the idea, stay overnight at any large motel or hotel near you. Look at what's on the floors and walls—that'll give you the right idea.

If the house you are considering doesn't already come equipped with the interior just described, you will probably have the expense of reoutfitting it correctly within a year or two. Since the average tenant stays for a year or slightly less, after one or two tenants a house without a "tenant-proofed" interior is going to need plenty of work.

> NOTE: Most tenants expect the owner to supply an oven and stove. In addition, some tenants do not have refrigerators, washers, or dryers, and thus owners that can supply these stand a better chance of renting their units.

4. *House size.* Since you plan to resell for your profit, you'll want a house big enough to attract many buyers. Ideally your house should have at least three bedrooms and two baths. However, this house also carries with it real rental problems. Most people who rent a three-bedroom house will have children, and children, delightful as they are, are the bane of the landlord. Being natural, good children, they tend to scuff walls, break windows, stain and damage carpeting and flooring, and in general put a rental unit through some very severe usage. The only thing harder on a rental than a child is a pet.

Ideally, a two-bedroom unit would make the best rental for you could normally expect to rent it to a couple with no more than one child. (Their smaller size is the reason that two- to fourplexes often make good rentals.) Consequently, when buying a house for rental purposes look for the smaller units, preferably one with no more than three bedrooms.

5. *Occupancy.* When buying a duplex or larger piece of rental real estate that is not new and is already occupied, the purchaser faces an additional problem that has to do with actual versus fictional occupancy and price.

The price of large real estate investment projects is usually determined on the basis of the income produced. As a quick means of comparing units available on the market *income multipliers* are used. These are simply convenient numbers handled in this fashion: Within a given area, past experience with sales leads brokers and investors to realize that a building will sell, for example, for six times its gross annual income after deducting for vacancies. Thus the gross income multiplier in that area is 6. When considering the purchase of an apartment building, a wise buyer will take the gross annual income, deduct for vacancies that are likely to occur, and multiply by 6. That will give a reasonably close estimate of value. Of course, the prospective buyer may want to deduct from this price for poor maintenance or add to it for exceptional features such as a swimming pool or size of units. Gross income multipliers of between 5 and 7 are commonly used in today's rental market.

Some investors feel that the gross annual income method is inaccurate and instead prefer to use a monthly net income multiplier. For this the income from the units for one month is used after all expenses (exclusive of mortgage costs) are deducted. The monthly rental income is usually multiplied by a figure between 110 and 120 to give a sales price.

Finally, some investors looking for a specific return on their investment use the *capitalization* method of figuring price. There are several equations that are used here, but all involve the price of the property, the return rate on investment, and the income. For example, the investor who wants a 10 percent return would find the price by dividing 10 percent into the estimated future annual income of the building after all expenses had been paid. Thus, if the building brought in a net income of $10,000 a year, the investor would divide this by 10 percent and would come up with a figure of $100,000 as the correct price. For the convenience of the reader, here are the three commonly used capitalization equations:

$$\text{Value} = \frac{\text{income}}{\text{interest rate}}$$

$$\text{Interest rate} = \frac{\text{income}}{\text{value}}$$

$$\text{Income} = \text{value} \times \text{rate}$$

Regardless of what method is used, it should be clear that the potential buyer must first learn one critical piece of information: What is the building's income? Herein lies the great pitfall. Since the price is determined by the income, many sellers try to get a higher price by falsely increasing it. One method used is to charge the tenants one rent and refund a portion of it under the table so they are in reality paying a lower price. A simpler method is to lie about the actual rental both in the books and in conversation. In some areas with high vacancies, sellers have been known to disguise the vacancy rate (and resulting low income) by filling the units up with nonpaying friends and relatives.

What is a buyer to do to determine correct income? There are two steps to finding income. First, check around with other apartment buildings (contact both landlords and tenants) and find what a comparable unit *should* rent for and how high vacancies *should* be. Then, go to *each* tenant and verify that tenant's rent as well as possible. Ask to see rent receipts and ask whether any relatives or friends of the owner are living in the building. Now, by comparison, you should come close to knowing the actual net income.

It is positively amazing how often buyers do not bother to check out rental buildings. Usually the bother and the tiring footwork discourage them. Don't let a difficult task stop you from determining actual income. Just think how difficult it will be to meet those monthly payments if you don't have adequate income from tenants.

6. *Tenant's confusion.* One final pitfall when buying an already occupied rental building should be noted. Often it is difficult to know exactly what the terms of the tenancy are with each tenant—whether they're on a lease, month-to-month, or whatever. An *offset statement* is often used to overcome this difficulty. If the buyer properly specifies that offset statements must be included in the purchase agreement, the seller must see to it that all tenants deposit into escrow a statement of their rights of possession. Then, when ownership changes hands, the tenants won't have any surprises, and neither will the buyer.

Buying a house for a rental is at best a compromise. You'll tend to do much better in renting with two to four units which are built to be rentals. But, your biggest appreciation for dollar invested will probably come from the single-family house. Be prepared to have some headaches and to spend quite a few weekends fixing plumbing and finding tenants. If you've bought wisely, it'll all seem worth it in the end when you sell and get that fat check.

30

Answers to Tenant Trouble

It should go without saying that the best way to avoid problems with tenants is to get good tenants in the beginning. Who are good tenants? They are simply those people who will pay their rent on time, not damage your property while they are living in it, and leave at a time you and they have agreed upon. Basically, they are people who will live up to their word.

How do you select good tenants from the many prospective renters? The two essential characteristics of a good tenant are: first, the *desire* to fulfill an agreement, and second, the *ability* to do it. Taking these matters separately, let's begin with ability.

You may rent your property to a tenant who has a sincere desire to avoid damaging it in any way. This tenant, however, may be prevented from fulfilling this desire by two things: children and pets. Normal, well-adjusted children tend to occasionally mark or even poke holes in walls. They may tear up a few shrubs in innocent play outside. A softball driven through a window is not an uncommon occurrence. Dogs and cats, when they are kept inside, have their own little problems. There is always the chance they may stain the carpet or scratch doors or walls.

This is not, of course, to condemn children or pets, but merely to point out what you as a landlord should be prepared for. There are many families where the pets and children are so well behaved that no damage whatsoever is done to the property, but these tend to be in the minority. A general rule followed by many successful landlords is to rent to tenants with as few pets and children as possible.

Finding a tenant with a desire to live up to a rental agreement is a bit more difficult. Consider the case of Mrs. Clemens. She bought a home to rent out and for the first time in her life was looking for tenants. A number of people answered her ad, and soon two sisters wanted to rent the house. They wanted to give Mrs. Clemens only a first month's rent, but she insisted on a $50 cleaning deposit. They agreed, a brief tenancy agreement which Mrs. Clemens had picked up at a stationery store was signed, and the sisters moved in.

About a week later, Mrs. Clemens drove by her house. She was surprised to see five cars of varying types and ages parked in the driveway and on the lawn. Being a little bit snoopy, she decided to stop by and see what was going on. Upon knocking at the door, she was allowed to enter the house and found there were at least eleven children from the ages of a few months through seventeen years living there. The sisters had even fixed up the garage as a dormitory to house some of the children.

Mrs. Clemens was shocked, but the sisters pointed out that they had never denied having children and besides, they would take care of the place and pay their rent, so there was no need to worry. Mrs. Clemens was skeptical, but decided to give them a chance.

It was an unwise decision, for the tenants had no intention of giving Mrs. Clemens any chances. They never paid another month's rent, and three months later, when Mrs. Clemens had finally paid a lawyer to have them evicted, the place looked as if a herd of camels had lived there. Mrs. Clemens lost not only several months' rent, but the money it cost, which was considerable, to repaint and repair to get her house ready to rent again. Needless to say she checked out her next tenants more carefully. Here's what she did:

The next tenants to come by were a couple with one child and a dog. They said the three-year-old child and the dog were well behaved and would not damage the house and that the rent would be paid on time. Mrs. Clemens said that if that was so, the couple wouldn't mind if she ran a credit check on them and got in touch with their last landlord. They agreed.

Mrs. Clemens got their written permission for a credit report and took it to a local credit agency. For $15 she received a credit history on the tenants. (Many credit agencies require an initiation fee of $50 to $100, but credit reports then usually cost only $2 or $3.) She found that they always had paid their bills on time. Next, she called their former landlord. He verified that they had lived in the apartment for two years and that when they moved, the place was spotless.

Mrs. Clemens then went to a lawyer and had a lease drawn up spelling out exactly what she expected of the tenants. She also had them put up the first and last months' rent as well as a $100 cleaning deposit. Then Mrs. Clemens rented to the couple. She never regretted it. They paid their rent on time and kept the premises in good condition.

The rule here is to select your tenants carefully. Remember, they will be living in your house (or apartment).

One final word of caution should be given. While it is normally the prerogative of *private* landlords to select tenants, *public* landlords are much more restricted in this selection. A public landlord is someone who has built or owns property largely as the result of government help. These are usually landlords who are renting property under the 1937 Public Housing Act, but in the past some few private landlords who built large projects on urban renewal sites using FHA mortgage assistance and receiving property tax relief were also included. Finally, no landlord can refuse to rent property on the basis of the religion, color, or national origin of the prospective tenant. For a full discussion of the Open Housing Act see Chapter 26.

HABITABILITY

At one time a landlord in any part of the United States could offer to rent any shack whether or not the roof leaked, it had running water or sanitary facilities, or it was ready to fall down. In some areas of the country this rule still applies, but not in most. Today, in nearly every state and locality a house or apartment offered for rent must meet certain minimum requirements. The property must meet the state and local building codes with regard to health and safety standards. If a piece of property that grossly does not meet these standards is rented out and something happens, for example, a floor collapses, the landlord could be sued by the tenants. Further, if direct negligence can be shown on the part of the landlord criminal charges might be filed. For example if the landlord refused to fix a leaking gas line after being notified of the leak by a prospective tenant, the landlord might be found guilty of criminal negligence if an explosion occurred in which someone was hurt. Once the tenant has accepted the habitability of the property, however, many states hold that it is up to the tenant to fix and repair.

This does not mean, however, that the rental property must be clean or in good shape. After a bad tenant moves out, the home or apartment often needs a complete repainting. A landlord may offer the next tenant a slightly reduced rental fee for a few months and free paint if the tenant will move in and then paint the premises while living there.

Some landlords today use the following technique to solve habitability and related problems. They warrant (guarantee) that the property they are offering for rent is clean, safe, free from rodents and pests, and in a sanitary condition, and they have the tenants sign a statement that they have inspected the property and found it to be as the landlord has indicated. Now, if a problem develops in the property after a few weeks or more of occupancy by the tenant, the landlord can point to this signed statement and say with much truth that it must have occurred after the tenant moved in and was possibly caused by the tenant. Therefore, it is the tenant's responsibility to correct it.

LEASE VERSUS MONTH-TO-MONTH TENANCY

Many landlords are torn between the lease and a month-to-month agreement, unable to decide which gives better protection. There is something to be said for both, but in either case, I always have a tenant sign a rental agreement so that the tenant understands what I, as a landlord, am offering and what the tenant is expected to do.

A lease specifies a certain length of time (in nearly every state leases for a year or more must be in writing) for a tenancy and a total amount of money to be paid. For example, a lease might run for twelve months for $300 a month. It would specify that the tenant (called the lessee) would pay the landlord (called the lessor) a total of $3600 at $300 a month and give the exact starting and termination date. It might also specify that the first and last months' rent be paid in advance. For landlords, the advantages of a lease are that they know the amount of time the property will be rented, the amount of the rent, and that the money will come in on a regular basis. It also has these disadvantages: Rent can't be raised during the period of the lease unless a specific increase is mentioned. (Usually such increases are specified only in commercial leases and are tied to gross sales or other indicators of business health.) If the tenant moves out and refuses to pay, the landlord's usual recourse is to sue for lost rent. Normally, suit can only be brought as the rent comes due, that is, as each monthly payment is not met. Further, it is the landlord's usual duty to mitigate damages, that is, to try to rerent to a new tenant in order to regain some of the lost rent.

To avoid having to sue each month as the rent comes due, some states allow landlords to include an acceleration clause in the lease which states that if one monthly payment is missed, the entire lease amount immediately is due.

As you can see, the disadvantages of a lease often outweigh the advantages *unless* the tenant is financially solvent. If the tenant has valuable assets such as a car, bank account, stocks, and property, you can sue and get lost rent and in many cases recover all your attorney and court costs as well. However, if your tenant is a transient with few assets who leaves town without paying and you don't know where to begin looking, your lease is worthless. This is the reason that leases tend to be used heavily in high-rent property but seldom in low-rent real estate.

Month-to-month tenancy specifies a rental amount, but indicates that the condition of tenancy applies for only one month. Upon notice either party may terminate the tenancy. Usually the notice required is equivalent to the time between rent payments; thus if rent is paid every two weeks, two weeks' notice must be given; if rent is paid every month, thirty days' notice is necessary. Further, upon notice the landlord can raise or lower the rent or change other terms of the tenancy.

The month-to-month agreement provides greater flexibility for the landlord, but does not offer a long-term assurance of rental.

Some states have a third type of tenancy called a *tenancy-at-will*. This simply means that a landlord gives a tenant permission to rent until a specific event takes place, for example, until the property is sold. In these states after a lease expires, the tenancy usually becomes a tenancy-at-will rather than a month-to-month tenancy.

THE LEASE

The minute you become a landlord you become a professional in real estate. And as a professional it will behoove you to act like one. When first renting out property, many landlords will go to the nearest stationery store and pick up a prepared lease agreement. In my opinion these agreements are too often not worth the paper they are written on. At best, they contain a legally accurate though very general lease agreement. At worst, they are written to flatter landlords (it's always the landlord who buys them, never the tenant) and purport to give landlords rights that they may not have. In the latter case, the lease may be so one-sided in favor of the landlord that in a lawsuit it would not hold up. It should be noted, however, that some landlords, particularly those in low-rent areas, prefer these one-sided leases. They know full well that they never will be able to take a tenant to court and collect, and they want the scariest possible lease to intimidate the tenant.

A professional landlord will start not at the stationery store but at a lawyer's office. There the landlord will have a lease prepared specifically for that area of the country in accordance with all local laws (many lawyers already have a standard form prepared). This may cost $50 to $100 or more, but over the course of years, the landlord can use copies of the lease over and over again, and it will much more than pay for itself in headaches avoided and money not lost. Besides, the cost is usually tax deductible.

While your lawyer will prepare your lease, there are certain features that you should know about.

1. *Minimum requirements.* The usual minimum requirements for a lease are *an agreement to lease* in which you agree to give the tenant possession of your property and the tenant agrees to take possession of it; an accurate *description* of your property; the *term* of the lease (in some states leases may not run for over 100 years); the rate of *rent*, where and when it will be paid, and the full amount to be paid over the term of the lease; the *capacity* of the parties—you can't sign a lease with a minor or an incompetent, such as someone who is senile. In addition, you can't use force or fraud to get someone to sign.

2. *Access.* It is necessary for the landlord to be able to inspect the house or apartment. In case there is an emergency such as a fire, there is a need to be able to get in. A wise landlord will also want to have the right to occasionally inspect the premises to be sure the tenant is not doing damage. However, contrary to popular opinion, landlords do not normally have the right to barge in on their tenants any time they choose. A tenant has the right to "quiet enjoyment" of the premises. Therefore, I always include in my leases a provision that the landlord has the right to inspect the property at reasonable hours and upon giving advance notice to the tenant. Failure by the tenant to let the landlord inspect becomes grounds for breaking the lease.

3. *Subletting.* Unless the landlord specifically prohibits it, tenants may normally sublet a rental. For example, if you rent a house to someone for $300 a month, that person could then sublet it to another tenant for $350 and pocket the difference. The disadvantages to the landlord are more than just money lost. The sublet tenant may not meet the landlord's criteria for a good tenant: the family may be too large, the credit history poor, the income inadequate to meet rental payments. To prevent such a situation from developing, I always include a paragraph specifically prohibiting any tenant from subletting my property.

4. *Destruction.* In some areas destruction of the property is not considered sufficient cause for the tenant to stop paying rent. To be practical, however, you cannot really expect a tenant to continue to pay rent on a house that has burned down. A problem arises, however, with regard to partial destruction. For example, a fire might destroy one bedroom or part of a kitchen. Must the tenant now pay rent? I always include a clause specifying that in the event of partial damage, the tenant must continue to pay rent unless the premises are uninhabitable as determined by local building and safety codes. For example, if the house is still habitable, there is no reason a tenant should not pay rent if one wall in the kitchen is gutted by fire. I, as landlord, would make every effort to get the wall repaired as quickly as possible and the tenant would have to bear with the inconvenience. This is not as harsh as it may sound since in many cases localized fires are caused by the tenant.

5. *Maintenance.* When renting a house, I always insist that the tenants agree to maintain the grounds in the same condition as they found them. In a house or apartment I also insist that this apply to the inside of the unit. Many landlords insert a clause stating that upon expiration of the lease the tenant is required to return the premises in the same condition as they were found, excepting reasonable and normal wear and tear. As a landlord you should not expect that the property will come back exactly as you gave it. When anyone lives in a house or apartment for a period of time, there will be some damage to paint, flooring, appliances, etc. You should expect this and figure it in as part of your operating costs. You should not, however, have to pay for unreasonable or abnormal wear and tear by a tenant.

When renting a piece of property with a yard, unless I have contracted for a gardening or maintenance service, I always agree to pay for at least the water. Tenants who are responsible for maintaining the yard are much more likely to do a thorough job if they aren't worrying about running up a water bill. Even if I have to occasionally pay a high water bill, it is worth it to keep the yard green.

In some areas of the country, particularly the Midwest and Northeast, landlords also must provide heat and hot water during the cold winter months. You should check with your lawyer to see if your local codes insist upon this.

6. *Security and cleaning deposits.* A cleaning deposit is probably the single greatest bone of contention between landlord and tenant. The problem arises out of a misunderstanding. Landlords often assume that they can use the tenant's cleaning deposit to pay for *any* cleaning of the rental after the tenant moves out. Tenants often assume that if the rental is left fairly clean, *all* their deposit should be returned. Since in almost every case some cleaning is required by the landlord, one party or the other is bound to feel injured.

As the landlord, you have the most to say about the deposit since it is in your bank account. (Landlords in most areas are required to keep this deposit *separate* from their other monies, preferably in a separate bank account. In some few areas they may be required to pay the tenant interest on the money when it is returned.) Some landlords have derived a compromise; taking a $100 deposit, they specify that half of it is a security deposit to be returned providing the tenant leaves the premises in reasonably good shape and that the other $50 is a nonrefundable cleaning fee that will be used to pay for cleaning the property when the tenant moves out.

The problem with this arrangement is that many tenants who agree to it make no effort to clean up the place when they move out, figuring that they've already paid $50 to have it done. As any landlord knows, $50 will not go far in cleaning up a rental, and so the plan often backfires.

One better idea that I have seen successfully used is this: When the tenant moves out, the property is cleaned and the costs are carefully itemized. Then percentages attributable to normal wear and tear and to real tenant-caused damage are calculated. If the rental is particularly clean, there may be no damage fee. If it is particularly dirty, there may be no refund. Usually there is a split, with some of the deposit going back to the tenant and some being retained. The landlord then goes over the list with the tenant and explains the distribution of funds.

Sometimes tenants will disagree. If they have valid arguments, I will change the figures in their favor. If not, I will explain that someone has to pay the costs, and since they did the damage, it is only right that they should be the ones.

Some landlords refer to the cleaning deposit as a security deposit or take a security deposit in addition to one for cleaning. They do this so that they can apply the deposit to other areas of the lease besides clean up. They may insert a clause providing that if a tenant fails to pay rent on time, brings in a pet against the lease provisions, or alters the property without permission, the deposit is forfeited.

The usual reason for doing this is to intimidate the tenant by implying that real money can be lost if the lease is not strictly adhered to. In many cases landlords use this clause as an excuse for not giving back the deposit when the tenant moves out, claiming some infraction of the lease. If you do this and the tenant goes along with it, you're ahead. But if the tenant pursues the matter to court, you could lose.

If you apply the security deposit as liquidated damages toward unpaid rent, you probably are on solid ground (provided you made an attempt to mitigate losses by rerenting). If, however, you retain the security deposit for the tenant's improper keeping of pets, altering of the premises, or other such infraction, the court might hold that the deposit was in reality a prepaid penalty, which in some areas is not enforced. Check with your attorney for the law in your area.

7. *Alterations and repairs.* One thing you do not want your tenants doing is altering your rental. You don't want them knocking out the wall between a living room and bedroom to make a family room. You may not like the new arrangement, and you have no idea whether they can do a professional job. My leases always include a clause specifying that the tenant may make no alterations, including changing walls, windows, appliances, and even painting, without the specific written consent of the landlord.

Repairs can be an even more serious matter. Consider, for example, the case of the leaking water heater. Mr. Freed owned a house that he rented out. The water heater, which was located in the garage, began to leak, and the tenants complained. Mr. Freed inspected and found the leak to be minor. Further, it was causing no damage to the tenants' possessions; it was just running along the floor and out the back door of the garage. Since Mr. Freed was paying for the water anyway, he decided to wait. If the old heater held out another half year, that was six months more before he had to pay for a new one.

The tenants disagreed. They were afraid the heater would suddenly burst during the night, flooding the garage and damaging some articles they had stored there. Taking matters into their own hands, they had a new heater put in and deducted the cost from their rent.

Needless to say, Mr. Freed was outraged, particularly since he could have gotten the heater installed for much less than it cost the tenants.

Mr. Freed refused to allow the tenants to deduct the cost of the water heater from their rent. The tenants now became outraged and moved out owing one month's rent, which was more than the water heater cost. Mr. Freed might have gone to court and sued for the money owed by the tenants. In most states tenants may not deduct from rent the cost of making repairs. (In some states, such as California, certain deductions may be made when the repair affects the health or safety of the tenants.) The moral here, however, is that it is probably better to fix the water heater than to lose the tenant.

8. *Attorney's fees.* If a tenant breaks a lease without cause, as mentioned earlier, the landlord may take that tenant to court to force payment. However, even if the landlord wins the case, there undoubtedly will be legal fees to pay. My leases always include a clause providing that in the event of a suit to regain rent or to force eviction, the tenant will be liable for the landlord's attorney's fees.

31

Collecting Rent and Eviction

All landlords should realize at the beginning that they are involved in a business and that the goal of every business is to make money, not to lose it. In renting real estate the way to make money, or at least to make ends meet, is to collect the rent when it is due. There are *no* good excuses for late payments, not even illness. If rent is not paid exactly when due, the landlord should *immediately* begin considering evicting the delinquent tenants.

That is the best advice you can get as a landlord, even though it may sound very harsh. Renting property is not an easy job, and to do it successfully sometimes requires the cold heart of a Scrooge. Being harsh is, however, necessary, since in almost all cases today the owner has payments as high as or higher than the rent, and to not collect it means that you the owner, have to make up the tenant's rent money out of your own pocket. If you have a kind heart and couldn't bear to be harsh with a nonpaying tenant, it might be wise for you to consider a different investment.

If you let tenants be late even a few days with payment, they will figure that if things get tight, they can pay some other bill first because you're willing to wait. Don't let your tenants think this. Make yourself so demanding that your tenants make somebody else wait.

There is an even more important reason for getting your rent on time. Some tenants will be a day or so late, at first. This may turn into a week, then two, and pretty soon a month. When you finally harden up and demand the rent, the tenant may skip out. Your laxity may cause you to lose a month's rent. In other cases tenants may not be able to pay, but, rather than admit it, they will beg for a few more days to come up with the rent. You might allow the time and then discover the tenants still do not have the rent. Now you'll have to start eviction proceedings, which may take up to three weeks. You'll lose not only the time it takes for the proceedings, but also the time before you started the proceedings.

Eviction usually comes about because a tenant fails to pay rent or because of *gross* violations of the rental contract. When the reason is nonpayment of rent, the procedure is usually very straightforward. When the reason is a violation of a lease clause, there may occasionally be a court trial.

At one time many states allowed "self-help" evictions if they were done peaceably. This simply meant that the landlord could go in and evict the tenant. However, these evictions were usually merely covers for illegal forceful evictions, in which the landlord physically (and sometimes brutally) evicted the tenant. Today they have been outlawed in almost all areas. To get a tenant evicted today normally involves a court action and requires the services of an attorney. If you find an eviction is necessary, be prepared to pay the costs. In some locales the landlord is also required to put up a bond of $300 or more to pay for any damages the tenant may ultimately receive against the landlord and a fee to cover the removal of the tenant's personal possessions and their storage.

Often, however, a costly eviction can be avoided by the simple threat of it. Almost all states require that a prior *notice of default* be given to the tenant. This is a notice that tells the tenant what the problem is (nonpayment of rent, keeping of pets, damage, etc.) and demands that the tenant pay up, correct the problem, or quit the property. The actual form of this notice and its legal requirements vary from state to state. In California, for example, a three-day written notice to quit is required. In New Jersey, simply giving a proper oral notice is sufficient. Some areas require that written notices be personally delivered, while other states require that they be affixed to the front door. You should consult your attorney to get the proper notice for your area. (You might do this when you get your lease form.)

This notice makes the tenant aware that you mean business and are willing to pay the costs for an eviction. In most cases this threat is enough to get the tenant to pay or move out.

If the tenant still refuses to pay, move out, or correct a problem, your attorney will have to get a court order. In the case of nonpayment of rent, eviction proceedings are rarely contested and are handled quite quickly, perhaps within three weeks or less. You'll get a judgment for the rent owed and costs (if provided in your lease) and an order for eviction, which you will take to your marshal or sheriff, who will finally evict the tenant.

If, however, the tenant contests your eviction, usually because an interpretation of some clause in the lease other than rent payment is involved, the process could be lengthy. The tenant in most states is entitled to due process of law on initial hearings and a jury trial if demanded. Usually, the jury considers only disputed questions of fact. The judge decides on the law and may overrule a jury in favor of the tenant or landlord.

A jury trial may result in a delay of many months, during which time the tenant may not pay rent. I have seen obstinate tenants insist on all their time-consuming legal rights even when they were totally in the wrong and in the end lost the case. And even though the landlord received a judgment for all costs, the tenants were judgmentproof, that is, they had insufficient assets to collect upon.

Eviction is the last resort of the landlord and should be used with discretion. It is also a complex subject. Some states, for example, prohibit the eviction of a pregnant woman past the sixth month of her pregnancy. Others prohibit eviction of those seriously ill. Eviction is the realm of an attorney, and any landlord would be wise to use one in such matters.

SIX

Protect Yourself When You're a Tenant

32

The Renter's Rights

Being a tenant is a little like being a pedestrian on a turnpike. If you don't keep out of the way of cars, you can get run over. Historically, the law in this country has always favored the landowner over the renter. But times are changing, and more and more the rights of tenants are being upheld. Today, when they are in the right (and sometimes even when in the wrong), tenants can force landlords to change their ways. In all areas of residential tenancy, the renter's voice is becoming louder and clearer.

But, in order to exercise this new-found power, limited though it may still be, the tenant must first be able to identify the problem and then use an appropriate solution. In this chapter the five areas that most frequently cause problems are listed and protections that other tenants have successfully used are outlined.

The reader should note carefully, however, that while some areas of the country are very progressive in landlord-tenant relationships, others remain quite backward. When considering any action that could jeopardize a lease or other tenancy agreement or that could result in a lawsuit or other legal problem, the reader should first consult with an attorney familiar with the landlord-tenant situation in the reader's part of the country. This chapter should not be construed as providing legal advice.

THE LEASE OR RENTAL AGREEMENT

Once you've found a place you want to rent and the landlord has agreed to rent it to you, you will almost always have to sign a rental agreement. (A landlord cannot refuse to let you sign or, indeed, refuse to rent to you on the basis of color, religion, or national origin. See Chapter 26 if you have a problem.) This agreement informs you of how the landlord expects you to act while a tenant; it specifies where, when, and how much you are to pay and requires your agreement to pay; and it often includes many paragraphs listing the dire consequences if you fail to pay or to live up to terms of the agreement—it intimidates.

Why do landlords usually insist that tenants sign such an agreement? There are two reasons: First, the landlord is putting into your care a very expensive item, a house or apartment that in today's market may be worth $40,000 or more and that could be almost demolished by an irresponsible tenant. Second, today almost all landlords have high mortgages, taxes, and other expenses on their rental property, which means that any amount they have to pay to repair a damaged unit often comes out of their own pocket.

Knowing that you will undoubtedly have to sign a rental agreement if you want to rent a landlord's property, it behooves you to try to get one that is as favorable to you as possible. Most landlords, particularly those who rent out one house or a few apartment units, will simply go to a local stationery store to pick up a rental or lease form. If the form says they have the right to barge in on the tenant any time they please, they may assume they do have that right. If the form says they can evict a tenant simply by carrying his or her furniture out onto the street, the landlord again may think that right exists. Such landlords may not have consulted with an attorney, as they should have, to find out just what they can and can't do to a tenant.

What should you, as a tenant, do when a landlord wants you to sign an agreement?

You should have your attorney look at it. It is unfortunate that few residential tenants do this. You should carefully read the form and question any item that seems out of line. Don't be afraid to change or add in new conditions. If the form says the landlord has the right to inspect at any time and you don't want your landlord barging in without warning day or night (and you certainly shouldn't), you might suggest that he or she be given the right to inspect the property occasionally, at reasonable hours, and upon first giving you advance notice. You should also insert a clause specifying that you can be evicted only by due process of law. No landlord should object to this. If there is a clause prohibiting you from fixing, repairing, or altering any part of the property without the landlord's written consent, you could try to insert a provision that the landlord will fix anything that breaks or wears out because of age or defect. If possible, you should insert a clause that allows you to fix and deduct from your rent the cost of repairing any item the landlord refuses to fix after you've given notice of its disrepair. (Few landlords will allow such a clause in a lease.) If a deposit is mentioned, you should be sure the lease specifies a reasonable method for its return to you. If the lease specifies that a certain portion of a cleaning deposit is not refundable, you should understand that this is probably an *advance fee* and not a deposit. In certain areas of the country, particularly the Northeast, when signing a rental agreement for an apartment in a building of many units, you should get the landlord to agree to supply heat, hot water, and cold water.

The landlord is usually in the driver's seat when it comes to these agreements. If you don't sign, you probably won't get the rental. Consequently, it may not be possible for you to change even the most obnoxious terms of the rental agreement. If this is the case, you might want to consider renting some other place. If enough tenants turned away from such landlords, they would be forced into using more reasonable leases.

Perhaps, however, you need to rent a particular apartment or house and you sign the agreement with the bad terms. You are not entirely lost. The landlord cannot get away with acts which are illegal, such as bodily throwing you out into the street for failure to pay rent, even if you both agree to them in a rental agreement. Further, if such an agreement is entirely out of balance in favor of the landlord, it probably would not be enforceable in a court of law. Many judges will simply throw out one-sided agreements.

You will, however, normally be required to perform with regard to the rent payment part of the agreement, so you should be sure you understand it. There are basically two types of rental agreements—the month-to-month agreement and the lease.

In the month-to-month agreement you have a very tenuous hold on the property. Your right to the tenancy, in effect, expires at the end of every month, and the landlord, with or without cause, can terminate the rental with short notice. The period of notice may be specified in the rental agreement. If not, it is usually equal to the period between rent payments, that is, if you pay once a month, thirty days' notice usually is required. You, of course, have the same option. You can leave for any reason after giving the proper notice. This type of agreement is ideal if you do not know how long you will be renting. Perhaps you're planning to leave the area, or buy a house, or move to a better apartment. If so, this type of agreement is probably what you will prefer.

The lease, on the other hand, ties you, the tenant, to a piece of property for a specific period of time. Leases are usually written for one year or longer. There are many advantages for you in having a lease. The landlord can't raise the rent during the lease term unless the lease specifically provides for increases, and this is not usually done in residential property. Further, the landlord usually can't end the tenancy *without cause* during the term of lease. Finally, even if the landlord should sell the property, you normally will retain your tenancy unless a specific provision terminating the lease upon sale is inserted.

The disadvantage of the lease is that you can't simply pull up stakes and move any time you want. You are committed to paying a certain rental every month for a fixed period of time.

If you do sign a lease, you should be sure to check what provision is made for your continued tenancy after the lease expires. Many leases provide that you may continue as a tenant, but at a higher rent. If no provision is made, it is usually assumed that you may continue to rent on either a month-to-month or a tenancy-at-will basis at the old rental figure.

THE LANDLORD WHO WON'T FIX OR REPAIR

Perhaps you've rented a house and after a few months, the water faucet in the kitchen begins leaking very heavily. Since you happen to be paying the water bill, you're concerned. You call the landlord, Mr. Smith, and ask him to fix it. He replies he'll be out as soon as he can. Weeks go by, and he doesn't come to fix it. You call him again and again. Eventually it becomes apparent that Mr. Smith doesn't intend to fix the faucet. What should you do?

If I were the tenant, I would put a new washer in the faucet and forget it. If you're at all handy, fixing a faucet is not much more difficult than changing a spark plug.

But what if the water heater burst, leaving you without water? When fixing requires the expenditure of a good sum of money, it is time for serious consideration.

If your rental agreement contains a clause specifying that the *landlord shall be responsible for making repairs* and, after notice, the landlord refuses, you have several options.

You can sue the landlord for the cost of repairs.

Suit against the landlord in this circumstance need not sound formidable. Every state has provision for small claims court to handle civil suits for low amounts, usually under $200 or $500. For a small filing fee you can usually get a speedy trial. At this trial you need not be represented by a lawyer, and as long as you present a logical, brief case, using the lease to back up your claim that the landlord is responsible, and evidence of the damage, such as photos, you have a good chance of winning. Winning, however, does not always mean you can collect. Many excellent books are available on the advantages and disadvantages of small claims court. A particularly readable one is *Sue the Bastards* by Douglas Matthews (New York: Arbor House, 1973).

Not wanting the trouble of a court suit, some tenants have tried making repairs themselves and then deducting the cost from their rent. There's a problem with this method, however. The landlord may not see it their way and may regard the deduction of money from rent as a failure to pay the full rent and, if really angry, may bring an adverse possession suit (eviction) against the tenant. Thus the tenant might have to go to court anyhow just to avoid losing the property.

There is, of course, the method of getting repairs made that Larry and Gail used. During a severe windstorm, a window in a house they were renting blew in. While the breakage did not harm Larry, Gail, or the apartment, it was certainly inconvenient having a big hole in the side of one wall. Repeated attempts to get the landlord to fix it got no results. It was summertime in an area where it never rained in summer. Larry and Gail got the impression from talking to the landlord that he figured they would fix it themselves to protect the security of the house, that is, to keep burglars from simply climbing in and walking off with their possessions.

Finally, in desperation, they hit upon a plan. Gail called the landlord one last time. She told him she absolutely would not fix the window and further, that she would not be responsible for any water damage caused by the hole in the wall. The landlord chuckled and asked what water damage she was speaking of, surely it would be four months before the earliest rain. She replied the damage that accidently occurred when Larry was watering the shrubs outside. The last time he watered, she fibbed, the walls and floors (they were hardwood) had absorbed an enormous amount of water. The next day, a new window was installed by the landlord. While this method is not necessarily recommended, it did get results for Larry and Gail.

If the lease has no provision for the landlord to repair damages and, even worse, if the lease requires you to fix them, or if the problem does not make the premises uninhabitable, you probably don't have any alternatives. Your chances of successfully deducting the repair costs from the rent would be doubtful in most states. In certain states, notably California, if certain conditions were met, usually involving the health and safety of the occupants, you might be able to repair and deduct and rely on state law to uphold your claim. (In California, provisions in a rental agreement *waiving* your rights to those sections of the Civil Code which provide for repairing and deducting by the tenant under special circumstances are usually not enforceable.)

There are other extreme alternatives open to a tenant whose landlord refuses to repair a house or apartment, and they apply mostly when the problem makes the apartment uninhabitable. It should be noted, however, that before resorting to these, a tenant should consult with an attorney.

Rent Abatement. This simply means the withholding of payment of rent. Several states, notably Massachusetts, Pennsylvania, and New York, have passed legislation allowing for rent abatement in certain limited cases. In almost all instances these involve the property being unfit for human habitation coupled with a long period of noncorrection by the landlord. In New York, for example, the problem must be a *serious* violation of the housing code (serious is usually taken to mean threatening the life, health, or safety of the occupants); the proper housing authority must be notified and agree that there is a violation; and the owner-landlord must be given six months within which to repair, after being notified of the problem. Even then, the landlord may win by proving that the problem was caused by the tenant.

Rent Escrow. This is a device whereby rent is paid to an independent third party. The money held can then be used to make repairs once the action gets to court. The rent escrow can be used legitimately only in those states, notably New York, which have provided for it in the law. Use of a rent escrow should not be attempted without legal aid.

Tenant Unions. A tenant union should *never* be considered as an alternative by tenants without first consulting an attorney. In certain areas of the country, principally New York and San Francisco, tenant unions have had some success in dealing with intractable landlords. A tenant union is much like any other union. Its power comes from the rent strike—the ability to withhold rent payment by a large number of tenants from a single landlord. The problem with tenant unions has always been the difficulty in getting them organized. Unless there is an immediate and pressing problem, tenants have been reluctant to join. Most tenants seem to resent the paying of union dues and many drop out of the organization once the immediate problem has been solved. Further, the mobility of apartment dwellers threatens the stability of such a union. Nonetheless, given a specific cause, tenants have risen up in the past to successfully challenge landlords.

Once organized, the tenants often try to enter negotiations with a landlord. Very often the landlord will refuse to negotiate, or the negotiations will lead nowhere. The tenant union may then suggest a rent strike. All the tenants will be asked to withhold rent or pay their rent to an independent third party until the landlord corrects the problem. In the past, many rent unions have failed at this test. A good percentage of the tenants, fearing eviction, have failed to go along with the rent strike, making the union ineffectual.

In those cases where the tenants held together in a strike, the landlord has almost invariably first threatened and then proceeded with eviction. However, in states where rent abatement or rent escrow is allowed, eviction may not be an alternative for the landlord.

Some strong landlords have their own methods of retaliation. They may selectively evict only the leaders of the strike, hoping to break the union. They may cut off utilities to the building, although in some areas this is no longer a legitimate response. They may sue the entire union collectively and the tenants individually. If the landlord is immovable and the tenants persistent, the matter may get to court, in which case the outcome is doubtful. Some courts have held with landlords, others with tenants.

THE NOSY LANDLORD

What should you do about the landlord who won't stay away, who keeps dropping in to see how you're doing?

This usually happens where a landlord is living very close by. The landlord may be motivated by a desire to see that the property is being well maintained. Often, however, it is simply a case of a lonely landlord. In this circumstance you should probably treat the landlord as you would any other person who desires too much of your company. Ask him or her to stop bothering you, to come by less often.

Occasionally, the landlord's visits will be of a more serious nature. Landlords have been known to simply walk in on tenants at any time of the day or night—when the tenant was giving a party or asleep in bed. There have even been cases of male landlords who have dropped in on female tenants with more on their mind than watching out for their real property. Usually the landlord is aided in this nosing around by the possession of a passkey.

What should you do if you are so bothered?

First, you should tell the landlord you object to his or her actions. Never overlook the possibility, slight though it may be, that the landlord simply isn't aware that you object.

Next, if it is legally within your rights, you might try to change the lock on your door. You may not, however, have the right to do this if your rental agreement prohibits you from making any alterations in the unit.

When faced with a new lock, many landlords will point out that they need to be able to get into the apartment or house in case of an emergency, such as leaking gas, and that thus they need the use of the passkey. You might counter this with the argument that in the event of leaking gas, the fire department or gas company, not the landlord, might be the best choice of help. If your agreement requires you to fix and repair you might be able to use this provision against the landlord. In such agreements there is normally no provision for the landlord to make repairs. In the absence of a permitting clause, the landlord normally has no right to enter to effect a repair.

In any event, changing the locks usually alarms landlords. In order to get you to put the old lock back, the landlord might agree to leave you alone.

Third, you could consider calling the police if a landlord knocked on your door demanding entry late at night with no apparent emergency and no prior request. The landlord would probably be sufficiently discouraged by the notoriety to not attempt bothering you again. Some tenants in this situation have called for police help, claiming they were afraid it was a burglar. When everything was straightened out, the tenants remained indignant. They pointed out that they were entitled to the quiet enjoyment of the premises and they requested the police to keep an eye on the landlord. (In such cases, unless there is some kind of violence, the police rarely intervene.) On occasion, this method has been particularly effective when used by women tenants bothered by overly aggressive male landlords. If you do call the police (or even change the door lock), however, you should be prepared to have your landlord retaliate by asking you to move.

Finally, if all else fails, you should move. There are always other rentals, and if none of these methods has kept a nosy landlord away, you're undoubtedly better off living somewhere else.

EVICTION AND BREAKING A LEASE

Eviction is the most severe power a landlord has over a tenant. Yet like most power, it is a double-edged sword. Evicting a tenant costs money. The landlord must pay an attorney's fees and often other fees for marshals and storage of the tenant's possessions, not to mention the loss from unpaid rent during the eviction period. A landlord is never anxious to evict and only does it as a last resort.

As a tenant, you should never want to be evicted, either. An eviction carried all the way through will result in marshals coming into your rented apartment or house, using force if necessary, and physically moving you onto the sidewalk. They will also move out your furniture and other possessions and in some cases may auction or hold it until you pay back rent and costs.

Eviction is often played like a game of chicken between some landlords and tenants. The landlord threatens to evict, and the tenant pays only that amount of the rent that the tenant feels will temporarily satisfy the landlord, guessing just how far the landlord can be pushed before threats turn into action.

If you find that you are unable to pay your rent, you should immediately begin looking for other quarters. If you are morally callous, you may want to stall the landlord as long as possible, to lie, to say anything to forestall eviction proceedings. It may be possible to gain a week, perhaps a month or more of free rent by doing this.

In almost all states, you normally can't be evicted until the landlord has given you an initial default notice. This gives you notice of the amount due and usually offers you a few days (usually from three to fourteen depending on the state) to pay up or get out. Many tenants mistakenly assume that this is always a court order. It often is not. It often is a notice from the landlord *prior* to starting court action.

If you do not move under the threat of a default notice, and the landlord determines that you are not going to get out or pay rent without eviction proceedings, he or she will usually, reluctantly, start the proceedings. Eviction proceedings, usually called *unlawful detainer* actions, vary from state to state. Usually they involve the court sending the tenant a summons or notification that proceedings are underway. Unfortunately, because the servers are often poorly paid, they may throw the summons in the sewer rather than bother to make delivery.

The summons usually tells the tenant the date for a court hearing. At the hearing the landlord will plead his or her case and the tenants will normally have the opportunity to give their version. Then a verdict will be rendered and if it's against the tenants, the landlord can usually have marshals conduct an eviction in a few days.

I have seen tenants move after receiving their initial default notice and before court action and get away without ever having to pay the rent they owed. If it's a small sum, many landlords do not want to bother going to small claims court to get a judgment, particularly if they don't know where the tenants have gone. The tenants, however, still owe the money.

If you wait until eviction proceedings have begun, the landlord will probably proceed whether you move or not and secure a judgment against you. This may tie up just your immediate possessions, such as furniture, or it may apply to all your assets. (In some areas it is illegal to remove your possessions from a rental until you have made full payment, although this is mainly applied to hotels and motels.)

Thus far we have been talking about evictions involving failure of the tenant to pay rent. Suppose, however, that you and the landlord disagree over a provision of the rental agreement, such as the keeping of pets or the maintenance of the yard. What is the landlord likely to do?

Most landlords try to intimidate the tenant. They bring out the rental agreement and point to the clause you are accused of violating. They look very stern, and if you fail to comply with their wishes, they may threaten to evict you.

In many cases, that's about all the landlord may really do. Eviction based on breaking a provision of the rental agreement *other than payment of rent* may or may not be successful. About half the time the landlord wins, and about half the time the tenant who fights the case wins.

Some landlords who are aware of this and who want a tenant out may refuse to accept rent payment. They will not come by for the rent, and they will refuse to cash checks sent to them. Then, they will start eviction proceedings based on failure to pay rent. If you feel you are in the right, you could fight such an eviction proceeding. Be sure you have made every attempt to make rent payment, such as sending the landlord registered letters with cashier's or bank checks enclosed. Once you've convinced a judge or jury that the proceeding is based on something other than failure to pay rent, it's a whole new ball game. Of course, by the time you get to court you will probably need an attorney and you may not get your attorney's fees paid, even if you win. The threat of this is just one more weapon in the landlord's arsenal.

While eviction is the proceeding a landlord uses to oust a tenant, it sometimes happens that a tenant is the party that wants to leave. No problem is likely to occur in a month-to-month agreement. The tenant gives notice as discussed earlier and moves out. (Simply mailing the landlord the key is not giving proper notice.) On the other hand, the situation is not so simple if there is a lease involved and the landlord does not want to release the tenant from the agreement. By moving out before the agreed-upon date and failing to pay rent, the tenant is breaking the lease agreement. The landlord may now sue for each month's rent as it becomes due or for the entire amount in states that permit the lease to contain an acceleration clause. If the agreement was properly drawn, the landlord stands an excellent chance of getting a judgment against the tenant.

How do you avoid this?

The usual method is for the tenant to try to show that in reality it was the landlord who broke a condition of the lease, leaving the tenant no alternative but to move out. For example, if the landlord agreed to provide hot water, but the water was not even warm, the tenant might argue that the landlord failed to live up to his or her end of the bargain.

The purpose of the "leasebreaker" tactic as used by most tenants is to convince landlords that the tenant will fight any lawsuit to collect rent. Once the landlord is convinced of the tenant's determination, the renter can then negotiate with the landlord on a settlement.

In many states it is the responsibility of the landlord to mitigate damages, that is, to try to rent the property to someone else. You might encourage and even help the landlord to rerent.

If the landlord does rent the premises to another party and only a few months' rent are lost, you might pay that sum or agree to split it. Most landlords will take any reasonable amount to avoid going to court.

As a final alternative, some tenants simply move out. Although no figures are available, I would guess that in residential rentals better than a third of the time the landlord simply forgets about the old tenant and finds a new one. It's easier to rerent than to bother with the hassles and costs of a court action.

GETTING BACK SECURITY AND CLEANING DEPOSITS

If you've rented much, you've probably run into a problem similar to this:

Diane and Leon rented a small one-bedroom apartment on a year's lease. They gave the owner a $100 cleaning deposit. At the end of the year's lease they bought a home. Just as they finished moving, Leon was injured in an auto accident and was hospitalized. Diane, who at the time was seven months' pregnant, needed money badly both because of the costs of moving into a new home and because of Leon's hospital costs. After their furniture was moved, she rented a carpet cleaner for $15 and cleaned all the carpets in the apartment. Then she repainted two walls that had been slightly marked. The paint cost her an additional $5. Finally, she scrubbed and washed the floors in the kitchen and the bathroom and washed away the accumulated grease from the oven and stove.

When she asked the landlord for the deposit money, he said that he would come by and look at the place after they were completely moved out and that they would receive a check in a week or so if everything was okay.

A week went by, then two. When Diane called, the landlord told her there were some spots on the carpet. He had called in a cleaning service, and since the cost was more than $100, she had no money coming. She pleaded and begged. He refused.

Several months later when Leon was well, he called the landlord and threatened to take him into court. He knew there were no spots on the floor. The landlord was not intimidated. He claimed to have receipts for $140 from a cleaning service. In the end, Leon and Diane just gave up and counted the money as lost, all $120 of it (remember, they spent $20 themselves on cleaning up).

A conscientious landlord will be reasonable about cleaning costs. If there is no damage beyond normal wear and tear, you'll get your cleaning deposit back.

If, however, your landlord is similar to the one Diane and Leon had, you won't. If you run into difficulties, you might consider taking the landlord to small claims court to recover your deposit. Several tenants who have used this tactic have reported they needed at least two elements to their case in order to win. The first was proof that they paid a deposit and that the intent was to have it returned if they left the rental in as good a condition as they found it. A lease or rental agreement with the proper terms usually sufficed here.

Secondly, they had to show that they did leave the property in good condition. Two techniques were used. In one instance the tenants borrowed a camera and photographed the rental before they moved in and again after they moved out, paying special attention to damaged areas such as stains or cracks. They had a friend along to verify when the photos were taken. In another instance the tenants invited several friends over before they moved in and showed them the rental, pointing out any damage. Then they invited them back when they moved out. Once they got to small claims court the photos and witnesses were a potent weapon in reinforcing their claims about the condition of the rental.

In several states, abuses have been so flagrant that penalties have been enacted against landlords who wrongfully refuse to return a deposit. In Pennsylvania, for example, the landlord must pay double the deposit. Further, the statute requires the *landlord* to prove that the rental was not returned in good shape and that there were damages. In New Jersey it may be a criminal act to wrongfully retain a tenant's deposit.

The other method of getting back the deposit is the fait acompli. This is doing exactly what it sounds like: The tenant simply deducts the deposit from the last month's rent.

The landlord may scream and howl and threaten to take the tenant to court, even to have the tenant evicted. But all this means time, and within thirty days the tenant moves out anyhow, leaving the landlord with a fait acompli. Even if there's real damage, it's now up to the landlord to go through the hassle of going to court. I have known tenants who believe in never giving a landlord a chance to take advantage of them. They always clean up the apartment and deduct the deposit.

A word should be said about security deposits. A security deposit is often just a pseudonym for a cleaning deposit in a rental agreement. If both sides understand what the deposit is for, there usually isn't any problem. In some cases, however, the landlord wants to make the deposit security against the tenant failing to live up to any of the other terms of the agreement. In this case, the deposit in reality is a prepaid penalty in the event the tenant breaks a condition of the lease—or if the landlord decides arbitrarily that the tenant broke the lease. Since, over the course of a tenancy, every tenant breaks at least some small covenant, particularly in a strict rental agreement, it is very easy for the landlord to claim a right to the deposit. (In many states, however, such a prepaid penalty is not enforceable in a court of law.)

I would not agree to rent if a security deposit were defined as a penalty. The opportunity for the landlord to cheat is simply too great. If I were forced to, however, and I thought the landlord really didn't mean to return the money, I would consider using the fait accompli to get it back.

The thing that landlords know and that renters often overlook or forget is that being a tenant is not easy. There is a basic security in living in a piece of property that you own and a basic insecurity in living in property that someone else owns. Given the opportunity, a landlord will probably play on your fears. When you're renting, the threat of eviction, which involves finding a new place to live, getting your furniture out, having your credit rating damaged (this rarely happens), and all the other problems involved in moving can be truly intimidating. If, however, you keep your head, know when you are right and don't give in, admit it when you're wrong and change, you have much less to fear from landlords.

SEVEN

Protect Yourself When You Buy Bare Land from Developers

33

"Have I Got a Deal for You!"

DANGERS OF A LAND INVESTMENT

There is an old saying that used to be very popular around the turn of the century: "You can't go wrong buying land." Of course, in those days bare land far away from urban areas sold for only a few dollars an acre and it really was hard to go wrong. The purchase price was rarely a hardship for the buyer, and taxes were often only a few dollars a year. The buyer could easily afford to wait ten, twenty, or more years for a return. If the area finally developed, the purchaser could sit back and take compliments on making such a shrewd investment decades earlier.

Today, it's a different story. While this country still has millions of square miles of undeveloped land, most of it is inaccessible. Each year, however, small amounts of it are developed and offered for sale. It is these developments that account for the vast majority of bare land purchases, a $4 billion business as estimated by the Department of Housing and Urban Development.

A good deal of bare land that was sold in the last decade has, in fact, skyrocketed in value. This is particularly true where recreational facilities developed nearby. Success stories are told of individuals who bought land for a song in the mountains and then had ski resorts go up. This has also happened with lucky individuals who bought near lakes, both artificial and natural, and in areas where airports or commercial developments went in. Prices have jumped year after year, and large profits were made. The success stories are told and retold. Unfortunately, the failures are seldom mentioned.

Land today cannot be purchased for a few dollars an acre. It sometimes goes for more than $25,000 a half acre (although usually the cost is lower). And taxes on the land also tend to be more than a few hundred dollars a year.

Today's buyer can only rarely afford to purchase and then sit back and wait decades for the value to appreciate. Many professional land investors figure that bare land must *double* in value every five years in order to make investing in it worthwhile. If it doesn't double that fast, you can do better investing your money in other types of real estate.

In addition, today the buyer who purchases bare land from a developer is already paying top dollar, in fact, over top dollar. Developers add to the selling price, besides their profit, the original cost of the land and all the costs of developing it, such as bringing in water and electricity, paving roads, and building recreational centers. This alone would make the sales price high, but in order to find buyers, developers usually have to spend large amounts of money in advertising and promotion—sometimes as much as 40 percent of the other costs—and this too is added onto the price. The drawback to this really comes when it's time to resell. In many instances, new owners of bare land have discovered that they have to sell for less than they purchased because they paid such an inflated price.

Finally, there is the matter of reselling. When you buy, the developer often goes to great lengths to bring you and the property together. This can include a free bus trip or even plane ride to the land. It may include a free dinner and motel room at nearby accommodations. But when you want to sell, the shoe is on the other foot. Short of adopting the very costly promotional practices of the original developer, you may find it impossible to get anyone to look at or consider your property. Because of the distant location of much bare land, you may find it very difficult to get a broker to accept a listing or work at selling it. You may, in short, find the property extremely difficult to dispose of.

Should you, then, avoid buying bare land?

No, not at all. You should, rather, be fully aware of what you're getting into.

Unless you have some inside information that indicates an area is going to develop dramatically (and I don't mean information supplied by the developer as an inducement to purchase), you're taking a big gamble buying bare land as an investment. Yes, you might win big, but you could lose big too.

You could do well, however, if you're buying for reasons other than investment. People buy land today for a future retirement home, for a second home, or for a recreational "place to go." If you've personally inspected bare land and have one of these reasons for buying, you probably will be very happy with your purchase. As long as you're not buying to get rich quick, but, rather, because you enjoy the land, it truly is hard to go wrong.

PITFALLS TO AVOID WHEN MAKING
A BARE LAND PURCHASE

Developers of bare land may be honest and reliable. Unfortunately, some may be the opposite. When you are deciding to make a land purchase, you should be on the watch for certain areas where trouble is likely to occur. In order to avoid being taken, you should pay particular attention to these items:

1. *Misrepresentation.* Land sales are often conducted in a high-pressure atmosphere. In order to get you to buy, a salesperson may forget to mention certain facts or offer incomplete information about the lot you are considering. This often occurs with regard to conditions of the site that may not be readily visible. Perhaps there is no water available. Perhaps you are viewing the site in summer and the salesperson doesn't mention that in winter it is usually covered by twelve to fourteen feet of snow. Maybe there are restrictions on the use of the land, such as prohibition against your camping on the site while you're preparing to erect a building. A salesperson might claim that utilities such as water and electricity will soon be available at the site when in reality no plans for these have been made. A misrepresentation might be made with regard to the availability of sewer or septic tank service.

A misrepresentation might also be made with regard to the title to the property. This is a particular danger when you buy "$50 down and $50 a month." On such deals the buyer rarely gets title. Instead, a *land contract of sale* is used. This is for practical purposes an agreement to agree to buy. (See the end of this chapter for further details.) You, the buyer, pay so much a month until a certain date when you have established enough money for a down payment, at which time the seller transfers title. Unless, however, the document is properly recorded, the developer may be able to borrow or otherwise encumber the land even after you, seemingly, have bought it. Also, unless you've arranged for proper title search, there may already be other liens ahead of your title claim.

What can you do to protect yourself?

Many of the larger states require a subdivision report from a developer when parcels of land are sold. These are usually very comprehensive, but are subject to certain conditions, such as the size of the lots and the number sold. In California, for example, a report must be filed on almost all sales involving five lots or more unless the lots are larger than 160 acres.

In many cases these reports are quite extensive and a state inspector actually visits the site. They provide information on the availability of nearby roads, the location of recreational facilities, the availability of utilities and sewers, the mortgages and liens on the property, as well as other information. In some states they also include an opinion by the state on the advisability of purchasing. In California, for example, if the subdivision does not meet minimum standards, lots cannot even be offered for sale. Be sure you read a subdivision report before buying. *Don't* sign a statement that you've received the report and read it unless you actually have.

In addition, buyers are afforded some protection by the Interstate Land Sales Act of 1968. A developer who wants to offer for sale a project containing more than fifty unimproved lots by means of interstate commerce and under a common promotional sales plan (most developments are offered this way) must file a statement of record with the Department of Housing and Urban Development, which administers the act, and provide each buyer with a property report.

This property report includes much information that is vital for you as a buyer to know. It includes information on the title to the property, availability of utilities and water, future development plans for the area, maps, local ordinance information, and many other useful items.

While on the surface this property report may seem like a panacea, it does not solve all the problems for the buyer. First, there are a whole list of exemptions that developers may come under. Some of the developments which do not have to file the property report include:

1. Tracts with fewer than fifty lots or where no lot is less than 5 acres in size

2. Lots where the seller is obligated to construct a building in less than two years

3. Lots which exceed 10,000 square feet and sell for less than $100

4. Lots sold free and clear where the buyer inspects the lot and receives a deed within 120 days

Secondly, the HUD unit which administers the act, the Office of Interstate Land Sales Registration (OILSR), does not inspect the land, does not prepare the property report (the developer does), and does not verify the statements in it.

What good, you might reasonably ask, is the property report?

It does offer the buyer these protections: the developer in the report makes representations covering just about every area of the land. When you go to the site to inspect the land, it is often possible for you to verify what the developer has said about the physical attributes. A quick trip to the local recorder's office or title insuring company and check of documents will verify most title claims. It is much easier to check out these items when they are presented in a comprehensive document such as the property report than when dropped in sentences here and there by a salesperson.

In addition to the full disclosure aspect, you may have the right to *void a purchase contract* if the developer failed to register with OILSR as required or failed to give you an approved property report. You may even have the right to void the purchase agreement if the property report is not delivered to you at least forty-eight hours before you sign a sales agreement. One danger here is that it is permissible for the buyer to waive this forty-eight-hour cooling-off period. *Don't sign any waivers* of your right to a cooling-off period unless you are 100 percent positive you are going to buy.

Finally, if the developer has lied, made misstatements of fact, omitted important items, or engaged in fraudulent sales practice with regard to the property report, you may be able to sue the developer in court to recover any loss.

These are potent rights, and you as a buyer should exercise them. If you look at bare land and the developer does not give you a OILSR property report, ask for it. If the developer still refuses and you think the land qualifies, write to HUD/OILSR, 451 Seventh Street S.W., Washington, D.C. 20410. Give a description of the development as accurately as possible and include $2.50. If there is a property report, it will be sent to you. If there is no report, but it appears one should have been filed, OILSR will usually look into the matter.

If you have already purchased land and feel you were cheated, you can complain to OILSR and it may conduct an investigation. Write to the above address giving the name and location of the subdivision and the name of the developer and including copies of any documents you signed.

2. *Failure to keep promises.* As an inducement to buy, the developer may make certain promises to you which may not be kept at a later date.

On occasion a developer will sell land over the phone or by mail or even in person without the buyer ever seeing the property. In order to get you to purchase, the developer may include a promise to refund your deposit or even rescind the sale if the property is not completely as represented when you finally do inspect it. In the past some buyers upon inspecting their property found it was not as represented and demanded their money back. On occasion, developers have refused, saying the buyer misunderstood the claims for the property. In a few deals the developer even claimed the salesperson made the money-back guarantee without the knowledge and consent of the owner.

The best way to avoid this situation is to *never buy without first inspecting*. You'll have to visit the property eventually, so make sure you do it before you purchase. If you've already made a mistake, your best bet is to complain loudly to the developer and contact your state department of real estate and OISLR. There is a chance you can still get back your deposit if you can prove a misrepresentation was made.

As an inducement to purchase, the developer may promise to develop the area even further. This could include adding a marina, a golf course, a swimming pool, a recreation center, additional roads, regular transportation to and from the area, and many more items. After you buy, however, the builder may not go through with any of these plans. They may never, in fact, have been planned for, or the builder may face bankruptcy and not be able to complete them.

There is very little you can do about this after you purchase. Before you purchase, however, you should check to see that the builder is putting into a special escrow account enough money from the sale of each lot to cover planned future developments. If this money is not being put aside, you should find out where the developer intends to get it from.

The developer may promise to deliver deeds, title insurance, and other documents and then refuse to do so, or deliver them only after much insistence on your part and a long delay. When purchasing bare land, you should exercise all the cautions you would normally use when buying any real estate.

3. *"Forgotten" sales inducements.* In order to get you to the site to inspect the bare land, the developer may use a wide variety of sales inducements. These can include free trading stamps, gifts, bonds, etc. Once you're at the site, however, the inducements may be forgotten.

As long as the inducements are of a small nature, not receiving them is no great loss to the purchaser and the deception is fairly harmless. In some cases, however, the "forgotten" inducement may produce a more serious problem for the buyer. Occasionally an unscrupulous developer may offer a "free" vacation and not mention that strings are attached to the offer. The vacation is not really free, but contingent on the consumer buying the bare land. In other cases a free plane ride or bus ride to a development may be called a free vacation. In reality, the prospective buyer may be subjected to a barrage of high-pressure sales talk during the trip and later at a distant site be pressured by a salesperson trying to get a signature on a purchase agreement. This is hardly a vacation. In at least one case with which I am familiar, a salesperson, perhaps without the knowledge of the developer, insinuated that the prospective buyer would have to remain at the site until she agreed to purchase.

To protect yourself, you should remember that you usually have to pay for what you get. Someone who offers you a "free" vacation expects to get something out of it. An old griff show adage goes, "You can't cheat a man who doesn't expect to get something for nothing." The same applies to bare land sales. If you're truly interested in the property, arrange to see it for yourself. After all, once you've bought it, you're going to have to go there and back on your own.

4. *Bait and switch.* This tactic has two ploys. The first involves the price of the land offered for sale. A parcel is advertised at a very low price. When prospective buyers reach the sites, however, they are told that only more expensive sites are left. A variation of this trick involves the "discount coupon." Occasionally unscrupulous developers will advertise discount coupons worth $500, $1000, or more off the purchase price of a piece of bare land. The amount of the coupon, however, has been previously added to the price of the land; thus the purchaser who tries to cash in still ends up paying full price.

In the second ploy, the developer shows the beautiful recreational features of the development in advertisements. A pleasant green meadow surrounded by tall pines and with a clear stream running through it may be shown. Upon visiting the site, prospective purchasers may be told that all the pieces of land in the meadow have already been sold but there are some lots nearby. These are pointed out on a map and may indeed seem close. The buyer who makes a purchase without first inspecting the land in question, however, may be in for a startling surprise. The actual lot may be miles away, on a barren slope with no trees, no stream, and no grass. When confronted with the deception, the developer may offer a site close to the original view, but at a much higher price. This is a double bait and switch.

5. *Troublesome terms.* Often bare land is offered for sale at "$50 down and $50 a month" or similar easy terms. What the developer is usually offering is a *land contract of sale* (also known as articles of agreement for a warranty deed). This is not a conventional sales agreement because the buyer *does not* receive a deed to the property. Rather, it is an installment contract similar to the one used when purchasing a washing machine or television set. It is used primarily because no other types of financing are available.

Financing on land is very difficult to obtain. Most lending institutions won't loan money on bare land. Those lenders who will loan usually require the buyer to put up a substantial down payment, usually a third or more. On a $3000 lot, that's $1000 down. Yet, in order to get a sale, many developers find it necessary to offer easy terms, hence the land contract of sale.

The land contract of sale is an agreement between buyer and seller by which the buyer pays to the seller a certain sum each month until an agreed-upon amount of money is obtained. In our example the buyer would put down $50 and pay $50, often including interest, for as many months as required to reach the $1000 down payment (the number of months would depend on the interest rate charged). Then, if the land contract so read, the buyer would obtain a mortgage for the balance ($2000 in our example), either from an independent lender or from the seller, and would receive a deed to the property.

In practice, the land contract can lead to many severe problems. The major one is the seller who encumbers the land during the period of the contract. Most land contracts read that the seller cannot put any loans on the property while the buyer is making payments. An unscrupulous seller, however, might go ahead and arrange financing without telling the buyer. When the buyer finishes the contract and wants to receive the deed, an unpleasant shock may await—there may be a loan on the property for more than the buyer's equity in it.

CHECKLIST FOR BARE LAND PURCHASES

1. Don't buy "site unseen." Take a trip to the property before you sign any agreement.

2. Check the OISIR property report and/or state subdivision report. Don't sign a statement that you've received and read these reports unless you actually have.

3. Check to see what provision the developer has made for completing the development as stated. Has money been set aside in an escrow account to pay for future developments?

4. Check to see how large the development will eventually become. Will there be too many people for your liking? Will you be able to camp on the property while you build?

5. Has the builder made adequate plans for garbage collection? What about utilities?

6. When will the project be completed? When will construction begin? Are the dates truly reasonable?

---

7. Will you have to join a property owner's association to handle water and sewer service? Will there be a fee? Will the landowners or the developer control it?

8. Will there be a street leading right up to your property, or will you have to cross someone else's lot to get to yours? Will you have to get permission for this from your neighbor? If there are roads, who will pay to maintain them? Will they be dirt or paved?

9. Are you getting a true sale and deed or just a contract of sale? On a contract of sale, will you still receive title to the property if the developer goes broke?

10. If you're buying a waterfront lot, have you checked to see whether the lake is natural or artificial? Has the lake a history of receding? (If so, your waterfront lot could be hundreds of yards from the shore in a few years.) If it is artificial, is there a dam? Do you have to join a homeowner's association to pay for maintenance on the lake to have access to it?

11. Have you thought about the purchase carefully? Is this your first visit to the site? What is the developer's response to your request to wait until you get home and think it over before signing? (Remember, even if this particular parcel of land may be lost by waiting, there will always be other land available.) Is the developer or the salesperson using high-pressure tactics to get you to sign? Why not sleep on it overnight?

The buyer's best protection is to record the land contract document with a county or township recorder's office. Then the contract would show up when a prospective lender searched title before loaning the original seller any money and would, in effect, prevent the seller from obtaining a loan. In most areas, however, notarizing or witnessing of the seller's signature to the document is generally required before the document can be recorded. By avoiding this procedure, unscrupulous sellers can prevent unwary buyers from availing themselves of this protection. Before signing a land contract, you should check out your rights with an attorney and be sure you can record the document. (Some states have enacted laws providing that a land contract can be recorded with only the buyer's signature notarized or witnessed.)

A second problem that arises with the land contract is the unscrupulous seller/developer that refuses to turn over a deed after buyers have faithfully lived up to their terms of the agreement. The developer may try to confuse and intimidate buyers and in some instances maintain that the money the buyers have paid is really just an option to purchase, that if the buyers want to go through with the sale they must now come up with the full purchase price.

In this situation a buyer should be firm with the seller and if necessary go to court to enforce the contract. If an attorney was used by the buyer when drawing up the agreement and if it is properly drawn, there should be little difficulty in forcing the seller to comply with its terms. Often the threat of court action will be enough to force the seller to turn over the deed.

Finally, unscrupulous sellers may write into the contract unreasonable provisions for payment. For example, the land contract may call for the monthly payment to be delivered on a specific date each month and if it is not received by that date, the entire contract becomes void and all the money the buyer has paid in becomes liquidated damages. A dishonest seller might wait until the buyer had paid a majority of money due and then claim, either rightly or wrongly, that the buyer had violated the contract and had thereby lost his or her money and the property. The buyer's only recourse at this stage would be to take the seller to court, where the buyer might very well lose.

The best protection is to never sign a land contract of sale unless you have your own competent lawyer check it over. Since you don't receive a deed with the land contract, you are for practical purposes at the mercy of the seller, and this is not an enviable position to be in. Better still, don't fall for the "$50 down and $50 a month" ploy. Realize that in most cases the property you are buying will cost a lot of money and be prepared to pay it . . . or don't buy.

Appendix

HOW TO USE THE APPENDIX

The information in this appendix has been gathered by carefully examining real estate practices in each state. It is presented to give a comparison of real estate conventions across the country. The reader, however, should not construe this appendix as providing legal advice. For legal advice the reader should consult with an attorney.

The reader should also keep in mind that much of the material presented is condensed or summarized—it is not complete, and due to the difficulty of securing adequate information from every state and because laws are constantly changing, no guarantee can be given as to accuracy.

REAL ESTATE COMMISSION

Each state has a real estate commission which supervises the licensing of real estate agents. If you have a question or a complaint, you can write the main address listed below for your state. You will usually receive a prompt reply.

TRUST DEEDS

Historically, the method of borrowing money on real estate has been the mortgage. However, in recent years deeds of trust have replaced this older type of lien in many states. (For an explanation of the difference between the two see Chapter 15.) An indication of common usage by state is given here.

MAXIMUM INTEREST RATE

Most states set a limit on the amount of interest an individual (the laws are often different for corporations) may charge on a home mortgage. To charge more than the maximum rate is usury and may result in loss of the usurious interest, stiff fines, and/or criminal penalties. A summary of the maximum interest rate allowed by a contractual agreement is given here. (Usury laws are often lengthy; the material here shouldn't be regarded as complete.) In recent years interest rates have fluctuated dramatically and usury laws have been constantly updated. Therefore, the reader should check his or her state code to verify the most current rate.

TIME LIMIT FOR REDEMPTION

After a foreclosure sale, many states allow the original mortgagor a certain period of time to redeem the property by paying fees, costs, interest, penalties, debt, etc. The period shown here is for redemption after a court sale of a mortgage and does not apply to trust deeds. Redemption periods in many states are tied to numerous special conditions, and only a summary is presented here for a state-by-state comparison. For advice regarding the redemption period in a particular state, readers should consult their state civil codes and see an attorney.

TRANSFER REVENUE TAX STAMP RATES

Many states require the payment of a special tax when title to property is transferred. Typical amounts are indicated here.

STATE RECOVERY FUND

Some states have established a fund designed to compensate clients of an agent for damages. The conditions of payment vary, but often the client must have proved in court a case of fraud against the agent and have been awarded a money judgment which the agent was unable to pay.

HUD/FHA OFFICE

Field offices are given for each state. This information is supplied by the Department of Housing and Urban Development, Washington, D.C. 20410.

ALABAMA

State real estate commission office

Director
Alabama Real Estate Commission
Room 562, State Office Building
Montgomery AL 36104

Trust deeds

In use

Maximum interest rate allowable by individuals on real estate loans (usury rate)

8% (over $100,000—15%)

Time limit for the redemption of real estate after foreclosure sale of a mortgage (does not apply to trust deeds)

1 year

Transfer revenue tax stamp rate

$0.50 per $500 or fraction of value exclusive of remaining liens

State recovery fund

—

HUD/FHA state office

Daniel Building
15 South 20th Street
Birmingham 35233
FTS Tel. 229-1617
Commercial number: (205) 254-1617

ALASKA

State real estate commission office

Director
Division of Occupational Licensing
Alaska Department of Commerce
Pouch D, Juneau 99801

Trust deeds

In use

Maximum interest rate allowable by individuals on real estate loans (usury rate)

10% (unlimited on loans over $100,000)

Time limit for the redemption of real estate after foreclosure sale of a mortgage (does not apply to trust deeds)

12 months

Transfer revenue tax stamp rate

—

State recovery fund

Yes

HUD/FHA state office

Insuring office:
334 West 5th Avenue
Anchorage 99501
FTS Tel. (Dial 399-0150 and ask operator for 265-4871)
Commercial number: (907) 272-5561 Ext. 871

ARIZONA

State real estate commission office

Commissioner
Arizona Real Estate Department
1645 W. Jefferson, Phoenix 85007

Trust deeds

In use

*Maximum interest rate allowable by individuals
on real estate loans (usury rate)*

10% (12% if original balance exceeds
$25,000—does not apply to loans on one
and two-family houses)

*Time limit for the redemption of real estate after
foreclosure sale of a mortgage (does not apply to
trust deeds)*

6 months (unless abandoned or used for
agricultural purposes)

Transfer revenue tax stamp rate

—

State recovery fund

Yes

HUD/FHA state office

Insuring office:
244 West Osborn Road
Post Office Box 13468
Phoenix 85002

FTS Tel. 261-4434
Commercial number: (602) 261-4434

ARKANSAS

State real estate commission office

Secretary
Arkansas Real Estate Department
1311 W. Second Street
P.O. Box 3173
Little Rock 72201

Trust deeds

—

*Maximum interest rate allowable by individuals
on real estate loans (usury rate)*

10%

*Time limit for the redemption of real estate after
foreclosure sale of a mortgage (does not apply to
trust deeds)*

1 year

Transfer revenue tax stamp rate

$1.10 per $1000 (or any fraction) of
selling price (first $100 is exempt)

State recovery fund

—

HUD/FHA state office

Room 1490, One Union National Plaza
Little Rock 72201

FTS Tel. 740-5401
Commercial number: (501) 378-5401

CALIFORNIA

State real estate commission office

Chairman of State Real Estate
Commission
California Department of Real Estate
714 P Street, Sacramento 95814

Trust deeds

Used almost exclusively

*Maximum interest rate allowable by individuals
on real estate loans (usury rate)*

10% (most banks and savings and loan
associations are exempted)

*Time limit for the redemption of real estate after
foreclosure sale of a mortgage (does not apply to
trust deeds)*

1 year, no redemption on trust deeds

Transfer revenue tax stamp rate

$0.55 per $500 or any fraction of consideration

State recovery fund

Yes

HUD/FHA state office

2500 Wilshire Boulevard
Los Angeles 90057
FTS Tel. 798-5973
Commercial number: (213) 688-5973

1 Embarcadero Center
Suite 1600
San Francisco 94111
FTS Tel. 556-2238
Commercial number: (415) 556-2238

Insuring offices:
801 I Street, Room 147
Post Office Box 1978
Sacramento 95809
FTS Tel. 448-3471
Commercial number: (916) 440-3471

110 West C Street
Post Office Box 2648
San Diego 92112
FTS Tel. 895-5310
Commercial number: (714) 293-5310

34 Civic Center Plaza, Room 614
Santa Ana 92701
FTS Tel. 799-2451
Commercial number: (714) 836-2451

COLORADO

State real estate commission office

Director
Colorado Real Estate Division
110 State Services Building
Denver 80203

Trust deeds

In use

Maximum interest rate allowable by individuals on real estate loans (usury rate)

8% (specific exemptions)

Time limit for the redemption of real estate after foreclosure sale of a mortgage (does not apply to trust deeds)

75 days after July 1, 1965; 6 months before that time

Transfer revenue tax stamp rate

$0.01 per $100 of the consideration paid over $500

State recovery fund

Yes

HUD/FHA state office

Insuring office:
4th Floor, Title Building
909 - 17th Street
Denver 80202

FTS Tel. 327-2441
Commercial number: (303) 837-2441

CONNECTICUT

State real estate commission office

Executive Director
Connecticut Real Estate Commission
90 Washington St., Hartford 06115

Trust deeds

In use

Maximum interest rate allowable by individuals on real estate loans (usury rate)

12%; banks, trust companies, and private banks are excluded; real estate mortgages over $5,000 are exempted

Time limit for the redemption of real estate after foreclosure sale of a mortgage (does not apply to trust deeds)

Set by court

Transfer revenue tax stamp rate

$0.55 per $500

State recovery fund

Yes

HUD/FHA state office

999 Asylum Avenue
Hartford 06105

FTS Tel. 244-3638
Commercial number: (203) 244-3638

DELAWARE

State real estate commission office

Secretary
Delaware Real Estate Commission
State House Annex, Dover 19901

Trust deeds

Rarely used

Maximum interest rate allowable by individuals on real estate loans (usury rate)

10% (special exemptions)

Time limit for the redemption of real estate after foreclosure sale of a mortgage (does not apply to trust deeds)

No redemption

Transfer revenue tax stamp rate

2% of property value over $100

State recovery fund

Yes

HUD/FHA state office

Insuring office:
Farmers Bank Building, 14th Floor
919 Market Street
Wilmington 19801

FTS Tel. 487-6330
Commercial number: (302) 571-6330

DISTRICT OF COLUMBIA

State real estate commission office

Secretary
District of Columbia Real Estate Commission
614 "H" Street, N.W., Washington 20001

Trust deeds

Used exclusively

Maximum interest rate allowable by individuals on real estate loans (usury rate)

8%

Time limit for the redemption of real estate after foreclosure sale of a mortgage (does not apply to trust deeds)

No redemption

Transfer revenue tax stamp rate

0.05% of consideration paid

State recovery fund

—

HUD/FHA state office

Universal North Building
1875 Connecticut Ave., N.W.
Washington 20009

FTS Tel. 382-4855
Commercial number: (202) 382-4855

FLORIDA

State real estate commission office

Executive Director
Florida Real Estate Commission
State Office Building, West Morse Blvd.
Winter Park 32789

Trust deeds

In use

Maximum interest rate allowable by individuals on real estate loans (usury rate)

10%

Time limit for the redemption of real estate after foreclosure sale of a mortgage (does not apply to trust deeds)

No redemption

Transfer revenue tax stamp rate

$0.30 per $100 of consideration plus $0.55 per $500 of consideration surcharge

State recovery fund

Yes

HUD/FHA state office

Peninsular Plaza
661 Riverside Avenue
Jacksonville 32204
FTS Tel. 946-2626
Commercial number: (904) 791-2626

Insuring offices:
3001 Ponce de Leon Boulevard
Post Office Box 341099
Coral Gables 33134
FTS Tel. 350-6221
Commercial number: (305) 445-2561

4224-28 Henderson Boulevard
Post Office Box 18165
Tampa 33679
FTS Tel. 826-2501
Commercial number: (813) 228-2501

GEORGIA

State real estate commission office

Real Estate Commissioner
Georgia Real Estate Commission
166 Pryor St., S.W., Atlanta 30303

Trust deeds

Permitted

Maximum interest rate allowable by individuals on real estate loans (usury rate)

9% (VA and FHA loans exempted)

Time limit for the redemption of real estate after foreclosure sale of a mortgage (does not apply to trust deeds)

Up to 10 years if possession given to mortgagor

Transfer revenue tax stamp rate

$1 for the first $1000 of consideration or value, $0.10 for each additional $100 or fraction after first $100

State recovery fund

Yes

HUD/FHA state office

Peachtree Center Building
230 Peachtree Street, N.W.
Atlanta 30303
FTS Tel. 285-4576
Commercial number: (404) 526-4576

HAWAII

State real estate commission office

Executive Secretary
Real Estate Commission
1010 Richards St.
P.O. Box 3469
Honolulu 96801

Trust deeds

Not commonly in use

Maximum interest rate allowable by individuals on real estate loans (usury rate)

1% per month (does not apply over $750,000)

Time limit for the redemption of real estate after foreclosure sale of a mortgage (does not apply to trust deeds)

1 year if foreclosure was by entry and possession and meets other special conditions

Transfer revenue tax stamp rate

$0.05 per $100 of consideration (minimum is $1)

State recovery fund

Yes

HUD/FHA state office

1000 Bishop Street, 10th Floor
Post Office Box 3377
Honolulu 96813

FTS Tel. (Dial 556-0220 and ask operator for 546-2136)
Commercial number: (808) 546-2136

IDAHO

State real estate commission office

Executive Secretary
Idaho Real Estate Commission
State Capitol, Boise 83720

Trust deeds

Commonly used

Maximum interest rate allowable by individuals on real estate loans (usury rate)

10% (special limitations)

Time limit for the redemption of real estate after foreclosure sale of a mortgage (does not apply to trust deeds)

1 year, but may be reduced to 6 months by common agreement on parcels smaller than 20 acres

Transfer revenue tax stamp rate

—

State recovery fund

—

HUD/FHA state office

Insuring office:
419 North Curtis Road
Post Office Box 32
Boise 83707

FTS Tel. 588-2232
Commercial number: (208) 342-2711

ILLINOIS

State real estate commission office

Commissioner of Real Estate
Illinois Department of Registration &
Education
628 E. Adams, Springfield 62706

Trust deeds

Used extensively; however, power-of-sale
clause is ineffective—must be foreclosed
through court sale

*Maximum interest rate allowable by individuals
on real estate loans (usury rate)*

8–9½% on residential real estate loans
made before Jan. 1, 1977 (no prepayment penalty allowed if over 8%)

*Time limit for the redemption of real estate after
foreclosure sale of a mortgage (does not apply to
trust deeds)*

6 months

Transfer revenue tax stamp rate

$0.50 per $500 or fraction of value
exclusive of remaining liens (first $100 is
exempt)

State recovery fund

Yes

HUD/FHA state office

1 North Dearborn Street
Chicago 60602
FTS Tel. 353-7660
Commercial number: (312) 353-7660

Insuring office:
Lincoln Tower Plaza
524 South Second Street, Room 600
Springfield 62701
FTS Tel. 955-4414
Commercial number: (217) 525-4414

INDIANA

State real estate commission office

Executive Secretary
Indiana Real Estate Commission
1022 State Office Bldg., 100 N. Senate
Ave.
Indianapolis 46204

Trust deeds

In use, but power-by-sale clause is in-
valid; must be foreclosed through court
sale

*Maximum interest rate allowable by individuals
on real estate loans (usury rate)*

Special limits set by state code

*Time limit for the redemption of real estate after
foreclosure sale of a mortgage (does not apply to
trust deeds)*

No redemption

Transfer revenue tax stamp rate

—

State recovery fund

None

HUD/FHA state office

Willowbrook 5 Building
4720 Kingsway Drive
Indianapolis 46205
FTS Tel. 331-6303
Commercial number: (317) 269-6303

IOWA

State real estate commission office

Director
Iowa Real Estate Commission
1223 East Court (Executive Hills)
Des Moines 50319

Trust deeds

Allowed

Maximum interest rate allowable by individuals on real estate loans (usury rate)

9%

Time limit for the redemption of real estate after foreclosure sale of a mortgage (does not apply to trust deeds)

1 year (may be reduced to 6 months by agreement if property is under 10 acres)

Transfer revenue tax stamp rate

$0.55 per each $500 or fraction of consideration (the first $500 is excluded)

State recovery fund

—

HUD/FHA state office

Insuring office:
210 Walnut Street
Room 259, Federal Building
Des Moines 50309
FTS Tel. 862-4512
Commercial number: (515) 284-4512

KANSAS

State real estate commission office

Director
Kansas Real Estate Commission
535 Kansas Ave., Room 1212
Topeka 66603

Trust deeds

Rarely used

Maximum interest rate allowable by individuals on real estate loans (usury rate)

10%

Time limit for the redemption of real estate after foreclosure sale of a mortgage (does not apply to trust deeds)

12 months unless abandoned; court may reduce to 6 months

Transfer revenue tax stamp rate

—

State recovery fund

Yes

HUD/FHA state office

Two Gateway Center
4th and State Streets
Kansas City 66101
FTS Tel. 758-4355
Commercial number: (816) 374-4355

Insuring office:
700 Kansas Avenue
Topeka 66603
FTS Tel. 752-8241
Commercial number: (913) 234-8241

KENTUCKY

State real estate commission office

Chairperson
Kentucky Real Estate Commission
100 East Liberty St., Louisville 40202

Trust deeds

Used occasionally

Maximum interest rate allowable by individuals on real estate loans (usury rate)

Under $15,000, rate is 8½%; no limit over $15,000

Time limit for the redemption of real estate after foreclosure sale of a mortgage (does not apply to trust deeds)

1 year if sale does not bring at least two-thirds of value

Transfer revenue tax stamp rate

$0.50 per $500 or fraction thereof

State recovery fund

Yes

HUD/FHA state office

Children's Hospital Foundation Bldg.
601 South Floyd Street
Post Office Box 1044
Louisville 40201

FTS Tel. 352-5251
Commercial number: (502) 582-5251

LOUISIANA

State real estate commission office

Director
Louisiana Department of Occupational Standards
P. O. Box 44095, Capitol Station
Baton Rouge 70804

Trust deeds

—

Maximum interest rate allowable by individuals on real estate loans (usury rate)

8% (10% if secured by realty)

Time limit for the redemption of real estate after foreclosure sale of a mortgage (does not apply to trust deeds)

No redemption

Transfer revenue tax stamp rate

—

State recovery fund

—

HUD/FHA state office

Plaza Tower
1001 Howard Avenue
New Orleans 70113

FTS Tel. 682-2063
Commercial number: (504) 589-2063

Insuring office:
New Federal Building
500 Fannin, 6th Floor
Shreveport 71120

FTS Tel. 493-5385
Commercial number: (318) 226-5385

MAINE

State real estate commission office

Administrative Officer
Department Business Regulation
Real Estate Commission
Capitol Shopping Center, Western Ave.
Augusta 04330

Trust deeds

Not used

Maximum interest rate allowable by individuals on real estate loans (usury rate)

None (if in writing)

Time limit for the redemption of real estate after foreclosure sale of a mortgage (does not apply to trust deeds)

1 year

Transfer revenue tax stamp rate

$0.55 per $500 or fraction (first $100 is exempted)

State recovery fund

—

HUD/FHA state office

Insuring office:
Federal Building and Post Office
202 Harlow Street
Post Office 1357
Bangor 04401

FTS Tel. 833-7341
Commercial number: (207) 942-8271
Ext. 7341

MARYLAND

State real estate commission office

Executive Director
Maryland Real Estate Commission
One South Calvert St. (6th floor)
Baltimore 21202

Trust deeds

In use

Maximum interest rate allowable by individuals on real estate loans (usury rate)

10%

Time limit for the redemption of real estate after foreclosure sale of a mortgage (does not apply to trust deeds)

"Reasonable time" (No redemption after final sale)

Transfer revenue tax stamp rate

$0.55 per $500 or fraction of consideration plus transfer tax of 0.5% of consideration. Additional fee in Baltimore

State recovery fund

Yes

HUD/FHA state office

Two Hopkins Plaza
Mercantile Bank and Trust Building
Baltimore 21201

FTS Tel. 922-2121
Commercial number: (301) 962-2121

MASSACHUSETTS

State real estate commission office

Executive Secretary
Massachusetts Board of Registration
of Real Estate Brokers & Salesmen
State Office Bldg., Government Center
100 Cambridge St., Boston 02202

Trust deeds

Not normally used

Maximum interest rate allowable by individuals on real estate loans (usury rate)

—

Time limit for the redemption of real estate after foreclosure sale of a mortgage (does not apply to trust deeds)

3 years unless sold under a power-of-sale clause in mortgage deed

Transfer revenue tax stamp rate

After first $500, $1 for each $500 or fraction of consideration

State recovery fund

—

HUD/FHA state office

Bulfinch Building
15 New Chardon Street
Boston 02114
FTS Tel. 223-4111
Commercial number: (617) 223-4111

MICHIGAN

State real estate commission office

Commissioner of Real Estate
Michigan Dept. of Licensing & Regulation
1033 S. Washington Ave.
Lansing 48926

Trust deeds

Not in normal use

Maximum interest rate allowable by individuals on real estate loans (usury rate)

7% special rate for loans secured by first liens on real property

Time limit for the redemption of real estate after foreclosure sale of a mortgage (does not apply to trust deeds)

6 months when by court sale; 1 year on mortgages before Jan. 1, 1965, and meeting other conditions

Transfer revenue tax stamp rate

After first $100, $0.55 per $500 or fraction of total value

State recovery fund

—

HUD/FHA state office

Patrick V. McNamara Federal Building
477 Michigan Avenue
Detroit 48226
FTS Tel. 226-7900
Commercial number: (313) 226-7900

Insuring office:
Northbrook Building Number II
2922 Fuller Avenue, N.E.
Grand Rapids 49505
FTS Tel. 372-2225
Commercial number: (616) 456-2225

MINNESOTA

State real estate commission office

Commissioner of Securities
500 Metro Square Bldg.
7th & Robert St., St. Paul 55101

Trust deeds

Not used

Maximum interest rate allowable by individuals on real estate loans (usury rate)

Under $100,000—8%; over $100,000—no limit

Time limit for the redemption of real estate after foreclosure sale of a mortgage (does not apply to trust deeds)

6 months; prior to July 1, 1967, 1 year, providing special conditions are met

Transfer revenue tax stamp rate

$2.20 on first $1000; $1.10 for each additional $500 of consideration

State recovery fund

Yes

HUD/FHA state office

Griggs-Midway Building
1821 University Avenue
St. Paul, Minnesota 55104

FTS Tel. 725-4701
Commercial number: (612) 725-4701

MISSISSIPPI

State real estate commission office

Administrative Officer
Mississippi Real Estate Commission
505 Woodland Hills Bldg., 300 Old Canton Rd.
Jackson 39216

Trust deeds

In common use

Maximum interest rate allowable by individuals on real estate loans (usury rate)

10%

Time limit for the redemption of real estate after foreclosure sale of a mortgage (does not apply to trust deeds)

No redemption

Transfer revenue tax stamp rate

—

State recovery fund

—

HUD/FHA state office

101-C Third Floor Jackson Mall
300 Woodrow Wilson Avenue, W.
Jackson 39213

FTS Tel. 490-4703
Commercial number: (601) 969-4703

MISSOURI

State real estate commission office

Secretary
Missouri Real Estate Commission
222 Monroe St., Jefferson City 65101

Trust deeds

Commonly used

Maximum interest rate allowable by individuals on real estate loans (usury rate)

10% (special exceptions)

Time limit for the redemption of real estate after foreclosure sale of a mortgage (does not apply to trust deeds)

1 year on trust deed providing other conditions are met

Transfer revenue tax stamp rate

—

State recovery fund

None

HUD/FHA state office

210 North 12th Street
St. Louis 63101
FTS Tel. 279-4761
Commercial number: (314) 425-4761

MONTANA

State real estate commission office

Board Director
Department of Professional & Occupational Licensing, Board of Real Estate
Montana Real Estate Commission
42½ N. Main, Helena 59601

Trust deeds

In use

Maximum interest rate allowable by individuals on real estate loans (usury rate)

10% plus special conditions

Time limit for the redemption of real estate after foreclosure sale of a mortgage (does not apply to trust deeds)

1 year

Transfer revenue tax stamp rate

—

State recovery fund

—

HUD/FHA state office

Insuring office:
616 Helena Avenue
Helena 59601
FTS Tel. 585-5237
Commercial number: (406) 449-5237

NEBRASKA

State real estate commission office

Director
Nebraska Real Estate Commission
600 S. 11th. St., Suite 200
Lincoln 68508

Trust deeds

In use

Maximum interest rate allowable by individuals on real estate loans (usury rate)

11%

Time limit for the redemption of real estate after foreclosure sale of a mortgage (does not apply to trust deeds)

No redemption

Transfer revenue tax stamp rate

$0.55 per $500 of value

State recovery fund

—

HUD/FHA state office

Univac Building
7100 West Center Road
Omaha 68106
FTS Tel. 864-9301
Commercial number: (402) 221-9301

NEVADA

State real estate commission office

Administrator
Real Estate Division, Nevada Department of Commerce
111 W. Telegraph St., Suite 113, Carson City 89701

Trust deeds

In use

Maximum interest rate allowable by individuals on real estate loans (usury rate)

12% plus special conditions

Time limit for the redemption of real estate after foreclosure sale of a mortgage (does not apply to trust deeds)

1 year

Transfer revenue tax stamp rate

$0.55 per $500 or fraction of value exclusive of any remaining lien; first $100 is exempt

State recovery fund

Yes

HUD/FHA state office

Insuring office:
1050 Bible Way
Post Office Box 4700
Reno 89505
FTS Tel. 598-5356
Commercial number: (702) 784-5356

NEW HAMPSHIRE

State real estate commission office

Executive Director
New Hampshire Real Estate Commission
3 Capitol St., Concord 03301

Trust deeds

In use

Maximum interest rate allowable by individuals on real estate loans (usury rate)

None

Time limit for the redemption of real estate after foreclosure sale of a mortgage (does not apply to trust deeds)

No redemption

Transfer revenue tax stamp rate

$0.15 per $100; first $100 is exempt

State recovery fund

—

HUD/FHA state office

Davison Building
1230 Elm Street
Manchester 03101
FTS Tel. 834-7681
Commercial number: (603) 669-7011
Ext. 7681

NEW JERSEY

State real estate commission office

Secretary-Director
Division of the New Jersey Real Estate Commission
New Jersey Department of Insurance
201 E. State St., Trenton 98625

Trust deeds

Seldom used

Maximum interest rate allowable by individuals on real estate loans (usury rate)

8% up to 9.25% if determined by commissioner of banking on residences of 1–3 units; savings and loan associations and banks are exempted.

Time limit for the redemption of real estate after foreclosure sale of a mortgage (does not apply to trust deeds)

10 days

Transfer revenue tax stamp rate

After first $100, $1.75 per $500 of consideration or fraction; rate for certain exempted persons is $0.50 per $500 or fraction

State recovery fund

—

HUD/FHA state office

The Parkade Building
519 Federal Street
Camden 08103
FTS Tel. 488-5081
Commercial number: (609) 757-5081

Gateway 1 Building
Raymond Plaza
Newark 07102
FTS Tel. 341-3010
Commercial number: (201) 645-3010

NEW MEXICO

State real estate commission office

Executive Secretary
New Mexico Real Estate Commission
Room 1031, 505 Marquette Ave. N.W.
Albuquerque 87101

Trust deeds

In use

Maximum interest rate allowable by individuals on real estate loans (usury rate)

10%

Time limit for the redemption of real estate after foreclosure sale of a mortgage (does not apply to trust deeds)

9 months

Transfer revenue tax stamp rate

—

State recovery fund

None

HUD/FHA state office

Insuring office:
625 Truman Street, N.E.
Albuquerque 87110

FTS Tel. 474-3251
Commercial number: (505) 766-3251

NEW YORK

State real estate commission office

Director
Division of Licensing Services
New York Dept. of State
270 Broadway
New York 10007

Trust deeds

In use

Maximum interest rate allowable by individuals on real estate loans (usury rate)

5–8% determined by banking board

Time limit for the redemption of real estate after foreclosure sale of a mortgage (does not apply to trust deeds)

—

Transfer revenue tax stamp rate

$0.55 per $500 (some exemptions)

State recovery fund

—

HUD/FHA state office

Grant Building
560 Main Street
Buffalo 14202

FTS Tel. 432-3510
Commercial number: (716) 842-3510

666 Fifth Avenue
New York 10019

FTS Tel. 662-5290
Commercial number: (212) 399-5290

Insuring office:
Leo W. O'Brien Federal Building
North Pearl Street and Clinton Avenue
Albany 12207

FTS Tel. 562-3567
Commercial number: (518) 472-3567

NORTH CAROLINA

State real estate commission office

Secretary-Treasurer
North Carolina Real Estate Licensing
Board
813 B.B.&T. Bldg. P.O. Box 266
Raleigh 27602

Trust deeds

In use

Maximum interest rate allowable by individuals on real estate loans (usury rate)

10% on first mortgages if agreed to in writing (special exceptions)

Time limit for the redemption of real estate after foreclosure sale of a mortgage (does not apply to trust deeds)

No redemption

Transfer revenue tax stamp rate

$0.50 per $500 or fraction of consideration

State recovery fund

—

HUD/FHA state office

415 N. Edgeworth Street
Greensboro 27401
FTS Tel. 699-5361
Commercial number: (919) 378-5361

NORTH DAKOTA

State real estate commission office

Secretary-Treasurer
North Dakota Real Estate Commission
410 E. Thayer Ave., Box 727
Bismarck 58501

Trust deeds

Not normally used

Maximum interest rate allowable by individuals on real estate loans (usury rate)

9% plus special conditions

Time limit for the redemption of real estate after foreclosure sale of a mortgage (does not apply to trust deeds)

1 year (6 months if provided for in mortgage, if property less than 10 acres, and if other conditions are met)

Transfer revenue tax stamp rate

—

State recovery fund

Yes

HUD/FHA state office

Insuring office:
Federal Building
653 - 2nd Avenue N.
Post Office Box 2483
Fargo 58102
FTS Tel. 783-5136
Commercial number: (701) 237-5771

OHIO

State real estate commission office

Secretary
Ohio Real Estate Commission
33 North Grant Ave., Columbus 43215

Trust deeds

Not in use

Maximum interest rate allowable by individuals on real estate loans (usury rate)

8%

Time limit for the redemption of real estate after foreclosure sale of a mortgage (does not apply to trust deeds)

No redemption

Transfer revenue tax stamp rate

After first $100, $0.10 per $100

State recovery fund

—

HUD/FHA state office

60 East Main Street
Columbus 43215
FTS Tel. 943-7345
Commercial number: (614) 469-7345

Insuring offices:
Federal Office Building
550 Main Street, Room 9009
Cincinnati 45202
FTS Tel. 684-2884
Commercial number: (513) 684-2884

777 Rockwell
Cleveland 44114
FTS Tel. 293-4065
Commercial number: (216) 522-4065

OKLAHOMA

State real estate commission office

Secretary-Treasurer
Oklahoma Real Estate Commission
4040 No. Lincoln Blvd.
Oklahoma City 73105

Trust deeds

In use

Maximum interest rate allowable by individuals on real estate loans (usury rate)

Special rates depending on type of loan

Time limit for the redemption of real estate after foreclosure sale of a mortgage (does not apply to trust deeds)

No redemption

Transfer revenue tax stamp rate

After first $100, $0.55 per $500 or fraction of value excluding remaining liens

State recovery fund

None

HUD/FHA state office

301 North Hudson Street
Oklahoma City 73102
FTS Tel. 736-4891
Commercial number: (405) 231-4891

Insuring office:
1708 Utica Square
Tulsa 74152
FTS Tel. 736-7435
Commercial number: (918) 581-7435

OREGON

State real estate commission office

Commissioner
Real Estate Division, Department of Commerce
Commerce Building, Salem 97310

Trust deeds

Commonly used

Maximum interest rate allowable by individuals on real estate loans (usury rate)

10% (over $50,000, any rate)

Time limit for the redemption of real estate after foreclosure sale of a mortgage (does not apply to trust deeds)

1 year

Transfer revenue tax stamp rate

—

State recovery fund

None

HUD/FHA state office

520 Southwest 6th Avenue
Portland 97204
FTS Tel. 423-2561
Commercial number: (503) 221-2561

PENNSYLVANIA

State real estate commission office

Room 300, 279 Boas St.
Harrisburg, 17120

Trust deeds

—

Maximum interest rate allowable by individuals on real estate loans (usury rate)

6% up to $35,000 (special mortgage rates)

Time limit for the redemption of real estate after foreclosure sale of a mortgage (does not apply to trust deeds)

No redemption

Transfer revenue tax stamp rate

1% of value (Philadelphia, Pittsburgh, and Harrisburg have separate revenue taxes)

State recovery fund

None

HUD/FHA state office

Curtis Building
625 Walnut Street
Philadelphia 19106
FTS Tel. 597-2645
Commercial number: (215) 597-2645

Two Allegheny Center
Pittsburgh 15212
FTS Tel. 722-2802
Commercial number: (412) 644-2802

Special recovery office:
Lackawanna County Building
Spruce and Adams Avenue
Scranton 18503
FTS Tel. 592-8281
Commercial number: (717) 961-5351

RHODE ISLAND

State real estate commission office

Administrator
Real Estate Division
Department of Business Regulation
169 Weybosset St.
Providence 02903

Trust deeds

Infrequently used

Maximum interest rate allowable by individuals on real estate loans (usury rate)

21%

Time limit for the redemption of real estate after foreclosure sale of a mortgage (does not apply to trust deeds)

No redemption

Transfer revenue tax stamp rate

Over $100, rate is $0.55 per $500 or fraction of value excluding remaining liens

State recovery fund

—

HUD/FHA state office

Insuring office:
330 Post Office Annex
Providence 02903

FTS Tel. 838-4351
Commercial number: (401) 528-4351

SOUTH CAROLINA

State real estate commission office

Commissioner
South Carolina Real Estate Commission
900 Elmwood, Columbia 29201

Trust deeds

In use

Maximum interest rate allowable by individuals on real estate loans (usury rate)

8%; special rates for loans over $50,000

Time limit for the redemption of real estate after foreclosure sale of a mortgage (does not apply to trust deeds)

No redemption

Transfer revenue tax stamp rate

$1 per $500 (first $100 is excluded)

State recovery fund

None

HUD/FHA state office

1801 Main Street
Jefferson Square
Columbia 29202

FTS Tel. 677-5591
Commercial number: (803) 765-5591

SOUTH DAKOTA

State real estate commission office

Secretary
South Dakota Real Estate Commission
Box 638, Pierre 57501

Trust deeds

Rarely used

Maximum interest rate allowable by individuals on real estate loans (usury rate)

10%

Time limit for the redemption of real estate after foreclosure sale of a mortgage (does not apply to trust deeds)

180 days where power-of-sale clause is contained and property is under 30 acres; otherwise 1 year

Transfer revenue tax stamp rate

$0.50 per $500 of value or fraction exclusive of remaining liens

State recovery fund

—

HUD/FHA state office

Insuring office:
119 Federal Building, U.S. Courthouse
400 S. Phillips Avenue
Sioux Falls 57102
FTS Tel. 782-4223
Commercial number: (605) 336-2980

TENNESSEE

State real estate commission office

Executive Director
Tennessee Real Estate Commission
556 Capitol Hill Bldg., Nashville 37219

Trust deeds

Used extensively

Maximum interest rate allowable by individuals on real estate loans (usury rate)

10%

Time limit for the redemption of real estate after foreclosure sale of a mortgage (does not apply to trust deeds)

2 years (may be waived in trust deed)

Transfer revenue tax stamp rate

$0.26 per $100 of consideration or property value, whichever is greater

State recovery fund

—

HUD/FHA state office

One Northshore Building
1111 Northshore Drive
Knoxville 37919
FTS Tel. 854-1222
Commercial number: (615) 637-9300
Ext. 1222

Insuring offices:
28th Floor, 100 North Main Street
Memphis 38103
FTS Tel. 222-3141
Commercial number: (901) 534-3141

U.S. Courthouse, Federal Building Annex
801 Broadway
Nashville 37203
FTS Tel. 852-5521
Commercial number: (615) 749-5521

TEXAS

State real estate commission office

Administrator
Texas Real Estate Commission
P.O. Box 12188, Capitol Station
Austin 78711

Trust deeds

Used almost exclusively

Maximum interest rate allowable by individuals on real estate loans (usury rate)

10%

Time limit for the redemption of real estate after foreclosure sale of a mortgage (does not apply to trust deeds)

No redemption

Transfer revenue tax stamp rate

—

State recovery fund

Yes

HUD/FHA state office

2001 Bryan Tower, 4th Floor
Dallas 75201
FTS Tel. 749-1601
Commercial number: (214) 749-1601

Kallison Building
410 South Main Avenue
Post Office Box 9163
San Antonio 78285

FTS Tel. 730-6800
Commercial number: (512) 229-6800

Insuring offices:
819 Taylor Street
Room 13A01 Federal Building
Fort Worth 76102

FTS Tel. 334-3233
Commercial number: (817) 334-3233

Two Greenway Plaza East, Suite 200
Houston 77046
FTS Tel. 527-4335
Commercial number: (713) 226-4335

Courthouse and Federal Office Building
1205 Texas Avenue
Post Office Box 1647
Lubbock 79408

FTS Tel. 738-7265
Commercial number: (806) 762-7265

UTAH

State real estate commission office

Director
Department of Business Regulation
Real Estate Division
330 East Fourth St.
Salt Lake City 84111

Trust deeds

In use

Maximum interest rate allowable by individuals on real estate loans (usury rate)

Special rates (see state codes)

Time limit for the redemption of real estate after foreclosure sale of a mortgage (does not apply to trust deeds)

6 months

Transfer revenue tax stamp rate

—

State recovery fund

—

HUD/FHA state office

Insuring office:
125 South State Street
Post Office Box 11009
Salt Lake City 84147
FTS Tel. 588-5237
Commercial number: (801) 524-5237

VERMONT

State real estate commission office

Executive Secretary
Vermont Real Estate Commission
Seven East State St., Montpelier 05602

Trust deeds

Often used

Maximum interest rate allowable by individuals on real estate loans (usury rate)

8½%; special rates for residential real estate loans

Time limit for the redemption of real estate after foreclosure sale of a mortgage (does not apply to trust deeds)

6 months after Apr. 1, 1968; 1 year prior to that date; court may shorten period

Transfer revenue tax stamp rate

½% of sales price

State recovery fund

—

HUD/FHA state office

Insuring office:
Federal Building
Elmwood Avenue
Post Office Box 989
Burlington 05401
FTS Tel. 832-6274
Commercial number: (802) 862-6501
Ext. 6274

VIRGINIA

State real estate commission office

Director
Real Estate Commission
Virginia Dept. of Professional & Occupational Registration
2 South 9th St. (2nd floor)
P.O. Box 1-X, Richmond 23202

Trust deeds

Used almost exclusively

Maximum interest rate allowable by individuals on real estate loans (usury rate)

8%; special rates for first mortgages and for lending institutions

Time limit for the redemption of real estate after foreclosure sale of a mortgage (does not apply to trust deeds)

Up to court (often 6 months)

Transfer revenue tax stamp rate

$0.15 on $100 of the greater of consideration or value plus a grantor's tax of $50 for each $500 or fraction excluding remaining liens; city and counties also may impose tax

State recovery fund

—

HUD/FHA state office

701 East Franklin Street
Richmond 23219
FTS Tel. 925-2721
Commercial number: (804) 782-2721

WASHINGTON

State real estate commission office

Administrator
Washington Real Estate Division
P.O. Box 247, Olympia 98504

Trust deeds

In use

Maximum interest rate allowable by individuals on real estate loans (usury rate)

12%

Time limit for the redemption of real estate after foreclosure sale of a mortgage (does not apply to trust deeds)

1 year unless abandoned

Transfer revenue tax stamp rate

$0.50 per $500 of value excluding existing loans plus 1% of the gross sales price

State recovery fund

None

HUD/FHA state office

Arcade Plaza Building
1321 Second Avenue
Seattle 98101
FTS Tel. 399-7465
Commercial number: (206) 442-7456

Insuring office:
West 920 Riverside Avenue
Spokane 99201
FTS Tel. 439-4571
Commercial number: (509) 456-4571

WEST VIRGINIA

State real estate commission office

Executive Secretary
West Virginia Real Estate Commission
402 State Office Building #3
1800 E. Washington St.
Charleston 25305

Trust deeds

Used primarily

Maximum interest rate allowable by individuals on real estate loans (usury rate)

8%

Time limit for the redemption of real estate after foreclosure sale of a mortgage (does not apply to trust deeds)

No redemption

Transfer revenue tax stamp rate

$1.10 per $500 of consideration or fraction plus county tax of $0.55 per $500 of value or fraction

State recovery fund

None

HUD/FHA state office

Insuring office:
New Federal Building
500 Quarrier Street
Post Office Box 2948
Charleston 25330

FTS Tel. 924-1321
Commercial number: (304) 343-6181 Ext. 321

WISCONSIN

State real estate commission office

Executive Secretary
Wisconsin Real Estate Examining Board
819 North 6th St., Milwaukee 53203

Trust deeds

Used occasionally

Maximum interest rate allowable by individuals on real estate loans (usury rate)

12%

Time limit for the redemption of real estate after foreclosure sale of a mortgage (does not apply to trust deeds)

No redemption

Transfer revenue tax stamp rate

After $100, $0.10 per $100 of value

State recovery fund

—

HUD/FHA state office

744 North 4th Street
Milwaukee 53203

FTS Tel. 362-1493
Commercial number: (414) 224-1493

WYOMING

State real estate commission office

Commissioner
Wyoming Real Estate Commission
2219 Carey Avenue, Cheyenne 82002

Trust deeds

In use

*Maximum interest rate allowable by individuals
on real estate loans (usury rate)*

Special rates determined by state code

*Time limit for the redemption of real estate after
foreclosure sale of a mortgage (does not apply to
trust deeds)*

3 months except agricultural real estate

Transfer revenue tax stamp rate

—

State recovery fund

None

HUD/FHA state office

Insuring office:
Federal Office Building
100 East B Street
Post Office Box 580
Casper 82601

FTS Tel. 328-5252
Commercial number: (307) 265-5550

Index